Going far beyond telling the story of how the 1534 Bible came about, Jensen shows what drove and shaped the translation and publication. Through a careful examination of words and phrases that Luther chose to emphasize, Jensen illuminates Luther's theological agenda. This Bible sought to speak gospel, to give the experience of the life-giving Word to readers and hearers, and thereby to change their lives.
—Mary Jane Haemig, professor emerita of church history, Luther Seminary, St. Paul, Minnesota

Most authors long for one best-seller. Luther had several, but none more enduring than the 1534 Luther Bible. Jensen's book explores the results of the Wittenberg Bible project, noting how the remarkable translation effort, notable illustrations, and a few highlighted texts brought audiences not just a book but the living voice of the gospel (*viva vox evangelii*).
—Jeffrey Jaynes, Warner Professor of Church History, Methodist Theological School in Ohio

Gordon Jensen has written a broad history of the so-called Luther Bible. In clear and captivating prose, he tells the behind-the-scenes story of its creation by multiple Wittenberg figures who spent years translating and revising the Scriptures into a German that resonated with German speakers. Jensen captures the energy of this group, the convictions that motivated them to carry out this lengthy project, and the vitality they saw in the Word. Through humanistic learning and creative renderings, they created a dynamic translation that quickly became a classic.
—Anna Marie Johnson, associate professor of Reformation church history, Garrett-Evangelical Theological Seminary; author of *Beyond Indulgences: Luther's Reform of Late Medieval Piety*

This book describes how Martin Luther and his colleagues not only translated biblical languages into German but also sought to translate the gospel from written page to personal experience. In that way, this insightful historical study serves as a great resource for understanding the scriptural theology that drove the Lutheran Reformation.
—Martin J. Lohrmann, associate professor of Lutheran Confessions and heritage, Wartburg Theological Seminary

Martin Luther's passion for the Word and his creativity as translator have drawn ample scholarly attention. Dr. Gordon A. Jensen's discovery of Luther's decision to capitalize certain words in his Bible translation led to this delightful study that demonstrates both Luther's intentionality in communicating the gospel and his commitment to lead the reader to experience forgiveness. The book contributes to the study of the art of biblical translation and the themes of Luther's essential theology.

—Kirsi Stjerna, First Lutheran, Los Angeles/Southwest California Synod Professor of Lutheran History and Theology, Pacific Lutheran Theological Seminary, Berkeley

LUTHERAN QUARTERLY BOOKS

Editor

Paul Rorem, Professor Emeritus, *Princeton Theological Seminary*

Associate Editors

Timothy J. Wengert, Professor Emeritus, *United Lutheran Seminary (Philadelphia)*

Mary Jane Haemig, Professor Emeritus, *Luther Seminary, St. Paul*

Mark C. Mattes, *Grand View University, Des Moines, Iowa*

Lutheran Quarterly Books will advance the same aims as *Lutheran Quarterly* itself, aims repeated by Theodore G. Tappert when he was editor fifty years ago and renewed by Oliver K. Olson when he revived the publication in 1987. The original four aims continue to grace the front matter and to guide the contents of every issue, and can now also indicate the goals of *Lutheran Quarterly Books*: "to provide a forum (1) for the discussion of Christian faith and life on the basis of the Lutheran confession; (2) for the application of the principles of the Lutheran church to the changing problems of religion and society; (3) for the fostering of world Lutheranism; and (4) for the promotion of understanding between Lutherans and other Christians."

For further information, see www.lutheranquarterly.org.

The symbol and motto of *Lutheran Quarterly*, VDMA for *Verbum Domini Manet in Aeternum* (1 Peter 1:25), was adopted as a motto by Luther's sovereign, Frederick the Wise, and his successors. The original "Protestant" princes walking out of the imperial Diet of Speyer in 1529, unruly peasants following Thomas Müntzer, and from 1531 to 1547 the coins, medals, flags, and guns of the Smalcaldic League all bore the most famous Reformation slogan, the first Evangelical confession: The Word of the Lord remains forever.

For the complete list of *Lutheran Quarterly Books*, please see the final pages of this work.

Experiencing Gospel

Experiencing Gospel

*The History and Creativity of
Martin Luther's 1534 Bible Project*

GORDON A. JENSEN

Foreword by
Robert Kolb

FORTRESS PRESS
MINNEAPOLIS

EXPERIENCING GOSPEL
The History and Creativity of Martin Luther's 1534 Bible Project

Library of Congress Control Number: 2023012802 (print)

Cover design and illustration: Kristin Miller

Print ISBN: 978-1-5064-8294-1
eBook ISBN: 978-1-5064-8295-8

"May a merciful God preserve me from a Christian Church in which everyone is a saint! I want to be and remain in the church and little flock of the fainthearted, the feeble, and the ailing, who feel and recognize the wretchedness of their sins, who sigh and cry to God incessantly for comfort and help, who believe in the forgiveness of sin, and who suffer persecution for the sake of the Word, which they confess and teach purely and without adulteration." (LW 22:55)

This book is dedicated to the community of justified sinners with whom I rub shoulders and who have taught me so much: my students, my colleagues, the wonderful members of my family, and most especially Brenda, who, with countless others, continues to experience and live in the Living Word of God.

In gratitude for the support given by my parents while still on their earthly journey.

Contents

Foreword

Five hundred years ago Martin Luther's translation of the New Testament attracted its first purchasers. This epochal event provided a dress rehearsal for the publication of the translation of the entire Bible into German twelve years later. This translation has not only provided the biblical text for the German people over five centuries, and in the last century in several slightly altered forms, but also helped shape William Tyndale's English version of the New Testament, thus influencing English-language translations to this day. Furthermore, it has also formed expressions and interpretations of the Greek and Hebrew words and phrases in a significant number of other languages around the world.

As Gordon Jensen points out, Luther's was not the first vernacular translation into German, and John Wycliffe had stimulated translation of the Bible into English by his Lollard followers over a century before Luther's birth. Luther's translation commands so much attention because it brought a vernacular Bible into the hands of a much larger readership than had been the case with earlier translations, some of which remained in manuscript, others prohibitively expensive rather than just costly.

Above all, the "Luther Bible" of the Wittenberg team commands such tremendous respect because it reveals and reflects Luther's particular gifts in setting the text to tones that German speakers could embrace in their own way of speaking. He combined his vast grasp of the Vulgate text that he had absorbed in primary school, secondary school, university, and cloister with his ever-growing sensitivity to the meaning of both Hebrew and Greek. He attained his knowledge of the ancient languages through use of the latest tools provided by biblical humanists such as the Hebraist Johannes Reuchlin and the Greek scholar Desiderius Erasmus. His gift of communication in his own version of the German language caught the rhythm and tones of those whom he encountered in the marketplace, at the electoral Saxon court at the other end of Wittenberg's main street, and on the Saxon roads. Thus, his scholarly sensitivities to the text led to effective communication of its meaning for both common people and fellow scholars.

Luther's translation could make its impact because of its happy coincidence with an invention hardly a half-century old, the use of movable type in printing texts. Johannes Gutenberg died fifteen years before Luther was born, but the two made a perfect team, even without personally meeting. Luther had stumbled into the effective use of printing when an item usually difficult to sell, namely, his Ninety-Five Theses on Indulgences, opened his eyes to the use of the medium and impelled him to compose a German presentation of their content, his *Treatise on Grace and Indulgence*, in early 1518. It became a genuine best-seller.

The year 2022 marked also the five-hundredth anniversary of the launching of further work on the translation of Scripture, both in revisions of the New Testament translation and also in the composition of the translation of the Old Testament. Under Luther's leadership, a committee undertook the task, with a core of Wittenberg colleagues and a collage of others who were drafted into participation in the project. Like Luther, who believed that "nowhere can the Spirit be found more present and more active than in the very holy letters which he wrote"[1] and that "God is everywhere, but he is really to be found in the Holy Scriptures, in his Word, more than anywhere else,"[2] Melanchthon and others gathered in the consultations on the methodical work of translating the Old Testament regarded this work as a sacred task. Their work on the text provided another avenue for public confession of their faith, a new medium for their proclamation of new life in Christ.

The members of the committee did not meet regularly over the twelve years, but at times they gathered together and worked intensively. They were sensitive to the fact that just as the oral words of the prophets and apostles moved into written form, the written form was itching to return to oral form as well as to communication in other writings and in the sacraments with their promise of forgiveness, life, and salvation. The translators were convinced that they were bringing readers and hearers

1. "An Assertion of All the Articles of Martin Luther Condemned by the Latest Bull of Leo X (1520)," WA 7:97,2–3.
2. "Sermon for the First Sunday after Epiphany (1523)," WA 12:413,32–34.

into the presence of their Creator and drawing these consumers of the text into the experience of talking with God himself. Jensen helpfully highlights the experience of joy and delight that Luther and his colleagues wished to give readers and hearers through the text. Their translation was to convey the down-to-earth interest of God in the tiniest detail of his human creatures' lives and in the peace that forgiveness of sins and restoration of righteousness, their identity as God's children, deliver. This peace takes place in their lives as God's address of the gospel of Christ to them arises out of the biblical page through the proclamation and conversation of his people with others.

All this has fallen under the analytical eye of Gordon Jensen, who presents the results of several years of careful study of the Luther Bible as an effectively constructed material object as well as an effectively formulated vehicle of communication. Jensen's unparalleled investigation has led to a treasure trove of insights into the "how" of the construction of the 1534 Luther Bible and the "why" behind the decisions of Luther and his committee for specific formulations. With his firm command of the scholarship on the Wittenberg concepts of God's Word and Holy Scripture from the past century up to 2021, this study places itself squarely in the middle of ongoing interest in, and study of, the communication of God in Jesus Christ and through his people, led by the prophets and apostles.

Jensen also takes seriously that its first readers experienced the thick book as a material object. His examination of how the text as a printed object struck the eye of the person whose hands were holding it opens new vistas for the readers of this volume. Jensen's research and analysis highlights in pioneering fashion Luther's accentuation of certain phrases through the capitalization of every letter. His unfolding of the significance of four phrases provides fresh insights into the reformer's perceptive appreciation of the possibilities of communication in print. Jensen also provides helpful theological analysis of the phrases so accentuated: "the Word," "listen to him," "forgives sins," and "take" (in the Words of Institution of the Lord's Supper). Chapters 5 through 8, which provide this analysis, offer readers valuable insights into the heart and core of Luther's theology.

The five-hundredth anniversary of the publication of Luther's translation of the New Testament on the very day of my writing these words foreshadows the coming of the quincentennial of the appearance of the entire Bible in Luther's German twelve years later. Gordon Jensen sounds a call to dedicated and intensive delving into the biblical Word in this volume. His fruitful study of this event in the history of the church presents readers with an invitation to join him in pondering the continuing significance and impact of the Wittenberg effort that produced this translation. For this effort continues to broadcast God's address to people of every time and place, the witness to God's working in human history, above all, in the incarnation, death, and resurrection of Jesus Christ.

Robert Kolb

Mainz, Germany, the festival of Saint Matthew,

apostle and evangelist, 2022

Acknowledgments

While doing research one year in Wittenberg, I came across what I first considered a typographical or printing error in the 1534 Luther Bible. In Paul's Letter to the Romans, I noticed that every letter in the words "FORGIVES SIN" was capitalized in chapter 3 (before verse numbers were used). This soon led to leafing through the Luther Bible, page by page, looking for other instances of such capitalized words. To my surprise, I discovered seven different places where this occurred, and that led to exploring why these words, seemingly picked at random, were emphasized, and who was responsible. The results of my investigation are found in this book. In these highlighted words and phrases, one encounters the basic building blocks for Luther's reformational theology. Not only did Luther want people to read the Bible in a language they could understand, but he wanted them, even more so, to experience the gospel for themselves as they encountered the Living Word of God in the pages of Scripture.

The research and writing for this book took place during a sabbatical granted me by the Lutheran Theological Seminary (LTS) in Saskatoon. My colleagues, William Harrison, Kristine Ruffatto, and Kayko Driedger Hesslein, encouraged my research and filled in for me in various administrative tasks while I was immersed in my research. The LTS registrar, Colleen Rickard, also ably handled many of the Academic Dean's tasks that fell on her shoulders while I was away. I truly appreciated their support, questions, conversations, and their ability at knowing when to not bother me during the research and writing process. While originally planning for further research in Germany, and times of writing in a warmer clime to avoid the cold Canadian winters, the onset of Covid-19 led to a project carried out at home, in between shoveling snow. Paul Rorem, the editor of both the *Lutheran Quarterly* journal and the *Lutheran Quarterly Books*, provided much-appreciated support and encouragement for this project.

I am also deeply appreciative of the sharp eyes of Pamela Giles, Hugh Williams, and Brenda Jensen, masters of the English language. Each of them carefully edited initial drafts of this manuscript and made countless helpful suggestions. I am also indebted to Robert Kolb, who graciously agreed to write the foreword to this book, taking the time away from his own writing projects. It was also a delight to work with the people at the Reformationsgeschichtliche Forschungsbibliothek Wittenberg–Stiftung Luthergedenkstätten, who provided the photographs of the texts in question from their copy of the 1534 Luther Bible. Laura Gifford and Steven Hall, the editor and project manager of this volume at Fortress Press, were prompt and efficient in handling the manuscript, and I give credit to them and Fortress's hardworking staff for the thoughtful guidance and insights they have provided. Last, but not least, I thank Brenda for the support and encouragement she has given, even when I am immersed in the sixteenth century.

Gordon A. Jensen
500th anniversary of the publication
of Martin Luther's 1522 *Septembertestament*, 2022

Abbreviations

AC	Augsburg Confession (*Confessio Augustana*). *The Book of Concord*, ed. Robert Kolb and Timothy J. Wengert. Minneapolis: Fortress Press, 2000, 27–105.
Ap	Apology of the Augsburg Confession. *The Book of Concord*, ed. Robert Kolb and Timothy J. Wengert. Minneapolis: Fortress Press, 2000, 107–294.
BC	*The Book of Concord*, ed. Robert Kolb and Timothy J. Wengert. Minneapolis: Fortress Press, 2000.
BSELK	*Die Bekenntnisschriften der EvangelischLlutherischen Kirche. Vollständige Neuedition*, ed. Irene Dingel. Gottingen: Vandenhoeck & Ruprecht, 2014.
CR	*Corpus Reformatorum: Philippi Melanthonis opera quae supersunt omnia*, ed. Karl Brettschneider and Heinrich Bindseil, 28 Vols. Braunschweig: Schwetchke, 1834–1860.
DBW	*Dietrich Bonhoeffer Works*. 17 Volumes. Minneapolis: Fortress Press, 1996–2014.
Ep	Epitome of the Formula of Concord. *The Book of Concord*, ed. Robert Kolb and Timothy J. Wengert. Minneapolis: Fortress Press, 2000, 486–523.
FC-SD	Formula of Concord, Solid Declaration. *The Book of Concord*, ed. Robert Kolb and Timothy J. Wengert. Minneapolis: Fortress Press, 2000, 524–660.
LB Apoc	Apocrypha, *Biblia/ das ist/ die ‖ gantze Heilige Sch=‖rifft Deudsch.‖* Mart. Luth.‖ Wittemberg. Begnadet mit

Kurfurstlicher zu Sachsen freiheit. Gedruckt durch Hans Lufft. M.D.XXXIIII.

LB NT   New Testament, *Biblia/ das ist/ die* || *gantze Heilige Sch=||rifft Deudsch.*|| Mart. Luth.|| Wittemberg. Begnadet mit Kurfurstlicher zu Sachsen freiheit. Gedruckt durch Hans Lufft. M.D.XXXIIII.

LB OT   Old Testament, *Biblia/ das ist/ die* || *gantze Heilige Sch=||rifft Deudsch.*|| Mart. Luth.|| Wittemberg. Begnadet mit Kurfurstlicher zu Sachsen freiheit. Gedruckt durch Hans Lufft. M.D.XXXIIII.

LC   Large Catechism. *The Book of Concord*, ed. Robert Kolb and Timothy J. Wengert. Minneapolis: Fortress Press, 2000, 377–480.

LW   *Luther's Works* [American edition], ed. Helmut Lehmann, Jaroslav Pelikan, and Christopher Boyd Brown. 79 vols. Philadelphia: Fortress Press/St. Louis: Concordia Publishing House, 1955–1986. 2008–.

LW-CV   *Luther's Works, Companion Volume: Sixteenth-Century Biographies of Martin Luther,* ed. Christopher Boyd Brown. St. Louis: Concordia Publishing House, 2018.

MBWT   *Melanchthons Briefwechsel: Kritische und Kommentierte Gesamtausgabe. Texte,* ed. Heinz Scheible. Stuttgart-Bad Cannstatt: frommann-holzboog, 1977–.

SA   Smalcald Articles. *The Book of Concord*, ed. Robert Kolb and Timothy J. Wengert. Minneapolis: Fortress Press, 2000, 295–328.

SC   Small Catechism. *The Book of Concord*, ed. Robert Kolb and Timothy J. Wengert. Minneapolis: Fortress Press, 2000, 345–375.

TAL   *The Annotated Luther*, 6 vols, ed. Hans J. Hillerbrand, Kirsi I. Stjerna, and Timothy J. Wengert. Minneapolis: Fortress Press, 2015-2017.

Tr   Treatise on the Power and Primacy of the Pope. *The Book of Concord*, ed. Robert Kolb and Timothy J. Wengert. Minneapolis: Fortress Press, 2000, 329–344.

WA   Luther, Martin. *Luthers Werke: Kritische Gesamtausgabe*
            [*Schriften*], 73 vols. Weimar: H. Böhlau, 1883–2009.

WA BR   Luther, Martin. *Luthers Werke: Kritische Gesamtausgabe:*
            [*Briefwechsel*], 18 vols. Weimar: H. Böhlau, 1930–1985.

WA DB   Luther, Martin. *Luthers Werke: Kritische Gesamtausgabe:*
            [*Deutsche Bibel*], 12 vols. Weimar: H. Böhlau, 1906–1961.

WA TR   Luther, Martin. *Luthers Werke: Kritische Gesamtausgabe:*
            [*Tischreden*], 6 vols. Weimar: H. Böhlau, 1912–1921.

Introduction

"I want to acknowledge Christ as my Lord, and I do this not only out of Scripture but also out of experience, because the name of Christ has often helped me where no one else was able to help. So I have on my behalf the substance and the words—that is, experience and Scripture— and God has given both to me in very large measure."[1]

"The Word is not to sit lightly on the heart, like a swan on water . . . [Mary] said, 'I want God's Word so impressed upon my heart that it is a mark no one can remove.'"[2]

The year 2022 CE marked the five-hundredth anniversary of the publication of Martin Luther's German translation of the New Testament. Nicknamed the *Septembertestament* because it was first published in September of 1522, it quickly became a best seller among supporters of the Reformations sweeping through the land—and a lightning rod for its opponents. Luther originally undertook this project while in hiding at the Wartburg Castle, where he had fled after being declared an outlaw by the Emperor Charles V at the Diet of Worms in the spring of 1521. Luther's initial translation project was completed in a few months, and then it was reviewed and further polished by his colleagues in Wittenberg in the spring and summer of 1522. But the translation of the New Testament was only the beginning of his "Bible Project." While the ink was still drying on the first printing of the *Septembertestament*, he and his colleagues were already engaged in translating the rest of the Bible into an easily readable German. This project proved to be much more challenging, and it was

1. "Letter to the Christians at Strassburg (December 15, 1524)," LW 49:94; WA TR 1:240,6–10 (No. 518).
2. "Sermon on St. John's Day (27 December 1533)," WA 37:246,3–6.

1

not until September 1534 that the Wittenberg (or, Luther) Bible came off the presses—twelve years after the release of the New Testament. Nor was the publication of the 1534 Bible the end of the project. For the rest of his life, Luther and his colleagues continued to revise and update their translation. It was a work in progress. Despite this translation project's lengthy duration, the reason for taking it on remained the same. Luther wanted preachers, as well as the Bible's readers and hearers, to experience the gospel within the pages of Scripture.[3] How well did he succeed in this task? Perhaps the jury is still out.

Over fifty years ago, Heinz Bluhm authored a book titled *Martin Luther: Creative Translator*.[4] This title can be taken in quite different ways, however: negatively, in the sense of Luther's failure to provide a literal, word-for-word translation, or positively, because he sought to capture the meaning of the text in the best idiomatic German. On the one hand, for those who insist that translations must translate the Scriptures as literally as possible, to avoid error—even if it creates difficulty in understanding the text—creativity is a red flag, suggesting an undisciplined and irresponsible approach. This was one of the complaints, for example, that Luther's critics leveled against him when his translation of the New Testament came out in September 1522. A year later, after looking through Luther's creative translation, Jerome Emser, secretary and chaplain to Luther's opponent, Duke George of Saxony, claimed it had over fourteen hundred errors, with the biggest flaw in Luther's translation being his addition of *"allein"* (only) to Romans 3:28, since the word was not in the Latin or Greek texts.[5] Emser also felt that the graceful and "sweet sounding" translation made Luther's translation dangerous.[6] After all, his creative translations, which many of his contemporaries might call "loose" translations, deviated significantly from earlier German Bibles that had come off the presses since 1466. Unlike these earlier editions that were, for the most part, literal, word-for-word

---

3. Throughout this work, the terms "Gospel," and (Living) "Word," are capitalized wherever they refer specifically to Christ. "Bible" is also capitalized any time it refers to a specific edition of the Bible.

4. Heinz Bluhm, *Martin Luther: Creative Translator* (St. Louis: Concordia, 1965).

5. Martin Brecht, *Martin Luther: The Preservation of the Church, 1532–1546*, trans. James L. Schaaf (Minneapolis: Fortress Press, 1993), 107–8. For Emser's own critiques, see Hieronymus Emser, *Auß was gründ || vnnd vrsach || Luthers dolmatschung/ vber das || nawe testament/dem gemeinē man || billich vorbotten worden sey.|| Mit scheynbarlicher anzeygung/wie/wo/vnd || an wölchen stellen/ Luther den text vorkert/vnd || vngetrewlich gehandelt ... || hab.|| ... ||* (Leipzig: Wolfgang Stöckel, 1523). For Luther's justification on adding the word *"allein"* to the text, see "On Translating: An Open Letter (1530)," LW 35:188–89; WA 30.II:636,31–637,22.

6. Martin Brecht, *Martin Luther: Shaping and Defining the Reformation 1521–1532*, trans. James L. Schaaf (Minneapolis: Fortress Press, 1990), 53.

translations from the Latin Vulgate, Luther's *Septembertestament* of 1522 and his complete Bible of 1534 tried to translate the meanings of the text, not just from the official, Latin Vulgate but also from the Greek and Hebrew texts. His critics felt that Luther had crossed the line, from a careful, literal translation of the official Latin text to a liberal interpretation of the text used to justify his heretical theology.

On the other hand, many who read his creative translation were excited to find within its pages a translation that breathed life into the text, something that wooden, literal translations did not provide. Unlike the previous German translations, Luther's translation was, for the most part, "user friendly." In the rush to get the first edition out, there were still many rough spots that would need to be ironed out. But the sheer popularity of the Luther Bible in its various editions during Luther's own lifetime gave an indication of readers' appreciation for this lively, creative translation. By the time of Luther's death, over 430 partial or complete editions of his Bible had come off the presses, with over half of them printed outside Wittenberg, often without his explicit approval.[7] Copyright laws did not exist at that time, and printers throughout Europe took advantage of that. They knew a money-maker when they saw it!

Luther was a creative translator, however, not because he wanted something new and fresh, nor because he wanted something that was "sweet sounding" or simply "user-friendly." He wanted to translate so that people would encounter Christ within the pages of Scripture and through Scripture, thus driving Christ into their hearts and lives.[8] Encountering the Living Word leads to gospel living, as he himself had discovered. As Jaroslav Pelikan said, "[Luther] lived *by* the Word of God: [and] he lived *for* the Word of God."[9] The Living Word of God, who is none other than the Christ, was the One who enabled him to live by and for the Lord of Life. Luther wanted the gospel to be experienced. That was the purpose of his Bible translation project, and it's the intention that this book seeks to explore.

This book is divided into four general sections. The first, covering the first two chapters, explores Luther's theological understanding of the distinction between, and the interrelatedness of, the Scripture and the Word (chapter 1), which influenced how he interpreted and translated

7. Brecht, *Preservation of the Church*, 101–2.
8. "So I have on my behalf the substance and the words—that is, experience and Scripture." "Letter to the Christians at Strassburg (December 15, 1524)," LW 49:94; WA TR 1:240,9–10 (No. 518).
9. Jaroslav Pelikan, *Luther the Expositor: Introduction to the Reformer's Exegetical Writings*. Luther's Works Companion Volume (St. Louis: Concordia, 1959), 49.

the Bible (chapter 2). The second section shifts to an examination of the eighteen German language translations of the Bible that preceded Luther's New Testament of 1522 (chapter 3), and the work of Luther and the rest of his Wittenberg Circle in translating the rest of the Bible and revising the New Testament between 1522 and 1534 (chapter 4), when the first full edition of the *Lutherbibel* was published.

The third, main section of this book (chapters 5 to 8) explores one of the most fascinating, albeit often overlooked, features of the 1534 Luther Bible: his deliberate decision to highlight seven specific words or phrases, by means of using all capital letters that, when put together, give a concise summary of Luther's Reformation theology. These specifically highlighted words and phrases may seem at first glance to be underwhelming, since they do not even capture the reader's eyes when glancing at the pages of the 1534 Bible; however, like an iceberg, their value lies beneath the surface. Only by exploring how important these words and phrases were to Luther can one begin to understand why Luther felt it was so important to emphasize these particular words and phrases. No wonder the process of revising and highlighting of particular words, phrases, and verses of the Luther Bible continues to this day. The focus of these chapters, therefore, is not simply to identify the highlighted word or phrase on the pages of Scripture, but to explore the importance of that word or phrase in Luther's theology and writings. In chapter 5, an examination of the highlighting of "The Word" is studied in detail. Then Luther's emphasis on "Listen to Him," as found in the three transfiguration accounts in the Synoptic Gospels, is explored (chapter 6). The next chapter (chapter 7) examines Luther's deliberate capitalization of every letter in the words, "forgives sin" from Romans 3, which he considered the Gospel in a nutshell, or as Hartmut Hövelmann called them, "*Kernstellen* (core places)."[10] The last chapter in this section (chapter 8) explores Luther's highlighting, found in 1 Corinthians 11, of the word "Take" in the command of Christ regarding the Lord's Supper. Thus, the Word that people are called to listen to is the Word of forgiveness, proclaimed in Word and Sacrament. It is a gospel word—a word that breathes life into the individual and the community, a word that brings a person and a community into an experience of Christ and of the gospel. This Word is to be heard and tasted and experienced.

The final section of the book explores the revisions to the highlighted sections of the Bible in later editions of the Luther Bible during Luther's lifetime, and then after his death (chapter 9). The Conclusion explores how Luther's approach to the Word of God, which focused on experiencing the gospel as one encounters the Christ. This approach was radically

10. Harmut Hövelmann, *Kernstellen der Lutherbibel: Eine Anleitung zum Schriftverständnis.* Texte und Arbeiten zur Bibel, Deutschen Bibelgesellschaft, eds., Bd. 5 (Bielefeld: Luther-Verlag, 1989), 49–74.

different from an approach that emphasizes the literal inerrancy of the text of Scripture. Luther's method of translating placed ultimate authority on the Living Word, who is Christ, and not on Scripture itself. This emphasis on Christ the Living Word shows that Luther was committed to translating the Bible so that its readers and hearers would not just read or hear the words of the text, but so that they would experience and encounter the gospel. He was not interested in having a nice, polished text that was popular simply because his name was attached to the translated biblical text. That would not put a person in contact with "Christ and his benefits."[11] Rather, Luther wanted people to experience the Christ who speaks a Word of forgiveness to a people in need. His translation thus offered an alternative to a system of forgiveness that relied on purchasing indulgences, a system that made forgiveness and comfort for those Christians in purgatory a monetary transaction that decidedly favored those who could afford it. His alternative relied instead on an encounter with the One who is the Word, the One to whom all people are called to listen. In that encounter with the Living Word, the gospel is experienced as forgiveness is proclaimed and tasted. This is what made Luther's Bible translation project worthwhile. His focus on how he tried to translate the Bible into German in a way that helped people experience the gospel is the subject of this study.

---

11. Philip Melanchthon, "*Loci Communes Theologici*," *Melanchthon and Bucer,* Library of Christian Classics Vol. XIX, Wihelm Pauck, ed. (Philadelphia: Westminster, 1969), 21. See also Melanchthon's use of the phrase in AC XXIV, 24 (Latin text), BC, 71; BSELK, 145; as well as in Ap IV, 118, BC,139; BSELK, 316.

1.

Luther, Scripture, and the Word

"Lord keep us steadfast in your word;
curb those who by deceit or sword
would wrest the kingdom from your Son
and bring to naught all he has done."[1]

INTRODUCTION

Martin Luther was a professor of the Bible. His teaching career began with a course on the Psalms, and his major work near the end of his life was a decade of lectures on Genesis. In between, he and his colleagues translated the Bible into German. He was constantly immersed in the study of the Holy Scriptures and desired nothing more than to "sit in the middle of the Scriptures,"[2] something he recommended for preachers everywhere. Even as a child he encountered the Scriptures through artwork such as stained-glass windows and altarpieces, paraphrased bibles such as the "Bible of the Poor," and pamphlets with excerpts from the Bible.[3] His familiarity with the Bible was further developed by the monastic practice of the hours, where the monks worshipped and heard Scripture read multiple times each day. As Robert Kolb notes, Luther "settled into the life of the cloister, reciting psalms and prayers in the seven hours of prayer each day. Thus,

---

1. *Evangelical Lutheran Worship* (Minneapolis: Augsburg Fortress, 2006), Hymn number 517. See also LW 53:304–5.
2. "Sermon on the Nativity of the Lord (1520)." WA 9:664,17.
3. Robert Kolb, *Martin Luther as He Lived and Breathed*, Cascade Companions (Eugene, OR: Cascade Books, 2018), 36. See also Kolb, *Martin Luther and the Enduring Word of God: The Wittenberg School and Its Scripture–Centered Proclamation* (Grand Rapids: Baker Academic, 2016), 17–34.

the words of Scripture become so firmly implanted in his mind that he could not think in any other vocabulary."[4] As a monk, therefore, Luther heard the complete Psalter every two to three weeks. It is no wonder that his first lectures were on the Psalms.

Luther's practice of reading and meditating on the Bible sometimes caused his fellow cloistered monks to try to curb his "obsession" with Scripture. Johannes Mathesius, first a student and then a colleague of Luther's, reported that one time the brothers "took the Bible from him and pressed upon him their own sophistry and scholastic teaching, which he read diligently as an obedient brother. But when he found the right times, he hid himself in the cloister's library and stuck to reading his dear Bible devotedly and faithfully."[5] In these words of Scripture, he heard, and began experiencing, the Word of life.

The centrality of the Scriptures in his life is exemplified in his trial at the Diet of Worms. On April 18, 1521, he stood before the Emperor and declared,

> Unless I am convinced by the testimony of the scriptures or by clear reason . . . I am bound by the scriptures I have quoted and my conscience is captive to the Word of God. I cannot and I will not retract anything, since it is neither safe nor right to go against conscience. I cannot do otherwise, here I stand, may God help me, Amen.[6]

His conscience, as he notes, was "captive to the Word of God," for it was "the font of all wisdom."[7] Highlighting his defiant, and perhaps not original, statement, "Here I stand, I can do no other" overshadows, however, Luther's responsibility as a doctor of the faith to correctly interpret Holy Scriptures. Shortly after this trial in the city of Worms, while in his "exile" at the Wartburg Castle, Luther wrote in a sermon that "we could wish nothing better than that all books might simply be abolished and nothing but the pure, simple Scripture or Bible remains throughout the

---

4. Kolb, *Martin Luther as He Lived and Breathed*, 19–20.

5. Johannes Mathesius, *Historien, Von des Ehrwirdigen in Gott Seligen thewren Manns Gottes, Doctoris Martini Luthers/anfang/lehr/leben vnd sterben*, (Nuremberg: Ulrich Neuber, 1566), Via, as quoted in Kolb, *Martin Luther as He Lived*, 31.

6. "Luther at the Diet of Worms (1521)," LW 32:112; WA 7:838,2–9. The words, "Here I stand, I cannot do otherwise," are given in German in the Latin text upon which this translation is based. There is good evidence, however, that Luther actually said only, "May God help me!" See Adolph Wrede, ed., *Deutsche Reichstagsakten unter Kaiser Karl V, II. Band 1520–1521.* (Gotha: Perthes, 1896), 587. The addition of "Here I stand," does add a nice emphasis to the statement, however.

7. "Genesis Lectures (1535–1545)." LW 3:305–6; WA 43:93,40–94,3.

world, especially among Christians."[8] The Bible, as the Living Word, was the only book a person needed.

It is tempting to begin with an exploration of Luther's understanding of Scripture as a written text. To do so, however, would lead to misunderstanding the big picture, by focusing on the text of the Bible rather than giving pre-eminence to the Word of God. Rather, Luther's understanding of the Word of God, as found in the pages of Scripture, informed his conscience and grounded him in Scripture. Once the big picture is grasped, Luther's understanding of Scripture, including the defining phrase associated with him, *sola Scriptura* (Scripture only, or Scripture alone), and the subsequent questions about the inerrancy and inspiration of Scripture, fall into place.

THE WORD OF GOD

Many would see the Bible, Scripture, and the Word of God as simply different terms for the same thing. People talk about reading the Word of God, in an obvious reference to the Bible. Yet Luther had realized early in his career that the "Word" was not identical to the "Bible" or "Scripture." He used a vivid image to depict the difference between the Word and the Scriptures in his Preface to the Old Testament:

> Think of the Scriptures as the loftiest and noblest of holy things, as the richest of mines which can never be sufficiently explored, in order that you may find that divine wisdom which God here lays before you in such simple guise as to quench all pride. Here you will find the swaddling cloths and the manger in which Christ lies, and to which the angel points the shepherds [Luke 2:12]. Simple and lowly are these swaddling cloths, but dear is the treasure, Christ, who lies in them.[9]

As lofty as the Scriptures are, Luther makes the point that even in all their magnificence, the Scriptures are still only the swaddling cloths and the manger that hold the living Christ, who is the Word made flesh. The shepherds did not come to worship the manger; they came to worship the Christ child, lying in the manger.

Luther made two key distinctions between Word and Scripture. First, he applied the term "Scripture" to the written text, while the "Word" is audible. The "Word" is the voice that speaks, creates, heals, and gives life.

8. "Christmas Postil (1522)." LW 52:206; WA 10.I.1:627,16–18.
9. "Prefaces to the Old Testament (1545/1523)." LW 35:236; WA DB 8:12,2–8.

On this point, Luther followed St. John by insisting that the name for this Word is none other than Jesus the Christ, "the word made flesh, full of grace and truth" (John 1:14). In the opening words of his Gospel, John makes a grand statement about Christ as the Word: "In the beginning was the Word, and the Word was with God, and the Word was God." (John 1:1). John did not mean that "In the beginning was the Scriptures, and the Scriptures were with God, and the Scriptures were God." That would be blasphemy. Thus, the Word, as used by both John the evangelist and Luther the preacher, is quite different than Scripture. While Scripture contains the account of the ministry and words of Christ, it is still a document or text. The Word, on the other hand, is a living, breathing, speaking voice. The emphasis on the Word in Luther's writings, then, is really an emphasis on Christ and what Christ does in speaking the Word of the gospel. As Kolb notes, "God talks his way through the entire Scriptures."[10] When God talks, creation happens, as the first chapter of Genesis reveals. The Scriptures, or the Bible, on the other hand, can only report about this One who is coming and has come to give life. It is unable, however, to breathe life and salvation into a person's heart.[11] Luther makes the same basic point in his debate with Erasmus. Luther argued that "God [i.e., the Word] and Scripture are two things, no less than the Creator and creature are two things."[12] The Bible is a creation of God, while the Word speaks creation into being.

Second, this Living Word, Christ, speaks the *gospel*. Thus, the Word who is Christ is always a life-giving proclamation. This Living Word is nothing less than the Gospel that brings life into being. Whenever this Living Word speaks the gospel, salvation, life, and forgiveness of sins happen, as Luther's *Small Catechism* states.[13] As inspiring as Scripture is to read, the manger that holds Christ cannot breathe life into a person's heart. Only the Word can do that. Like John the Baptist, the Bible can point to the life-giving Christ and declare, "Here is the Lamb of God who takes away the sin of the world" (John 1:29), but it cannot take away those sins. Only Christ the Living Word can. The Word creates: it is not simply a report about what God has done.

Based on these two main distinctions, Hartmut Hövelmann has rightly noted that "Scripture is not identical to the Word of God. The Word is

---

10. Robert Kolb, *Martin Luther and the Enduring Word of God: The Wittenberg School and Its Scripture-Centered Proclamation* (Grand Rapids: Baker Academic, 2016), 46.

11. "Sermon on 1 Peter (1523)." LW 30:19; WA 12:275,5–11.

12. "Bondage of the Will (1525)." LW 33:25; WA 18:606,21–23.

13. "Wherever there is forgiveness of sins, there is life and salvation." SC, Sacrament of the Altar, 5–6. BC 362; BSELK 890.

the *viva vox evangelii*" (the Living Word of the gospel),[14] and the gospel is made incarnate in Christ, the Living Word. This Word makes the gospel real, something to be experienced. This is something that Scripture cannot do. Luther made this point when he stated that "the Gospel is not what one finds in books and what is written in letters of the alphabet; it is rather an oral sermon and a Living Word, a voice that resounds throughout the world and is proclaimed publicly, so that one hears it everywhere."[15] In other words, the Bible and Scriptures are written, historically recorded words, while the Word is a living voice, a voice proclaiming the Word of gospel, something that cannot be found in books or "written in letters of the alphabet."[16] In the words on the pages of Scripture, one encounters the Word, who brings people into an experience of life. It is only from this perspective, then, that a person can understand the relationship between the Scripture and the Word. The first records the story of God giving life, and the latter is the One who encounters the reader with an experience of life "for us and for our salvation," as stated in the Nicene Creed.

SCRIPTURE

Luther supposedly once described the Bible as the "Book, Scripture, and Word" (*Buch, Schrifft, Wort*),[17] although he generally used the term, Scripture, rather than Bible, to describe the written Word. In the Greek language, "Bible" (*Biblia*) literally means "book," and refers to the book containing the Holy Scripture. It is not Scripture, however, but the Word that involves a living relationship with God. This was the most important thing for Luther. Nevertheless, his emphasis on the oral nature of the Word, experienced especially in preaching, did not denigrate the role and authority of Scripture. Rather, Scripture was crucial for the life of the church. One finds in Scripture the clear, unequivocal record of the proclaiming Word. In Scripture one discovers Christ the Living Word and the gospel. Scripture was thus essential to the church because it describes what is central to the faith: the Word who is Christ. Thus, Hans-Martin Barth stated that for Luther, "The central content and decisive

---

14. Hartmut Hövelmann, *Kernstellen der Lutherbibel: Eine Anleitung zum Schriftverständnis.* Texte und Arbeiten zur Bibel, Deutschen Bibelgesellschaft, Bd 5 (Bielefeld: Luther Verlag, 1989), 37.
15. "Sermons on 1 Peter (1523)," LW 30:3: WA 12:259,10–13.
16. Hans-Martin Barth, *The Theology of Martin Luther: A Critical Assessment* (Minneapolis: Fortress Press, 2013), 439.
17. "Foreword to Luther's Second Collected German Works (1548)," WA 54:474,4–5. One must question, however, whether Luther actually stated this, or whether Georg Rörer put it into Luther's mouth.

criterion of Scripture is Christ: take Christ out of Scripture, and what is left that is in any way essential?"[18] The "entire Scripture deals only with Christ everywhere."[19] This is a bold claim! A sceptic would think such claims were stretching the point too far, as Luther himself would readily admit.[20] Nevertheless, Hans-Martin Barth could assert that for Luther, "Sacred Scripture is clear in both an external and an internal sense. The external clarity he sees as also founded in Christ, for he is the 'center of the circle . . . and all the stories in Holy Scripture, when regarded rightly, are about Christ,' [for they] have their goal in him."[21] Scripture plays the role of John the Baptist, pointing to Christ.

What about the Old Testament, or the Hebrew Scripture, however? Many would consider it inappropriate to impose Christ on the Old Testament. Luther, however, had no problem with a Christocentric reading of the Old Testament. He declared,

> Thus the books of Moses and the prophets are also Gospel, since they proclaimed and described in advance what the apostles preached or wrote later about Christ. But there is a difference. For although both have been put on paper word for word, the Gospel, or the New Testament, should really not be written but should be expressed with the living voice which resounds and is heard throughout the world. The fact that it is also written is superfluous. But the Old Testament is only put in writing. Therefore it is called "a letter." Thus the apostles call it Scripture; for it only pointed to the Christ who was to come. But the Gospel is a living sermon on the Christ who has come.[22]

In some ways, then, Luther placed more emphasis on the Old Testament than on the New. In a sermon for Epiphany, based on the story of the Magi visiting Jesus, Luther insisted that the New Testament was merely a continuation of the gospel message contained in the Old Testament:

> For the New Testament is nothing but an uncovering and a revelation of the Old Testament, [. . .]. That is why Christ did not write his doctrine himself, as Moses did his, but transmitted it orally, and also commanded that it should be orally continued giving no command that it should be written. Likewise the apostles wrote little, [. . .]. Those who did write, do no more than point us to the old Scripture [the Old Testament], just as the angel pointed the

---

18. Hans-Martin Barth, *The Theology of Martin Luther: A Critical Assessment* (Minneapolis: Fortress Press, 2013), 443. See also "The Bondage of the Will (1525)," LW 33:26; WA 18:606,29.

19. "Romans Commentary (1515–1516)," LW 25, 405; WA 56:414,15.

20. Barth, *The Theology of Martin Luther*, 443.

21. Barth, *The Theology of Martin Luther*, 445. Quote is from "Commentary on John (1537–1540)," LW 22:339; WA 47:66,23–24.

22. "Sermons on the First Epistle of Peter (1523)," LW 30:19; WA 12:275,5–15.

shepherds to the manger and the swaddling clothes, and the star pointed the magi to Bethlehem.[23]

Clearly, Luther was not a Marcionite who rejected the Old Testament. Instead, he considered only the Old Testament as Scripture, while the New Testament was "proclamation" (*kerygma*). As he stated, "it is the intention of all the apostles and evangelists in the whole New Testament to chase and drive us into the Old Testament, which alone is what they call 'Holy Scripture.' For the New Testament by its nature was supposed to be only physical, living words and not writing."[24] This was not a slight against the New Testament, or a questioning of its authority. Rather, he elevated the importance of the Old Testament, unlike his contemporaries, who treated the Old Testament as a collection of stories pertinent only to the people of Israel.[25] Luther also considered the Old Testament relevant for modern people because it served as a source of the apostles' teaching

> based on the Old Testament, and there is no word in the New Testament that does not look back into the Old Testament where it was first told. We have noted in the Epistle how the divinity of Christ is confirmed by the apostle from the Old Testament passages. For the New Testament is nothing but a revelation of the Old; it is as if somebody had a sealed letter and later on broke it open.[26]

Of course, Luther had justification for labeling only the Old Testament as Scripture, since Jesus and the Apostles also consistently referred to the Old Testament as the Scriptures. There was a difference between Scripture and *kerygma*, and this distinction reinforced his understanding of the difference between Scripture and the Word.

By distinguishing between the Old Testament as the written word and the New Testament as proclamation, Luther then observed their different target audiences. In a Postil for the fourth Sunday in Advent, he claimed that "the Old Testament or the Law was preached among the tents

23. "Gospel for Epiphany (1522)," LW 52:205–6; WA 10.I.1:626,2–15. See also Simon Kuntze, *Die Mündlichkeit der Schrift: Eine Rekonstruktion des lutherischen Schriftprinzips* (Leipzig: Evangelische Verlagsanstalt, 2020), 89–91. For Luther, the Hebrew Scriptures were the swaddling clothes which held the Christ Child. "A Brief Instruction on What to Look for and Expect in the Gospels (1521)," LW 35:122; WA 10.1.1:15,4–5.

24. "Advent Postil (1522)," LW 75:39; WA 10.1.2:34,27–35,3. See also William A. Graham, *Beyond the Written Word: Oral Aspects of Scripture in the History of Religion* (Cambridge: Cambridge University Press, 1987), 145.

25. See LW 75:39, note 36. See also Timothy J. Wengert, *Reading the Bible with Martin Luther: An Introductory Guide* (Grand Rapids: Baker Academic, 2013), 14.

26. "Christmas Postils (1522)," LW 52:41: WA 10.I.1:181,20–182,1.

at Mount Sinai to the Jews alone. But John's voice is heard in the wilderness, freely and openly, under the heavens, before all the world."[27] The Old Testament was an "in-house" document, while the New Testament was in the public domain, meant for all the world. As Simon Kuntze observes, "The oral Gospel is proclaimed loudly and publicly to the whole world; the written law is given only to the Jewish people."[28] Yet regardless of the different target audiences, both the written word of Scripture and the oral word of proclamation functioned the same: to reveal human sinfulness and the forgiveness, life, and salvation found in God. As Wengert notes, "For Luther, the entire Old Testament was filled with believers and sinners, with commands and promises, with terror and comfort. In this way, it is simply filled to overflowing with Christ, the Savior of the world, because it is filled with believers clinging to God's promises."[29] The Scriptures are overflowing with Christ, the Living Word.

SCRIPTURE ONLY (*SOLA SCRIPTURA*)

The slogan *sola Scriptura* (Scripture only) is one of the defining marks of the sixteenth-century reformation movements. Luther simply "presumed that Scripture held the ultimate authority for the proclamation of God's Word."[30] Perhaps he assumed too much, however, since the church often gave itself ultimate authority over Scripture, especially when it came to dealing with heresy. As B.A. Gerrish states,

> The only way to check heresy was by an appeal to an authority apart from Scripture, for (notoriously) the heretic makes use of Scripture no less than the orthodox. The Bible remained the professed authority, but in fact there was a second authority that controlled it. Augustine repeatedly declares that his supreme norm and standard is the Scriptures: yet it is the church that decides what is and what is not Scripture, and it is the church that guarantees their authority and interprets their meaning.[31]

Moreover, unlike the teachers of the church, Luther considered only Scripture as authoritative since it alone was pure. Thus, in his commentary on 1 John he could say, "it is very rare that there are pure teachers in

---

27. "Advent Postils (1522)," LW 75:184; WA 10.I.2:204,18–27.
28. Kunzte, *Die Mündlichkeit der Schrift*, 118.
29. Wengert, *Reading the Bible with Martin Luther*, 15–16.
30. Robert Kolb, *Luther and the Stories of God: Biblical Narratives as a Foundation for Christian Living* (Grand Rapids: Baker Academic, 2012), 13.
31. Brian A. Gerrish, *The Old Protestantism and the New: Essays on the Reformation Heritage* (Chicago: University of Chicago Press, 1982), 52.

the church. Only Scripture is pure."[32] Luther gives credence to this claim when he stated, "The Holy Spirit, as you know, has deposited God's wisdom and counsel and all mysteries into the Word, and revealed these in Scripture, so that no one has an excuse. Nor must anyone seek or search for something else or learn or acquire something better or more sublime than what Scripture teaches of Jesus Christ, God's Son, our Savior, who died and rose for us."[33] The scriptures were the most important source of the Christian faith. Yet even in this passage, Luther made an important distinction between Scripture and the Word. He insisted that it was not the scriptures themselves, but the Living Word that held God's wisdom, counsel, and all mysteries. The scriptures reveal the truth found in the Word. Scriptures are the clearest revelation of God given to humanity because they are the clearest "tool" or "means" by which Christ was revealed to humanity. What was most important was the focus on Christ as the Living Word and thus God's own self-revelation of God's nature.

Nor can one claim that *sola Scriptura* was a "Reformation Discovery."[34] The foremost scholastic Roman Catholic scholar, Thomas Aquinas, along with lesser lights such as the Carmelite Guido Terreni, Gerard of Bologna, and Thomas Netter, among others, insisted upon the primacy of Scripture over patristic decrees. After the Council of Constance (1414–1418), however, some scholars, including Nicolas of Cusa, started moving away from this position, leading eventually to the Dominican Sylvester Prierias claiming that "Holy Scripture draws its power and authority from the pope . . . to say otherwise is heretical."[35] It was no wonder, then, that by the time Luther met with Cardinal Cajetan in Augsburg in 1518, Luther could rightfully complain that some in the church were placing the pope above Scripture (*supra scripturam*).[36] The question of whether the church or Scripture had ultimate authority became the main issue at the 1519 Leipzig debates. At the beginning of the Reformation, then, the reformers were the ones taking the more traditional stance, upholding Scripture over tradition. They were not the "innovators"![37] The Leipzig debate between the

---

32. "Lectures on 1 John (1527)," WA 20:745,2–3.
33. "Commentary on 1 Corinthians 15 (1533)," LW 28:77: WA 36:501,11–16.
34. Ian Christopher Levy, "The Leipzig Disputation: Masters of the Sacred Page and the Authority of Scripture," in *Luther at Leipzig: Martin Luther, the Leipzig Debate, and the Sixteenth Century Reformations*, eds. Mickey L. Mattox, Richard J. Serina, Jr, and Jonathan Mumme, Studies in Medieval and Reformation Traditions 218, gen. ed. Andrew Colin Gow (Leiden: Brill, 2019), 124.
35. Levy, "The Leipzig Disputation," 126.
36. As noted by Levy, "The Leipzig Disputation," 126.
37. Brecht suggests that the Reformers were "in extreme tension with the dominant theory of the church at that time." Martin Brecht, *Martin Luther: His Road to Reformation 1483–1521*, trans. James Schaaf (Minneapolis: Fortress, 1985), 322.

Roman Catholic theologian Johannes Eck and Luther simply clarified the scriptural principle for the reformers. After studying the conclusion to this debate in Leipzig, Melanchthon laid out the "hermeneutical principle of 'sola Scriptura'" for the reformers,[38] even though he surprisingly never used the term himself.[39] Yet the Wittenberg reformers felt that where people encountered the gospel, the Bible alone provided the sure and trustworthy Word of Life. Other sources might not direct the reader or preacher to Christ in the clear fashion that did Scripture.

Even though Luther uses the term sola Scriptura, his focus was on the message that Scripture conveyed to its readers and hearers. Based on the frequency of the use of terms he defined with sola, it is clear that he focused much more on sola gratia (grace alone) and sola fide (faith alone) than sola Scriptura (Scripture alone). Studying the statistics, Wengert concluded:

> Using the critical Weimar edition of Luther's works online and its search engine, one can now determine how often Luther used these phrases in all their permutations in his Latin works. The results? Sola gratia: two hundred times; sola fide: twelve hundred times; sola Scriptura: twenty times. Twenty times! Moreover, a closer look at those twenty occurrences leads to even more surprises. Two are references not to Luther's writings but to his opponents. Both Cardinal Cajetan in 1518 and Erasmus of Rotterdam in 1524 offered to debate Luther (more or less) on the basis of sola Scriptura, using Scripture alone. So that leaves just eighteen cases.
>
> Of these remaining occurrences, some actually undercut the notion that Scripture was the only authority for Luther.[40]

Hövelmann echoes this conclusion, suggesting that for Luther, "the authority of the Scripture (sola Scriptura) is founded on the fact that God's word is the gospel of Jesus Christ alone (solus Christus) who justifies the sinful, condemned person by a word of grace through Christ himself (sola gratia) and it is acquired by faith (sola fide)."[41] Luther's use of sola Scriptura was thus only a part of the story and should not be taken by itself, apart from the other familiar "solas" of the Reformation tradition. When he used

---

38. Volker Leppin, "Papst, Konzil, und Kirchenväter. Die Autoritätenfrage in der Liepziger Disputation," in *Die Leipziger Disputation 1519*, Markus Hein and Armin Kohnle, eds. (Leipzig: Evangelische Verlagsanstalt, 2011), 117–24.

39. Timothy J. Wengert, *Word of Life: Introducing Lutheran Hermeneutics* (Minneapolis: Fortress Press, 2019), 53.

40. Wengert, *Reading the Bible with Martin Luther*, 16–17.

41. Hövelmann, *Kernstellen der Lutherbibel*, 37. See also Paul Althaus, "Der Geist der Lutherbibel," *Lutherjahrbuch* 16 (1934), 4.

the phrase, he was trying to make the point that the ultimate authority of the Word of God must always be Christ the Living Word as revealed in Scripture, over long-held traditions or mystical experiences. It would be more appropriate, therefore, claims Wengert, to replace *sola Scriptura* with *Solus Christus* (Christ alone) or even *solo Verbo* (the Word alone), "where 'the Word' was for Luther not simply the Bible but its proclamation."[42] It was the life-giving gospel that was most important.

The Roman theologians accepted the authority of Scripture, as has been already noted. But in matters of doctrine, it was considered one of the authorities, not the only authority. Despite the push for emphasizing papal authority over that of Scripture, in an attempt to condemn the writings of John Wycliff and Jan Huss at the Council of Constance, and led by Cusa, Prierias, and others in the years following, the church officially placed Scripture over authority. Canon law itself insisted that "papal decretals were authoritative only to the extent that they are in conformity with Holy Scripture."[43] What the Roman church feared, however, was that based on the principle of *sola Scriptura*, anyone would feel that they had the right to interpret Scripture for themselves, thus giving the individual as much authority to interpret Scripture as the church. Johannes Tetzel, Luther's bitter opponent in the indulgences debate that sparked the Reformation in 1517, and Johannes Eck, Luther's opponent at the 1519 Leipzig debate, both raised this very concern.[44] In response, they overemphasized the authority of the church and the pope over Scripture and insisted that the pope alone had the right to interpret Scripture. This was the same concern

42. Wengert, *Reading the Bible with Martin Luther*, 19. See also Willem Jan Kooiman, *Luther and the Bible*, trans. John Schmidt (Philadelphia: Muhlenberg, 1961), 42: "*Sola Scriptura* (Scripture alone) is the same as *solus Christus* (Christ alone), and that is again the same as *sola gratia* (grace alone) and *sola fide* (faith alone)."

43. "The canon *Sunt quidam dicentes* (C. 25. q. 1, c. 6) stated that whereas the pope is ordinarily entitled to make new laws, in those instances where Christ, the apostles, or the holy fathers have already clearly defined something, the pope cannot pass any new law, but must defend these precedents. And what is more, were the pope to attempt to undermine apostolic doctrine, his error would deprive his judgment of any force. For salvation consists in not deviating from the statutes of the fathers and preserving the rule of faith." (Causa 25, q. 1, c. 6; *Corpus iuris canonici*, Emil Friedberg, ed. 2 Volumes (Leipzig: Bernhard Tauchnitz, 1881. Reprint Graz: Academische Druck-u. Verlaganstalt, 1959), 1:1008.) Quote is from Levy, "The Leipzig Disputation," 127.

44. David Bagchi, *Luther's Earliest Opponents: Catholic Controversialists, 1518–1525* (Minneapolis: Fortress Press, 1991), 86. See also Michael Root, "The Catholic Reception of the Leipzig Disputation," in *Luther at Leipzig: Martin Luther, the Leipzig Debate, and the Sixteenth Century Reformations,* eds. Mickey L. Mattox, Richard J. Serina, Jr, and Jonathan Mumme, Studies in Medieval and Reformation Traditions 218, gen. ed. Andrew Colin Gow (Leiden: Brill, 2019), 297.

that the church had with vernacular translations of the Bible—anyone could claim that Holy Scripture supported their own interpretations and doctrines. Lost in the debate, however, was that the authority was found, not in any writing or any church official, but in Christ the Living Word.

CHRIST AT THE CENTER

Luther did not subscribe to a rigid *sola Scriptura* principle that located authority in a written text only and that shunned reason, tradition, and interpretive aids such as glosses, commentary, and marginal notes. All were helpful in properly understanding the text. Yet his foundational principle for the source and foundation of authority was "Christ the Living Word." It was the person of whom Scripture speaks who was the source of authority. Too often, however, authority is mistakenly located in the document that bears witness to the person who holds authority, rather than in the person with authority. For example, consider legal contracts. It is commonly assumed that a contract is valid because it is *signed*, thus making the transaction legal. However, legally signed documents only have authority because *the signatories stand behind the signed document*. Thus, handshake agreements also carry a certain legal weight because authority is located in the promises of each person in the agreement. That is how the reformers looked at the authority of Scripture. Scripture had authority because of the authority and promises of the Living Word standing behind it. God's promises in Scripture make it authoritative. In speaking these words of promise, God acts authoritatively to create new realities. It is a mistake, then, to focus all of one's attention on the authority of a document while overlooking the person making the authoritative promise. Thus, Luther and the Wittenberg circle recognized that Christ was at the heart of Scripture's authority. It led Luther to say, "take Christ out of Scripture, and what will you find left in them?"[45] Ten years earlier, in his Romans commentary, Luther had said much the same: "[T]he entire Scripture deals only with Christ everywhere."[46] While this is not technically true, as Luther himself realized,[47] the point he was making was that the Scripture points to God in Christ, just as John the Baptist pointed to the Christ (John 1:29). That is where one finds the voice of authority.

Carl Braaten has noted that Luther's grounding of authority in the person who speaks the reality-creating word of promise, rather than in a

---

45. "Bondage of the Will (1525)," LW 33:26; WA 18:606,29.
46. "Romans Commentary (1515–1516)," LW 25, 405; WA 56:414,15.
47. Barth, *The Theology of Martin Luther,* 443.

document, has too often been overlooked, in favor of granting authority to Scripture itself. Braaten states:

> Thus in Protestant orthodoxy a shift away from Luther occurs in the account of Scripture's authority. For Luther, as we have seen, its authority resides in its Gospel content. Scriptures are a means of grace. They are to be judged entirely in terms of Luther's famous formula *"was Christum treibt"* (what conveys Christ). For the seventeenth-century orthodox dogmaticians, Scriptures are authoritative because of their divine inspiration and inerrancy. Because this doctrine became the official teaching of almost all Lutheran and Reformed churches, and remains valid to this day, except where the historical-critical approach to Scripture has occasioned a new doctrine, it is well to consider some of the essential features of the doctrine of Scripture in Protestant orthodoxy.[48]

Braaten is right. In Luther's mind, Scripture was, first and foremost, the place where a person experienced Christ and Christ's life-giving Word. Scripture's authority is rooted in its author—not its own pages—and what the author does to a person when God speaks.

Luther vividly illustrated his focus on encountering the life-giving promises of Christ in his discussion about the Letter of James, when he insisted that the key was found in *was Christum treibet* (what pushes or drives Christ) into a person's heart.[49] While Luther labeled James as an epistle of straw,[50] considering it did give him an opportunity to clarify his scriptural hermeneutic. Wengert succinctly spells out how "what pushes Christ" is the "authoritative center" of Scripture: "This interpretive key to Scripture [*was Christus treibet*], best summarized by the phrase *solus Christus* (Christ alone), contrasts with Luther's reticence concerning and occasional rejection of the phrase *sola Scriptura* (Scripture alone), which some later Christians invoked to support more literalistic approaches to Scripture. Indeed, Luther was far more interested in God's Word *proclaimed* and not merely shut up in a book."[51] God's intent for Scripture was to clearly spell out where, and in whom, one could encounter the Living Word.

48. Carl E. Braaten, "Prolegomena to Christian Dogmatics," in *Christian Dogmatics*, ed. Carl E. Braaten and Robert W. Jenson, vol. 1 (Philadelphia: Fortress Press, 2011), 66.
49. "Preface to the Letters of James and Jude (1546/1522), "LW 35:396; WA DB 7:384,25–27. The LW translates *treiben* as "inculcate"—thus missing the force of Luther's statement.
50. "Preface to the New Testament (1522)," LW 35:362; WA DB 6:10,29–35. Wengert notes that in the 1534 preface to the New Testament in the Luther Bible, Luther drops these comments about James, and after 1539, these comments were also dropped from separate printings of the New Testament. Wengert, *Reading the Bible with Martin Luther*, 2.
51. Wengert, *Reading the Bible with Martin Luther*, vii–viii.

THE INERRANCY OF SCRIPTURE

Luther placed great stress upon the centrality of Scripture, since it was the manger and swaddling cloths that held the Christ. Yet he does not cling to an inerrant or even a literal interpretation of the Bible.[52] Scott Hendrix makes the case that:

> Luther was not a literalist in the mode of Christian fundamentalists who believe the infallible original of the text of the Bible can be determined and for whom every word is sacred. But neither was Luther a modern textual critic for whom the Old Testament was primarily or exclusively Hebrew Scripture. Instead, Luther treated Hebrew Scripture as the "Old Testament," the first part of the Christian Bible. In that regard, Luther was like the authors of the New Testament books, who cited or alluded to more than 300 "Old Testament" passages to illustrate or prove their points.[53]

Hans-Martin Barth echoes this, claiming that Luther "did not believe in a verbal inspiration of individual passages in Scripture. For him the very existence of the Bible was a stopgap measure; the 'putting into writing' of the gospel could be injurious to the living character of the message."[54] Scripture gained its prominence when it proclaimed the gospel. It could not "push Christ" into hearts if it remained a closed book.

With his governing principle of the Word driving the living and breathing Christ, and thus life, into people, Luther therefore had no trouble questioning whether certain books of the Bible, such as the Letters of Hebrews, James, and Jude, along with the Revelation of John, were worthy to be in the Bible. He felt that they too quickly emphasized law, works, or even fear, pushing the gospel into the background—unless they were read in the context of books such as Romans and John. Nevertheless, pushing his own personal feelings aside, he followed the tradition of the church and continued to include these "unworthy" books in the canon of Scripture while still making it clear that they were not of the same caliber as the other New Testament writings. To denote their lesser status, in both the 1522 New Testament and in the Luther Bibles published in his lifetime, these books were placed at the end of the New Testament canon and left unnumbered, as if they were appendices to the rest of the writings. That order has stayed to this day.

---

52. Graham, *Beyond the Written Word*, 146.
53. Scott H. Hendrix, *Martin Luther: Visionary Reformer* (New Haven: Yale University Press, 2015), 227.
54. Barth, *The Theology of Martin Luther*, 439.

Luther's willingness to question and even "categorize" certain books as less inspired than other books is not in line with a claim to the inerrancy of Scripture. The proclaimed Word's effect on believers' hearts, not questions of literal inerrancy, occupied his mind. Michael Reu felt that "Luther did not predicate inerrancy nor lack of contradiction with regard to the transmitted Hebrew or Greek text, but only with regard to the original documents of the prophets or the apostles, as for example, St. Paul, of the words they dictated."[55] While Reu's approach follows the arguments of Lutheran pietism in the nineteenth and twentieth centuries, it nevertheless makes the mistake of focusing on the authority of a document rather than the authority of the author and giver of the document. Literal inerrancy, in and of itself, does not guarantee an authoritative text.

Attempts to preserve the authority of Scripture by surrounding it with the fence of inerrancy are most often based on a definition of inerrancy as "being without error" (Latin, *in* + *erros*). This has been the predominant definition of the word in the last two centuries. According to Arthur Carl Piepkorn, however, "'Inerrancy' itself is a relatively young word. . . . in its etymological sense [inerrant] is actually a poetic, evocative, metaphorical term. It is appropriate to a person or a hypostatization, to the author of a book, but not to a book as a book. . . . As long as we realize that 'inerrancy' is used metaphorically of the Sacred Scriptures to describe them as 'not wandering away' from the truth, well and good."[56] The *Oxford English Dictionary* actually lists the English adjective "inerrant" (corresponding to the Ciceronian *inerrans*) in 1652 in technical astronomical reference to a fixed star. It was not until 1837, according to the same source, that "inerrant" was used in the modern sense of "exempt from error, free from mistake, infallible."[57] Thus, based on Piepkorn's argument, one could suggest that Luther would be able to say that Scripture inerrantly (without fail) works to push Christ into a person's heart, but he would not say that it was "without error." This idea is reinforced when the word "inerrancy" is compared to the similarly used word, "infallibility." Infallible, like inerrant, also has two meanings: it can be defined as "incapable of error (with regard to persons, their judgments, etc.)," but it can also be defined as "not liable to fail, unfailing (of things)." Thus, while the pope might be properly called infallible in matters of doctrine, in the sense of "without

55. Johann Michael Reu, *Luther and the Scriptures* (Columbus: Wartburg Press, 1944), 103.

56. Arthur Carl Piepkorn, *The Sacred Scriptures and The Lutheran Confessions: Selected Writings of Arthur Carl Piepkorn*, Volume 2, ed. Philip J. Secker (Mansfield: CEC Press, 2007), 29.

57. Piepkorn, *The Sacred Scriptures and The Lutheran Confessions*, 29. See also "inerrant, adj." in *Oxford English Dictionary*, 2nd ed, eds John Simpson and Edmund Weiner (Oxford: Clarendon Press, 1989).

error," when it comes to things (i.e., Scripture), infallible has the meaning of "not liable to fail, or unfailing"—in other words, Scripture unfailingly, or without fail, points to Christ and pushes Christ into human hearts.[58] This approach more closely reflects Luther's understanding of Scripture. Scripture, without fail, pointed to and pushed Christ the Living Word into the hearts of its hearers to transform them. Scripture was the Word of God, not because it was without error but because it "does God"[59] to humanity.

SUMMARY

Luther did not directly equate the "Word" with "Scripture." While the Word is found most clearly in Scripture, he understood the Word primarily as a living, life-changing person, Jesus the Christ. Using an example from Luke's story of the nativity of Christ, Luther observed that when the shepherds came to view the newborn, they worshipped the Christ child (the Word), and not the manger (the Scripture) that held the infant Jesus. As he stated it, "Simple and lowly are those swaddling cloths, but dear is the treasure, Christ, who lies in them."[60] The guiding question that was always on Luther's mind when reading and hearing Scripture, then, was "how is Christ being pushed or driven into human hearts?" How is Christ *experienced*? He was concerned with the Word that, in speaking and being spoken, created new realities. It was not just the written Word of Scripture that was important. Even more important was that people would experience and encounter the Word. As such, it would be inappropriate to describe Scripture as inerrant or infallible. Rather, the Holy Spirit, breathing through the Word, breathes into (Latin: *in-spires*) people and "does the gospel" in and for them. Holy Scripture is thus meant to drive people into relationship with God as Christ is driven into their hearts. Luther would have it no other way.

---

58. See "infallible, adj. and n." in *Oxford English Dictionary*.
59. Gerhard Forde, *Theology is for Proclamation* (Minneapolis: Fortress Press, 1990), 2–8. See also Wengert, *Reading the Bible with Martin Luther*, 10.
60. "Preface to the Old Testament (1545)," LW 35:236; WA DB 8:13,7–8.

2.

Luther the Interpreter and Translator

"I will go further with my boasting. I can expound psalms and prophets; they cannot. I can translate; they cannot."[1]

"I wanted to speak German, not Latin or Greek, since it was German I had undertaken to speak in the translation."[2]

INTRODUCTION

Luther considered himself a skilled translator, and he didn't mind boasting about it. Translation was an art that he finely honed with thousands of hours of practice. His very first published work, in fact, which came off the press early in 1517, was a German translation of the penitential Psalms.[3] He was committed to proclaiming the gospel, so that all could hear with their ears and eyes, in words and images, the life-giving Word. Translating was thus a high priority for him. But it was not enough to translate literally the text from Latin, Greek, and Hebrew. He wanted to translate in such a way that the Bible came alive for people. As Roland Bainton notes, "Judea was transplanted to Saxony, and the road from Jericho to Jerusalem ran through the Thuringian forest."[4] His whole career involved one translation project—or revision of a translation—after another. Even after the first edition of the *Lutherbibel* came out in 1534,

---

1. "On Translating: An Open Letter (1530)," LW 35:186; WA 30.II:635,20–21.
2. "On Translating: An Open Letter (1530)," LW 35:188; WA 30.II:637,3–4.
3. Timothy J. Wengert, *Word of Life: Introducing Lutheran Hermeneutics* (Minneapolis: Fortress Press, 2019), 20. The translation of these Psalms was accompanied by a commentary.
4. Roland H. Bainton, *Here I Stand: A Life of Martin Luther* (Nashville: Abingdon, 1950), 257.

he and his colleagues continued to make revisions and improvements to the translation and to the way the text appeared on the page. While he was busy with a multitude of other tasks, such as writing, teaching, and traveling to settle disputes—responding to opponents who felt he had taken the reforms too far or not far enough—he always had a translation project underway. At the most basic level, he translated because he felt that nothing was more important than people grasping the Gospel in their hearts, and that required hearing the Gospel in their own language.

INERRANT TRANSLATIONS AND THE BIBLE'S SELF-INTERPRETING FUNCTION

When translating the Bible, Luther sought not a word-for-word, literal translation, but a translation of the meaning of each verse of the Bible. One might describe this as a translation meant to help the reader or hearer experience the Living Word, rather than a translation of the written word. Wengert is thus inerrantly correct (in the sense of "without fail")[5] when he notes, "Before the term was invented, Luther was also a proponent of 'dynamic equivalencies' in translation. That is, he understood that one could not simply import Hebraic or Greek syntax and grammar into German and assume such literal translation was legitimate."[6] Luther's primary concern was to make the gospel, found everywhere in the Bible, clear to its readers and hearers. He wanted the Bible to breathe and speak and convey the gospel! Unlike the medievalists who were afraid they might not do justice to the sacred text if it were not a literal, word-for-word translation, Luther and his Wittenberg colleagues were willing to move away from a literal translation when it did not make the text's meaning as clear as possible.[7] In his "Preface to the Book of Job," for example, Luther observed that no one would understand the Bible if it contained only a literal, word-for-word translation.[8] If that were the case, the translation would be useless. Word-for-word translations are like the results obtained by rudimentary computer translation programs, where the meaning is often lost in the attempt to translate each word correctly. Translating meanings, on the other hand, requires trained translators grounded in theology so that the "living voice of the gospel" (viva vox evangelii) would be heard, without fail.

5. See Chapter 1, pages 21–22, for a discussion on the different meanings of "inerrant."
6. Wengert, Word of Life, 24–25.
7. Willem Jan Kooiman, Luther and the Bible (Philadelphia: Muhlenberg Press, 1961), 101.
8. "Preface to the Book of Job (1545/1524)," LW 35:252: WA DB 10.I:6,2–5.

Luther's insistence that Holy Scripture interprets itself (*scriptura sacra sui ipsius interpres*) is best understood in light of the constant, reverberating emphasis on the Living Voice of the gospel. Luther was constantly asking, "Where is the gospel found in this particular text?" The Gospel, embedded as it was in all Scripture, was the starting point for a proper translation of the message of the Bible. As Luther stated, "the Holy Scripture itself on its own, to the greatest extent possible, is easy to understand, clearly and plainly, being its own interpreter [*sui ipsius interpres*], in that it puts all statements of human beings to the test, judging and enlightening, as is written in Psalm 119[:130]."[9] Likewise, he insisted that Scripture "wants to be interpreted by a comparison of passages from everywhere, and understood under its own direction. The safest of all methods for discerning the meaning of Scripture is to work for it by drawing together and scrutinizing passages."[10] Thus, Hans-Martin Barth concludes that Scripture "interprets itself by articulating the witness to Christ so that it can be understood. Christ is, 'so to speak, the matter of Scripture in person.'"[11] Moreover, because Christ is in the midst of Scripture, not only does Scripture interpret itself, but it also goes on to investigate its readers, seeking to bring them into an experience of Scripture's message, even when readers, with their own agendas, think they are the ones doing the investigating. Luther made this very point in his First Psalms Lectures when he observed, "the strength of Scripture is this, that it is not changed into him who studies it, but that it transforms its lover into itself and its strengths."[12] Whenever the reader interprets Scripture in the way they want, said Luther, they were making a "wax nose out of Holy Scripture."[13] The reader, not the text, is examined and, in the process, transformed. The Holy Spirit, and not the reader, exegetes Scripture, claimed Luther,[14] and proclaims gospel to the reader. As Roy Harrisville states, with this approach Luther introduced a "radically different interpretive model, for now the roles of text and interpreter were reversed: The text, not the exegete, functioned as interpreter; the text interpreted the exegete."[15] Encountering the Gospel in the text meant that the reader, not the text, is investigated.

9. "Assertions Against the Bull of Leo (1520)," WA 7:97,20–24.
10. "Lectures on Deuteronomy (1525)," LW 9:21; WA 14:556,26–29.
11. Hans-Martin Barth, *The Theology of Martin Luther: A Critical Assessment* (Minneapolis: Fortress Press, 2013), 445.
12. "First Lectures on the Psalms (1513)," LW 10:332; WA 3:397,9–11.
13. "An Exposition of the Lord's Prayer for Simple Laymen (1519)," LW 42:63; WA 2:116,25–26.
14. The Holy Spirit, Luther claimed, is the "true exegete." "Sermon for the Gospel on Easter Monday (1534)," LW 77:57; WA 21:236,10–12.
15. Roy A. Harrisville, "Bible Interpretation," in *Dictionary of Luther and the Lutheran Traditions*, ed. Timothy J. Wengert (Grand Rapids: Baker Academic, 2017), 87.

The interpretation and translation of Scripture—by keeping the Gospel front and center or letting Scripture interpret itself—was not an easy task. Luther's struggle to emphasize the core of the Gospel in each text he translated is indicative of this difficulty. As Gerhard Forde noted, "The fact that scripture is to be understood as self-interpreting in no way means therefore that the interpreter has nothing to do. On the contrary, it makes the task of interpreting much more demanding and exacting,"[16] so that God's Word, and not human words, are heard and experienced. Thus, apart from understanding Scripture from its very heart—that is, the Gospel, where one encounters the life-giving Christ—it would be difficult to understand, let alone translate, scriptures in the way Luther intended.

An example of Luther's focus on translating meanings rather than words, and in a way that allows Scripture to interpret itself, is clearly illustrated in his addition of the word "*allein*" (in Latin, *solum*) to his translation of Romans 3:28. In defending this addition, Luther insisted that his addition best captured the important *idea* that one is justified by faith *alone*, even though such a translation was not literally word-for-word accurate. As he himself noted, "Here, in Romans 3[:28], I knew very well that the word *solum* is not in the Greek or Latin text; the papists did not have to teach me that. It is a fact that these four letters *s o l a* are not there. And these blockheads stare at them like cows at a new gate. At the same time they do not see that it conveys the sense of the text; it belongs there if the translation is to be clear and vigorous."[17] Adding the "alone" (*allein*) to the verse most accurately translated, without fail, the powerful idea of God's grace, even if it did not accurately translate, without error, the literal words of the Greek text.

TRANSLATING AS A TEAM PROJECT

Luther, like all who have taken up the task of translating, knew it was difficult work.[18] In his "Defense of the Translation of the Psalms," he quipped, "actually doing the translation is a wholly different art and task from that of simply criticizing and finding fault with someone else's translation."[19]

16. Gerhard O. Forde, *A More Radical Gospel: Essays on Eschatology, Authority, Atonement, and Ecumenism*, eds. Paul Rorem et al, Lutheran Quarterly Books (Minneapolis: Fortress Press, 2017), 74.
17. "On Translating: An Open Letter (1530)," LW 35:188; WA 30.II:636,31–637,2.
18. In a letter to Nicholas von Amsdorf on January 13, 1522, while working on translating the New Testament, he said, "I shall translate the Bible, although I have here shouldered a burden beyond my power." LW 48:363; WA BR 2:423,48 (No. 449).
19. "Defense of the Translation of the Psalms (1531)," LW 35, 223; WA 38:17,16–18.

The translation of a sacred book was thus best done by a team, who could together discern when a good translation required a fairly free translation and when a more literal or technical reading of the text was needed,[20] especially when important teachings of the church or the Gospel were being scrutinized.[21] Inspiration gained from a freer translation of ideas was not enough when heresy was at stake.

There were many reasons for Luther's reliance on a team to translate the Bible. First, the task was simply too much for any one person.[22] In a letter to his friend Nicholas von Amsdorf, while working on his translation of the New Testament, Luther wrote,

> I will not be able to touch the Old Testament all by myself and without the co-operation of all of you. Therefore if it could somehow be arranged that I could have a secret room with any one of you, I would soon come and with your help would translate the whole book from the beginning, so that it would be a worthy translation for Christians to read. For I hope we will give a better translation to our Germany than the Latins have. It is a great and worthy undertaking on which we all should work, since it is a public matter and should be dedicated to the common good.[23]

From the beginning, Luther saw translation as a team effort. Even with the *Septembertestament,* his translation of the New Testament into German, Luther consulted with others. He did the bulk of the work himself while still in the Wartburg castle, but when he returned to Wittenberg from his exile, he consulted with one of Germany's best Greek scholars, Philip Melanchthon. In a letter to Georg Spalatin in March of 1522, he wrote, "Philip and I have begun now to polish the whole thing. It will be (God willing) a worthy piece of work. We shall use your services sometime[s] for finding a right word, so be prepared. [But remember] to give us simple terms, not those [used at] the castle or court, for this book should be famous for its simplicity." In the same letter, he asked Spalatin

20. See, for example, "Defense of the Translation of the Psalms (1531)," LW 35: 209; WA 38:9,6–14.
21. "Defense of the Translation of the Psalms (1531)," LW 35:216; WA 38:13,3–4. See also his comments in Table Talks: WA TR 2 (No. 2771a); WA TR 3 (No. 3794); WA TR 5 (No. 5521); and Otto Albrecht's observations concerning Luther's way of translating, in WA DB 6:lxxv–lxxxiii. Wengert notes that "at many important points Luther made the translation more difficult by preserving Hebraisms and Hellenisms that earlier translations had often omitted." Timothy J. Wengert, "Martin Luther's September Testament: The Untold Story," *The Report: A Journal of German-American History* 47 (2017), 51.
22. This remains true today. English translations, from the 1611 Authorized (or King James) Version of the Bible to authoritative modern translations, are generally carried out by large teams of translators.
23. LW 48: 363; WA BR 2:423,50–56 (No. 449). "Letter to Nicholas Amsdorf, January 13, 1522."

to also find the German names of the gems mentioned in Revelation 21, using his resources in the elector's treasury.[24] Two months later, he again approached Spalatin, asking him for an understandable term in German for the word "eunuch."[25] He also asked Melanchthon to take on the task of converting and translating the coins mentioned in the New Testament and to provide a map of Palestine as an illustration, but that proved unsuccessful.[26] In letters to both Amsdorf and Melanchthon, dated January 13, 1522, he suggested that the Wittenberg scholars get together for a secretive "translating session," to deal with some of the more difficult texts, making them easier to understand for all Christians.[27] The work on the preparation, and then revision, of the German (Luther) Bible was also done by a committee, which Luther nicknamed his "Sanhedrin."[28] The translating team consisted of Johann Bugenhagen, Justus Jonas, Caspar Cruciger, Philip Melanchthon, and Matthäus Aurogallus, with occasional assistance from Johann Förster and Bernhard Ziegler, and with Georg Rörer as the recording secretary.[29] The task was simply beyond the ability of one person.

Second, Luther's biblical language skills, while honed over time, were not at the same level—at least in terms of formal grammar and the rules of linguistics—as the Greek and Hebrew language professors at the University of Wittenberg. As he himself admitted, he basically learned Hebrew by himself, by comparing the Hebrew text with the Latin.[30] He started learning Greek after mastering the basics of Hebrew, learning from his colleague and instructor Melanchthon.[31] It only made sense, therefore, to

---

24. "Letter to Spalatin, March 30, 1522," LW 49:4; WA BR 2:490,8–12 (No. 470). See also "Letter to Spalatin, May 10, 1522," WA BR 2:524,5–7 (No. 488).
25. "Letter to Spalatin, May 15, 1522," WA BR 2:527,37–39.
26. "Letter to Spalatin, March 30, 1522," LW 49:4: WA BR 2:490,12–15 (No. 470). Luther repeated this request to Spalatin in a letter of May 10. 1522. WA BR 2:524,5–7 (No. 488). See also Martin Brecht, *Martin Luther: Shaping and Defining the Reformation, 1521–1532*, trans. James L. Schaaf (Minneapolis: Fortress Press, 1990), 47.
27. "Letter to Amsdorf, January 13, 1522," LW 48:363; WA BR 2:423,51–55; and "Letter to Melanchthon, January 13, 1522," LW 48:372; WA BR 2:427,128–30 (No. 450).
28. "Sanhedrin," from the Greek word "sunedrion" literally means a "sitting together." In the New Testament it was commonly used to denote the Jewish judicial and administrative body of seventy elders.
29. "History of Luther, Sermons by Johannes Mathesius (1566)," LW CV 475. Chapter 4 will deal with this "editorial committee" in more detail. See also Stephan Füssel, *The Bible in Pictures: Illustrations from the Workshop of Lucas Cranach (1534)* (Cologne: Taschen, 2009), 25.
30. "Table Talks (1530)," WA TR 1:525,14–17 (No. 1040).
31. "Lectures on Galatians (1519)," LW 27:377; WA 2:595,18–20. Here, Luther humorously calls Melanchthon a youngster in body, but an "old man of great age" (*senex venerabili mentis canicie*) in intellect.

rely on others in the "Wittenberg team"[32] who were much more proficient in Greek and Latin than he was. Melanchthon was the Greek scholar at the University of Wittenberg, Cruciger the Chaldaean scholar, and Aurogallus (Goldhahn) the Hebrew scholar.[33] While Luther was more competent than many of the scholastic theologians beyond Wittenberg who attacked his theology and his translations, many of the humanist scholars had studied Greek and Hebrew in school while Luther was polishing his Latin.[34] In fact, Luther's translations came primarily from the Bible he was most familiar with, the Latin Vulgate—even though he himself had by then become familiar with Greek and Hebrew.[35] This was the Bible he grew up with and that he knew intimately from his time as a monk.

Third, a challenge that all translators—and not just the Wittenberg team—faced in the late fifteenth and sixteenth centuries was the lack of a standardized, common German language.[36] It was a language-in-progress. While Emperor Maximilian and other German courts were working toward a common, acceptable form of German that all could understand, it was a difficult task. Each territory thought their German dialect was the best. Centrally located in Germany, the Saxon territories thus had an advantage, in that their German could be more readily understood by both its northern and southern neighbors. The Saxon German was therefore a convenient starting point.[37] Luther commented, in one of his Table Talks, that "I speak in agreement with the way [German is used] in the Saxon court, and which is also favored by the princes and kings of Germany. It is therefore the most widely used version of the language. Maximilian [the Emperor] and Frederick [the Wise] have been able to unite all the local dialects from the entire territory of the empire into this one form. Consequently, I can now be understood in different parts of our country."[38] From Luther's own account, it was the developing court

---

32. The term is borrowed from Robert Kolb, *Martin Luther and the Enduring Word of God: The Wittenberg School and Its Scripture-Centered Proclamation* (Grand Rapids: Baker Academic, 2016), 210, and *Luther's Wittenberg World: The Reformer's Family, Friends, Followers, and Foes* (Minneapolis: Fortress Press, 2018), esp. 45–85.

33. Kolb, *Martin Luther and the Enduring Word of God*, 210. See also "History of Luther, Sermons by Johannes Mathesius (1566)," LW CV 593.

34. Willem Jan Kooiman, *Luther and the Bible* (Philadelphia: Muhlenberg Press, 1961), 92.

35. Kolb, *Martin Luther and the Enduring Word of God*, 211.

36. Kooiman states that "there was no single German language. Several local dialects were striving for supremacy." Kooiman, *Luther and the Bible,* 96. One gets a taste of the lack of standardization by reading the German of Ulrich Zwingli of Zurich, Martin Bucer of Strasbourg, and Luther. Add to that a Dutch version, and the challenge immediately becomes clear.

37. Kooiman, *Luther and the Bible*, 99.

38. "Table Talks (1530)," WA TR 1:524,42–525,4 (No. 1040).

language that shaped the German used by the translation team of the Luther Bible. The Wittenberg team did not create modern high German by its translation, but it did contribute to its standardization with the best-selling Luther Bible.[39] What set the Luther Bible apart from other, earlier translations was not its standardization of the German language, but the way it interpreted the diverse books and theologies of the Bible as a unified whole.

INTERPRETING IN ORDER TO TRANSLATE

To make a good, dynamic translation of the Bible, one must first understand the text. For the Wittenberg team of translators, this involved having a consistent theological interpretation. As Bluhm stated, "Luther the interpreter preceded Luther the translator."[40] Until the message of the text is understood, one cannot translate it properly. This is most certainly the case for the Wittenberg team. They were intent on clearly communicating the gospel message, which they saw as the heart of Scripture, in the language of the people. Ingenious plays on words and stellar grammatical structure did not mean a thing if the translation did not have a heart beating with the gospel message that Christ crucified and risen is given "for you."[41] In his Genesis lectures, Luther stated this bluntly: "Therefore we encourage fearful hearts in this manner: 'Believe that you have been baptized into Christ. I absolve you from your sins in the name of Christ,

39. Debate has raged over the question of whether Luther's Bible translation or the language of the court set the standard for high German. Volz, for example, argues that "In 1578, the language of the 1545 Bible became a guideline for the German language in the "*Grammatica germanicae linguae*" of Johannes Clajus." Hans Volz, *Martin Luthers deutsche Bibel: Entstehung and Geschichte der Lutherbibel* (Hamburg: Friedrich Wittig, 1978), 194. However, Gow, among others, strongly questions the claim that Luther and the Luther Bible single-handedly "created" the modern, high German language. Andrew Colin Gow, "The Contested History of a Book: The German Bibles of the Later Middle Ages and Reformation in Legend, Ideology, and Scholarship." *Analecta Gorgiana* (Piscataway: Gorgias Press, 2012), 274–76. See also Volker Leppin, "'Biblia, das ist die ganze Heilige Schrift deutsch,' Luthers Bibelübersetzung zwischen Sakralität und Profanität," in *Protestantismus und deutsche Literatur*, Münchener Theologische Forschungen 2, Jan Rohls and Gunther Wenz, eds. (Göttingen: Vandenhoeck und Ruprecht, 2004), 13–26.
40. Heinz Bluhm, "Luther's German Bible," in *Seven-Headed Luther: Essays in Commemoration of a Quincentenary 1483–1983*, ed. Peter Newman Brooks (Oxford: Clarendon Press, 1983), 186.
41. For excellent explorations of the importance of "heart" in Luther's writings, see Birgit Stolt, "Luther's Faith of 'the Heart:' Experience, Emotion and Reason," in *The Global Luther: A Theologian for Modern Times*, ed. Christine Helmer (Minneapolis: Fortress Press, 2009), 131–50; *Martin Luthers Rhetorik des Herzens*, (Tübingen: Mohr Siebeck, 2000), and "Luther's Translation of the Bible," *Lutheran Quarterly* 28 No. 4 (Winter 2014): 373–400.

who died for you and rose again, and said: "Because I live, you will live also" ' (John 14:19). This is solid and firm consolation. In it alone the godly can find rest."[42] This is the gospel in a nutshell. Simon Kuntze recognizes this when he states, "The task of the gospel, according to Luther, is the interpretation, opening, purification and public announcement of Scripture. The gospel clearly states what stands written in the Scripture."[43] The measure of a translation's greatness, according to the reformers, was how well the translation communicated this gospel message.

Luther described the proper understanding of the gospel in the heart of Scripture in many ways. First, the gospel is all about "justification by grace through faith." This was the message that Luther claimed he discovered in reading the letter to the Romans. He explained the importance of this teaching in his 1530 exposition of Psalm 117: "If this one teaching [on justification] stands in its purity, then Christendom will also remain pure and good, undivided and unseparated; for this alone, and nothing else, makes and maintains Christendom. Everything else may be brilliantly counterfeited by false Christians and hypocrites; but where this falls, it is impossible to ward off any error or sectarian spirit."[44] Only a year later, in his *Warning to His Dear German People*, he reiterated this assertion about justification: "This doctrine, I say, they will not tolerate under any circumstances. We are able to forgo it just as little; for if this doctrine vanishes, the church vanishes. Then no error can any longer be resisted."[45] Thus, "it is nothing to be trifled with."[46] In the same time period, Luther stated, ". . .if this [first, and chief article on justification] stands, the Church stands; if it falls, the Church falls."[47] Luther stood on

---

42. "Genesis Lectures (1535–1545)," LW 8:189; WA 44:717,17–20. Luther revels in this imagery in his Sermons on John (LW Volumes 22–24).

43. Simon Kuntze, *Die Mündlichkeit der Schrift: Eine Rekonstruktion des lutherischen Schriftprinzips* (Leipzig: Evangelische Verlagsanstalt, 2020), 91.

44. "Exposition of Psalm 117 (1530)," LW 14:37: WA 31.I:255,5–10. In the 1546/1522 preface to the New Testament, Luther stated that "The gospel, then, is nothing but the preaching about Christ, Son of God and of David, true God and man, who by his death and resurrection has overcome for us the sin, death, and hell of all men who believe in him." LW 35:360; WA DB 6:7,22–26. See also Eberhard Jüngel, *Justification: The Heart of the Christian Faith. A Theological Study with an Ecumenical Perspective*, trans. Jeffery F. Cayzer (Edinburgh: T & T Clark, 2001), 17.

45. "Warning to His Dear German People (1531)," LW 47:54; WA 30.III:319,30–32. Luther also quipped, "for if we lose the doctrine of justification, we lose simply everything." "Galatians Commentary (1535)," LW 26:26; WA 40.I:72,20–21.

46. "Galatians Commentary (1535)," LW 26:112: WA 40.I:201,27.

47. "Psalms of Ascent (1532–33)," WA 40/III.352,3. In the Schmalkald Articles, Luther calls justification the first and chief article, on which "stands all that we teach and practice against the pope, the devil and the world." SA II.1.5; BC 301; BSELK 728.

the shoulders of St. Paul and his interpretation of the gospel, and for them, Romans was the very center for all Scripture. Luther went so far as to say, "This epistle is really the chief part of the New Testament, and is truly the purest gospel."[48] No wonder Bluhm argued that:

> Luther's heart and mind are permeated with Pauline theology: and it is this that gives the Luther Bible what is perhaps its most characteristic aspect, its unity. In this remarkable unity, the German Bible is quite different from the Hebrew and Greek originals and even the Christianizing Vulgate, as well as virtually all other translations into European languages. Other translations retain unchanged the diverse and sometimes unreconciled religious ideas of individual Biblical authors. Only Luther unified this book of several theologies into one integrated whole.[49]

Bluhm correctly sees Paul's theology as central to Luther's interpretative approach to translating. The focus on God's actions alone in justifying, or bringing, people into relationship with God's very self is of utmost importance. Salvation is completely dependent on God's actions. This was the "fixed star" that guided the translations of the Wittenberg team of translators.

Second, the Reformers clarified and illustrated this gospel of justification by grace through faith through the language and imagery of law and gospel.[50] Luther delighted in juxtaposing law and gospel in his writings. In the English critical edition of *Luther's Works*, for example, one finds these two terms in tension with each other over 1,800 times. Philip Melanchthon recognized the importance of these two words for Luther's theology in the oration he gave at Luther's funeral in Wittenberg on February 22, 1546. Melanchthon stated, "He showed the distinction between Law and Gospel" and then succinctly defined how Luther used these two terms.[51] Luther himself stated that whoever "masters the art

---

48. "Preface to Romans (1546/1522)," LW 35:365; WA BR 7:3,3–4.
49. Bluhm, "Luther's German Bible," 186. Wengert has argued that for Luther, "what gives interpreters authority and what gives Scripture authority is one and the same thing: the witness to Christ." Wengert, *Word of Life*, 46.
50. For two excellent explorations of Luther's understanding of Law and Gospel, see Kolb, *Martin Luther and the Enduring Word of God*, 119–25; and Timothy J. Wengert, *Reading the Bible with Martin Luther: An Introductory Guide* (Grand Rapids: Baker Academic, 2013), 29–34.
51. LW CV 43; CR 11:726–34. In the "Preface to the Second Volume of the Complete Edition of Luther's Latin Writings (1546)," Melanchthon wrote, "Here [Luther] pointed out the essential difference between Law and Gospel; here he refuted the error which was prevalent at that time in the schools and in the pulpits, which teaches that human beings merit forgiveness of sins by their own works and that human beings are righteous before God by virtue of keeping a particular mode of life, as the Pharisees taught [cf. Matt 15:1–9]. Luther thus summoned

of exact distinction between the Law and the Gospel should be called a real theologian [doctor]."[52] Preaching, at its core, was about proclaiming the proper distinction between law and gospel.[53] Luther even preached a sermon on New Year's Day in 1532 on "How Law and Gospel Are to Be Thoroughly Distinguished," and another on the second Sunday of Lent in 1539 that dealt with the Antinomian controversy.[54] In both cases, Luther insisted that there had to be a distinction—but not separation—between the two. Both are needed. Thus, it would be wrong to see them as "two stages in salvation history," but rather, "two words from God that continually address human beings in their daily lives."[55] In simplest terms, he said, "the true and proper use of the Law is to accuse and kill, whereas that of the Gospel is to give life."[56]

This distinction between law and gospel also applied to translating the Bible. In the summer or autumn of 1532, Luther stated that in translating Scripture, he followed two basic rules. The first rule involved the proper distinction between law and gospel: "First, if some passage is obscure, I consider whether it treats of grace or of law, whether wrath or the forgiveness of sin [is contained in it], and with which of these it agrees better. By this procedure I have often understood the most obscure passages. Either the law or the gospel has made them meaningful, for God divides his teaching into law and gospel."[57] The crucial point in interpreting and then translating Scripture, then, was to be clear on whether a passage was accusing and killing or promising and life-giving to the one who hears the message. Second, Luther was clear that only God could breathe life into a person—the function of the gospel, accomplished by the Holy Spirit who is the "breath of life." Attempts to use the law to accomplish the gospel end only in failure. The law cannot be used to do something it was not designed to do. The law cannot breathe life into people, to effect

people's minds back to the Son of God, and, like the Baptist, he pointed to the Lamb of God, who takes away our sins [John 1:29]. He showed that sins are forgiven freely, for the sake of the Son of God, and that this favor must be received by faith." LW CV 65; This preface can be found in CR 6:155–70 and MBWT 15:296–311 (No. 4277).

52. "Sermons on John (15)," LW 23:271 WA 33:431,17–20.

53. See, for example, "First Psalm Lectures (1513–1515)," LW 11:160; WA 4:9,28–31.

54. "Afternoon Sermon on New Year's Day (1532)," LW 57:64–76; WA 36:8–23, and "Sermon for the Second Sunday in Lent (1539)," LW 58:16–30; WA 47:671–78.

55. Kolb, *Martin Luther and the Enduring Word of God*, 119–20. This echoes Luther's "Treatise on the Last Words of David (1543)," where he suggested that there are two preaching offices, one of law, and one of gospel, which must "stand side by side even though their objectives are different." LW 15:331; WA 54:82,18–19.

56. "Luther's Address Prior to the First Disputation Against the Antinomians (1537)," LW 73:71; WA 39.I:363,19–20.

57. "Table Talks (1532)," LW 54:42; WA TR 1:128,4–9 (No. 312).

the resurrection of the dry bones in the valley that Ezekiel witnessed (Ez. 37:1–14).[58] Only the Spirit, through the proclamation of the gospel, breathes life.

The Wittenberg reformers also carefully avoided simply labeling the Old Testament as "law" and the New Testament as "gospel." The words *law* and *gospel* have nothing to do with "specific books of the Bible and whether they were written before or after Christ."[59] Luther understood that the books of Moses and the prophets, for example, also contained gospel, along with the New Testament writings.[60] They both had to do "with God's Word spoken for the old creature (law) or for the new (gospel)."[61] Thus, while the Wittenberg reformers could talk about Moses as the Lawgiver and Christ as the bestower of gospel, both had the same ultimate focus: life in Christ.

Third, the distinction between law and gospel was not based on the literal words themselves, or even on the old creature and the new creature, but on what they *did* to the hearers of the Word.[62] This is most easily discovered in Luther's phrase, *was Christum treibet* (what drives Christ) into the human heart so that they might have life. Wengert calls this little phrase "the authoritative center of Scripture as Luther experienced it."[63] The lack of this authoritative center in the Letter of James explains why Luther had so many problems with that book. While he admitted it was a "good book" that "vigorously promulgates (*treibet*) the law of God"[64] rather than human doctrines, its major shortcoming was that it simply did not proclaim the gospel. It was all about works righteousness, pushing (*treiben*) the law, rather than Christ.[65] On top of that, Luther, along with many others, questioned whether the letter was apostolic.[66] Luther commented, "Whatever does not teach Christ is not yet apostolic, even

---

58. Surprisingly, Luther does not make any reference to the valley of dry bones in Ezekiel 37 in his prefaces to the Book of Ezekiel in the 1534 Bible; nor does he make any marginal notations in this chapter.

59. Wengert, *Reading the Bible with Martin Luther*, 30. Wengert adds (30, n. 6), that "Heinrich Bornkamm deals with this confusing terminology in *Luther and the Old Testament*, trans. Eric W. and Ruth C. Gritsch (Philadelphia: Fortress, 1969), 81–87.

60. "Sermons on the First Epistle of Peter (1523)," LW 30:19; WA 12:275,5–15.

61. Wengert, *Reading the Bible with Martin Luther*, 31.

62. Wengert, *Reading the Bible with Martin Luther*, 31.

63. Wengert, *Reading the Bible with Martin Luther*, vii.

64. "Preface to the Epistles of St. James and St. Jude (1546/1522)," LW 35:395; WA DB 7:384 and 385,4–5.

65. Wengert, *Reading the Bible with Martin Luther*, 11.

66. The Early Church theologians Eusebius and Jerome, for example, questioned the authorship of James (see LW 35:395, n. 47), as did Luther's contemporaries and opponents Cardinal Cajetan and Erasmus of Rotterdam. Wengert, *Reading the Bible with Martin Luther*, 3–4.

though St. Peter or St. Paul does the teaching. Again, whatever preaches Christ would be apostolic, even if Judas, Annas, Pilate, and Herod were doing it."[67] To properly interpret and translate the Bible, the translator must properly understand the apostolic message—that is, what God in Christ is *doing to us* "for us and for our salvation."[68] This summarized not just Luther's theology and understanding of the Word of God, the Gospel and God's actions of justification, but that of the entire translation team in Wittenberg.

Without this basic foundation upon the gospel, variously described by Luther as justification, law and gospel, and the hermeneutic of "what pushes Christ," and letting Scripture interpret itself, a translation can obscure or even contradict this good news. As Luther stated, "Ah, translating is not every man's skill as the mad saints imagine. It requires a right, devout, honest, sincere, God-fearing, Christian, trained, informed, and experienced heart. Therefore I hold that no false Christian or factious spirit can be a decent translator."[69] One of Luther's criticisms of Erasmus of Rotterdam's Greek and Latin New Testament, which he relied upon, was that Erasmus had "translated the New Testament, but he had not felt it."[70] He also criticized a German translation of the prophetic books done by the Anabaptists Hans Denck and Ludwig Hätzer, published in Worms in 1527, a year before his own translation of the Prophets hit the shelves. He felt that this work by the "Worms Prophets" was antitrinitarian and disputed Christ's deity, even though it also had some redeeming qualities.[71] Likewise, Luther's criticism of Sebastian Münster's Bible, published in 1534–1535 (around the same time as the 1534 Luther Bible), was that it still made "too many concessions to the rabbis."[72] It reinforced his argument, therefore, that wrongly interpreting the gospel—including the gospel found everywhere in the Old Testament (and to which he reserved

---

67. "Preface to the Epistles of St. James and St. Jude (1546/1522)," LW 35:396; WA DB 7:384 and 385,29–32.
68. Nicene Creed. See here BC 23; BSELK 49. Luther also quotes this phrase in a "Sermon for Christmas Vespers (1544), in LW 58:193; WA 49:633,9. It also echoes the *für euch* (for you) in the Small Catechism's explanation of the Lord's Supper, which Luther identifies as the important words to remember. SC Sacrament of the Altar, 7–10; BC 362–63; BSELK 890.
69. "On Translation: An Open Letter (1530)," LW 35:194; WA 30.II:640,25–29.
70. "*Novum testamentum transtulit et non sensit.*" "Sermons on 1 John (1527)," WA 20:728,6. The English Translation in *Luther's Works* attributes these actions not to Erasmus, but to Satan, who "tries to divest them [Scriptures] of their power." LW 30:286.
71. "On Translation: An Open Letter (1530)," LW 35:194, n. 59. Because Luther considered the translation by Denck and Hätzer anti-Trinitarian, he felt it might have been influenced by Jewish scholars. LW 35:194; WA 30.II:640,28–32.
72. "Table Talks (Winter 1542–1543)," LW 54:445–446; WA TR 5:218,8–11 (No. 5533).

the term, "Holy Scriptures")[73]—led to poor, and perhaps even dangerous, translations.

Based on Luther's foundational starting point in the gospel, Helmar Junghans has argued that Luther had three interpretive goals that shaped his translation agenda: *docere* (informing/teaching), *movere* (inspiring), and *delectare* (delighting). Delighting was prominent, because his basic aim was propaganda; he wanted to win the listeners or readers of the Word to the gospel. Thus, he not only wanted to inform (*docere*) but also stir up feelings (*delectare*) and move them toward decisions, even if, in the last analysis, this movement was work of the Holy Spirit alone.[74] Hans-Martin Barth is also correct in saying that "Luther's Bible translation is 'partisan'—we might say it corresponds perfectly to his theology."[75] Luther would not be offended by the claims that his translation was partisan, however. It was supposed to be partisan to the gospel. It worked from "a common denominator: they explain and justify Luther's theology in each and every case to everybody. Luther's translation is theologically motivated, and the results are theologically oriented."[76] His theological orientation toward the gospel, therefore, was not just a theological orientation, but it was to be experienced and felt in the heart. No wonder Birgit Stolt could say that "Luther's translation is distinguished from all later Bible translations by its emotional depth."[77] He translated for a purpose: so that Christ could

---

73. "Thus the books of Moses and the prophets are also Gospel, since they proclaimed and described in advance what the apostles preached or wrote later about Christ. But there is a difference. For although both have been put on paper word for word, the Gospel, or the New Testament, should really not be written but should be expressed with the living voice which resounds and is heard throughout the world. The fact that it is also written is superfluous. But the Old Testament is only put in writing. Therefore it is called 'a letter.' Thus the apostles call it Scripture; for it only pointed to the Christ who was to come. But the Gospel is a living sermon on the Christ who has come." "Sermons on the First Epistle of Peter (1523)," LW 30:19; WA 12:275,5–15.

74. Helmar Junghans, "Interpunktion und Großschreibung in Texten der Lutherzeit," *Lutherjahrbuch* 74 (2007), 178. See also Birgit Stolt, *Martin Luthers Rhetorik des Herzens* (Tübingen: Mohr Siebeck, 2000), 49–75. Compare the three Latin verbs *docere, movere* and *delectare* (teaching, inspiring, delighting) with Luther's comment that *meditatio, oratio,* and *tentatio* (meditating on the Word, prayer, and faithful tribulation) makes one a theologian. "Preface to the Wittenberg Edition of Luther's German Writings (1539)," LW 34:285–87, and the manuscript note, WA 48:276.

75. Hans-Martin Barth, *The Theology of Martin Luther: A Critical Assessment* (Minneapolis: Fortress Press, 2013), 447.

76. Sönke Hahn, *Luthers Übersetzungsweise im Septembertestament von 1522. Untersuchungen zu Luthers Übersetzung des Römerbriefs im Vergleich mit Übersetzungen vor ihm.* Hamburger philologische Studien 29 (Hamburg: Helmut Buske Verlag, 1973), 228.

77. Birgit Stolt, "Luther's Faith of 'the Heart:' Experience, Emotion and Reason." in *The Global Luther: A Theologian for Modern Times,* ed. Christine Helmer (Minneapolis: Fortress Press, 2009), 132.

be driven, or pushed, into the heart of the believer. No wonder understanding the heart of Scripture and properly interpreting this gospel was a prerequisite for translating.

ENHANCING THE TRANSLATION

The Wittenberg translators did not rely only on the translated text of the Bible itself to communicate the gospel. In order to supplement their translation—which was already shaped by how they interpreted the Bible—the Wittenberg team made use of tools such as glosses, marginalia, annotations, illustrations, capitalizations, punctuation, and even paragraph breaks, to push home their message.[78] Thus, "Luther's choice of words and style, the accessibility of ideas briefly put, the visual signals of pamphlets with an increasing design homogeneity—was in many ways as important as the message."[79] The Reformer wanted the hearers and readers of Scripture to experience the gospel, and he appealed to the senses to accomplish his goal.

The New Testament of 1522 and the Wittenberg Bibles, beginning in 1534, were not completely innovative with the addition of the many interpretive aids Luther and his colleagues added to the text of Scripture. For example, all but the first two complete Bibles published in German contained woodcut illustrations. These earlier bibles also often contained prefaces to the various books of the Bible, often by Jerome or Nicholas of Lyre.[80] The Wittenberg translations, however, replaced the woodcuts from earlier Bibles with their own illustrations, pictures that better highlighted the gospel and the oral nature of the proclamation of the Word that they wanted to accomplish. Likewise, dissatisfied with the prefaces written by Jerome, and Erasmus, because they tended to focus on works and the law rather than the theme of gospel that Luther and his colleagues felt permeated the Scriptures,[81] Luther wrote his own prefaces for each of the books of the Bible. These prefaces were often summaries of each book,

---

78. Junghans, "Interpunktion," 154–65.
79. Andrew Pettegree. *Brand Luther: How an Unheralded Monk Turned His Small Town Into a Center of Publishing, Made Himself the Most Famous Man in Europe–and Started the Protestant Reformation* (New York: Penguin Books, 2015), 334.
80. See Chapter 3 for a more detailed description of these early printed Bibles. See also Kenneth Strand, *German Bibles Before Luther: The Story of 14 High German Editions* (Grand Rapids: Eerdmans, 1966), 26–28, and *Early Low-German Bibles: The Story of Four Pre-Lutheran Bibles* (Grand Rapids: Eerdmans, 1967), 23–26.
81. "Table Talks (April 1, 1533)," LW 54,189; WA TR 3:200,1–9. See also the Editor's Introduction to the Prefaces of the Bible, LW 35:231.

reminding the reader of the unity of Scripture as well as its variety,[82] with a special emphasis on how each book highlighted God's actions in Christ, the gospel, the Word, grace, and forgiveness.

SUMMARY

Luther's project of translating of Holy Scripture—his most common name for the Bible—was a "public works" project for preachers and a largely illiterate people, so that the Word could be proclaimed and heard with their ears and their hearts. Hartmut Hövelmann observes that "The reformer and his friends invested a considerable part of their creative life's work in the translation and revisions of the Bible. The reason might be evident. They were persuaded that they could establish their theological understandings in their Bible translation."[83] His focus, then, was not on an impeccable literal translation that would be closest to the original Hebrew and Greek texts, but on letting the Word in the written text speak and come alive. His translation was full of passion and emotion; it was personal and even subjective,[84] because he was describing, first and foremost, an all-consuming relationship between God, humanity, and all creation. When the written Scripture is spoken, Luther saw and discovered God the Spirit breathing life into people as they came face-to-face with Christ. As Wilhelm Stählin concludes, "Luther's great contribution to the understanding of Holy Scripture lies not just in the fact that he has given a German version of the book to us, but above all in the fact that he has taught us to understand the Bible from its living core."[85] That living core of the gospel was what drove him, and that was what the preaching office was all about: creating opportunities for people to encounter the good news of new life in God as a totally underserved gift of grace. Everything else was secondary.

---

82. Hartmut Hövelmann, *Kernstellen der Lutherbibel: Eine Anleitung zum Schriftverständnis,* Texte und Arbeiten zur Bibel, Deutschen Bibelgesellschaft, Vol. 5 (Bielefeld: Luther Verlag, 1989), 47.

83. Hövelmann, *Kernstellen der Lutherbibel,* 17–18.

84. Junghans, "Interpunktion," 179. See also Birgit Stolt, "Martin Luthers Rhetorik des Herzens," 97–112, esp. 101, and "Luther's Faith of 'the Heart,'" 132; and Heinz Bluhm, "Luther's German Bible," in *Seven-Headed Luther: Essays in Commemoration of a Quincentenary, 1483–1983,* ed. Peter Newman Brooks (Oxford: Clarendon Press, 1983), 184.

85. Wilhelm Stählin, "Die Einheit der Bibel," in *Freiheit und Ordnung,* Symbolon 4, ed. Reinhard Mumm (Frankfurt: Evangelische Verlag Werke, 1980), 46.

3.

German Bibles before Luther: So Many Myths!

"In our day . . . so many are busying themselves with translating that history may repeat itself and there may be so many Bibles in the course of time and so many wiseacres who claim a mastery of the Hebrew tongue that there will be no end to it."[1]

INTRODUCTION

There are many myths about Martin Luther the Bible translator that are used to justify Luther as a German hero. The myths were used to elevate his significance among all Germans, and not just to his evangelical supporters. These myths emphasized Luther as the creator and shaper of the German language and culture. But these myths were also used to justify his reformation agenda. This is perhaps best expressed by Hans Holbein in his 1523 depiction of Luther as the Roman god Hercules, slaying medieval philosophers and inquisitors while championing God's truth for the common people.[2] While Luther's heroic image among the common people was tarnished by his writings about the peasants' uprisings two years later,[3] the portrayal of Luther as David in a battle with the Roman Catholic Goliath allowed Luther's supporters to continue to associate him with a prophetic hero. Luther's mythical status further developed as he was represented as

---

1. "Treatise on the Last Words of David (1543)," LW 15:267; WA 54:28,10–13.
2. Robert Kolb, *Martin Luther as Prophet, Teacher and Hero: Images of the Reformer 1520–1620* (Grand Rapids: Baker Books, 1999), 75–86.
3. See, for example, Luther's three 1525 treatises: "Admonition to Peace: A Reply to the Twelve Articles of the Peasants in Swabia (1525)," LW 46:3–43; WA 8:291–334; "Against the Robbing and Murdering Hordes of Peasants (1525)," LW 46:45–55; WA 18:357–61; and "Open Letter on the Harsh Book Against the Peasants (1525)," LW 46:57–85; WA 18:384–401.

the first and the best in everything that he did. This is particularly true when it comes to Luther's greatest accomplishment in the eyes of many: his translation of the Bible into a contemporary German. But the myths are not always true, even if they do reflect perceptions of truth.

There are four persistent myths about Luther's Bible translations that have prevailed over the centuries. The first myth is that Luther was the first person to translate the Bible into German from the Hebrew and Greek. The second myth claims that Luther's Bible was the best translation into German ever made. The third myth is that Luther single-handedly standardized the nascent German language. The fourth myth claims that the Roman Catholic Church banned the translation of the Bible into the vernacular (the language of the people), but Luther the heroic translator "freed the Bible"[4] and made it available to everyone by translating it into their own language.

Despite the challenges posed by these four myths about the importance of the Luther Bible translation, Luther and his colleagues contributed significantly to the availability and readability of the Bible in Germany. The value of Luther's New Testament and Bible translations, however, are not because they were the first or the best translations—at least from historical and linguistic standpoints—but because of the deliberate theological impact for which they were designed.[5] Studying the history and quality of German Bibles prior to Luther's translations helps us discern the myths from the reality.

MYTHS CONCERNING THE FIRST GERMAN BIBLE

Contrary to much popular perception, Luther's Bible was not the first Bible translated into a Germanic language, nor was it the first to be translated from the Hebrew and Greek into German. Those honors go to Ulfilas (c. 311–80 CE) and his colleagues.[6] Remarkably, Ulfilas completed his Gothic German translation before Jerome had finished his more famous "Vulgate,"

---

4. Andrew Colin Gow, "The Bible in Germanic: German and Netherlandish Bibles to the Advent of Printing," *New Cambridge History of the Bible: Volume 2: From 600 to 1450*. Four Volumes. Eds. Richard Marsden and E. Ann Matter (Cambridge: Cambridge University Press, 2012), 211.

5. See Chapter 2.

6. Wilhelm Streitberg, *Die Gotische Bibel*, reprint (Charleston: Nabu Press, 2010). See also M.J. Hunter, "The Vernacular Scriptures: The Gothic Bible," in *The Cambridge History of the Bible*. Three Volumes. Ed. G.H.W. Lampe (Cambridge: Cambridge University Press, 1969), 2: 338–62. The Old Testament books were translated primarily from the Septuagint (a Greek translation of the Old Testament), rather than the Hebrew Bible.

a Latin translation that became the standard Bible in the Roman Catholic church.[7] Moreover, Ulfilas' translation was influential in establishing the basic Germanic vocabulary[8] that was used and developed by Luther and his contemporaries. Other complete or partial translations of the Bible also sporadically appeared during the reign of Charlemagne,[9] who made theological education a priority. However, Bibles in the language of the people did not become as popular as one might expect. The Latin Vulgate Bible was the standard, since Latin was the language of the Roman church, beginning in the fourth and fifth centuries. Bibles, liturgies, and theological discourse in Latin were the norm. Even Jerome's Latin Bible—known as the Vulgate (meaning "the common language")—was in the people's language. Commissioned by Pope Damasus I, it was based on portions of earlier Latin translations of the Bible, to which Jerome added his own translations. Scholars continued to revise the Vulgate throughout the medieval era in an attempt to make the text more readable and easier to comprehend.[10] Yet the Vulgate did not become the *official* text of the Bible for the Roman Catholic Church until the Fourth Session of the Council of Trent on April 8, 1546—two months after Luther's death.[11] It is still used as the official text of the Bible by the Roman, "Latin" church today.

Yet for most people in the Holy Roman Empire,[12] the dominant language was German, and the development of German Bibles did for the German speaking populace what the Vulgate had done for the people of the Western Mediterranean: it allowed them to hear the Word of God in their own language, and in an idiomatic way that the common people

---

7. Johannes Mathesius, Luther's student and then colleague, actually notes this as the first Bible in German. LW CV 471.

8. Paul Arblaster, Gergely Juhász, and Guido Latré, eds., *Tyndale's Testament* (Turnhout: Brepols, 2002), 116. Fragments of this early Gothic German text still survive in the University of Uppsala library in Sweden. See here Stephan Füssel, *The Bible in Pictures: From the Workshop of Lucas Cranach (1534)* (Cologne: Taschen, 2009), 7.

9. Gow, "The Bible in Germanic," 200–204.

10. For details, see Frans van Liere, "The Latin Bible, c. 900 to the Council of Trent, 1546,"in *The New Cambridge History of the Bible: Volume 2: From 600 to 1450. Four Volumes. Eds. Richard Marsden and E. Ann Matter (Cambridge: Cambridge University Press, 2012), 2:93–109.

11. Two canons were approved regarding Scripture. The first, *"Sacrosancta,"* defined the inspiration of the Bible and formally canonized the accepted books of the Bible. The second, *"Insuper,"* made the Vulgate the authentic and official text of the Bible for the Latin rite. Norman P. Tanner, S.J., ed., *Decrees of the Ecumenical Councils: Volume II Trent to Vatican II* (Washington: Georgetown University Press, 1990), 663–65.

12. The Holy Roman Empire, founded by Emperor Charlemagne (Charles the Great) in the late eighth century, basically encompassed modern day Germany, Poland, parts of Austria, and the western part of France along the Rhine River. It was surrounded by the young states of Spain, France, and England.

could understand. This was also the goal of the German Bibles, including Luther's. As Bluhm notes, "Luther's splendid attempt to employ only idiomatic language was anticipated, pretty successfully, on the whole, by the creators of the Vulgate."[13] The vernacular bibles were simply following in the great tradition of Jerome's Vulgate.

The availability of German Bibles rapidly increased with the newly invented moveable type printing press in the last half of the fifteenth century. With Johannes Gutenberg and others in Europe in the 1450s, printing became a major industry and with it came a proliferation of Bibles printed in German. After the publication of the Latin Gutenberg Bible in 1454,[14] the first vernacular Bible in any language other than Latin to come off the printing press was Johannes Mentel's (or Mentelin's) translation in Strasbourg in 1466.[15] Counting this first printed German Bible, a total of eighteen German Bibles came off the press before the appearance of Luther's 1522 *Septembertestament*. But they were not the only sources that provided access to the Bible. As Stephan Füssel notes,

> Up to the 12th century, the Bible was usually not published in its entirety; instead portions of individual translations were copied, such as the Four Gospels, the Psalter or the Gospel Lectionaries (the assigned Sunday Gospel texts in a prescribed calendar series), which were then retranslated for their intended audience and made accessible to a wider public.[16]

The appearance of German translations of the Bible suggests that these German language Bibles were in demand for both official and personal reasons. The preface of the 1480 Cologne Bible stated that "all 'good hearts,' clerics and laypeople, who see and read this Bible should unite themselves with God and ask the Holy Spirit, master of this text, to help them to understand this translation according to His will and for the salvation of their soul."[17] The printers were quick to capitalize on

13. Heinz Bluhm, *Martin Luther: Creative Translator* (St. Louis: Concordia, 1965), 4.

14. Stephan Füssel, *Gutenberg and the Impact of Printing,* trans. Douglas Martin (Aldershot: Ashgate, 2005), 21.

15. Andrew Pettegree, "Publishing in Print: Technology and Trade," in *The New Cambridge History of the Bible. Volume 3: From 1450 to 1750*, ed. Euan Cameron (Cambridge. University of Cambridge Press, 2016), 3:166; and Euan Cameron, "The Luther Bible," in *The New Cambridge History of the Bible. Volume 3: From 1450 to 1750*, ed. Euan Cameron (Cambridge: University of Cambridge Press, 2016), 217. Luther's colleague Johannes Mathesius called this Bible the "un-German German Bible," since it was so difficult to understand. LW CV, 472.

16. Füssel, *The Bible in Pictures,* 7.

17. Gow, "The Contested History of the Book," 278. See also Wilhelm Ludwig Krafft, *Die deutsche Bibel vor Luther: sein Verhältnis zu derselben und seine Verdienste um die deutsche Bibelübersetzung* (Bonn: Carl Georgi, 1883), 6.

this demand. Always on the lookout for best sellers, they recognized the potential profits from easily understandable Bibles printed in the language of the people—even though it could take up to two years to print such a massive book.[18] Unlike specialized academic books, however, the Bible appealed to a large audience, justifying the risk of time and money that was involved in printing such a large book.

All eighteen German versions prior to Luther's Bible were translated from the Vulgate. Ten of the high German bibles were published between 1475 and 1490, with only two published before 1475 (in 1466 and 1470), and two published afterward (in 1507 and 1518).[19] Of these eighteen Bibles, fourteen were printed in high German and four in low German.

A majority of the early Bibles appeared in high German, since high German was used in the courts and in commerce,[20] while low German was the language spoken on the streets.

The last Bible to be published prior to Luther's *Septembertestament* was Halberstadt's Bible, printed in July 1522, two months earlier. Geographically, the cities publishing the high German Bibles were in the southern half of the German speaking lands, while the low German bibles were published in cities more to the north, reflecting, to some degree, the popular usage of the two versions of spoken German in the Holy Roman Empire.

The Low German Bibles were published between 1478 and 1522.[21] They were in demand in northern Germany, since low German was used by the Hanseatic League, which included the Nordic Countries and northern Germany. These Bibles also appealed to the Brothers and Sisters of the Common Life, a laity movement that arose in the fourteenth century in the Netherlands and quickly spread to northern Germany. Committed to the education of the common folk, this movement invested heavily in

18. Pettegree, "Publishing in Print," 163.

19. Hans Volz, *Martin Luthers deutsche Bibel: Entstehung und Geschichte der Lutherbibel* (Hamburg: Friedrich Wittig Verlag, 1978), 20. Three High German Bibles were published in Strasbourg (1466, 1470, 1485), nine in Augsburg (1475, 1476, 1477,1480, 1487, 1490, 1507, 1518), and two in Nuremberg (1476, 1483). See Appendix 1 for a chart of these earlier German Bibles.

20. Hartmut Hövelmann, *Kernstellen der Lutherbibel: Eine Anleitung zum Schriftverständnis.* Texte und Arbeiten zur Bibel, Deutschen Bibelgesellschaft, Bd 5 (Bielefeld: Luther Verlag, 1989), 18. See also Hulda Hagen, *Die Spreche des jungen Luther und ihr Verhältnis zu Kanzleissprache seiner Zeit.* Diss. Phil. Greifswald, 1922.

21. Cameron, "The Luther Bible," 218. For more detail about these initial German printed Bibles, see Volz, *Martin Luthers deutsche Bibel*; Kenneth A. Strand, *German Bibles Before Luther: The Story of 14 High German Editions* (Grand Rapids: Eerdmans, 1966); and *Early Low-German Bibles: The Story of Four Pre-Lutheran Bibles,* (Grand Rapids: Eerdmans, 1967), 23, 33. Two of the four Low German Bibles were printed in Cologne (1478, 1479), with one each published in Lübeck (1494) and Halberstadt (1522).

education. Luther claimed to have attended a school run by the Brethren of the Common Life in Magdeburg, although there is no record of such a school in that city. He did live in a Brethren house, however, while attending the cathedral school in Magdeburg.[22] Part of their curriculum was daily Bible readings. Their founder, Geert Groote, had translated portions of the Bible into Low German.[23] Low German was also often the first language for most of the students attending the University of Wittenberg, at least initially.[24] Whether one understood low or high German, there was a Bible translation available.

The early versions of printed German Bibles had many things in common. They were generally printed in two columns of 50–60 lines per page and bound in two volumes.[25] The Apocrypha is included in all the German Bibles printed before 1522, and the books of the Bible were in the same order as that found in the Vulgate. Thus, as Kenneth Strand notes, "The Prayer of Manasses is placed after Chronicles in all but the Mentel and Eggestein editions, in which it is lacking; . . . [while] in the New Testament , the apocryphal Epistle to the Laodiceans follows Galatians, and the Book of Acts is placed after the Epistle to the Hebrews."[26] As Strand notes, following the practice of the Vulgate, they all had the customary prefaces to the books of the Bible, generally written by Jerome and/or Nicholas of Lyra.[27]

These early German Bibles also displayed a remarkable diversity. Besides the difference between the use of high or low German, there are a variety of other differences that gave each Bible its own distinct character—a tradition that the Luther Bibles continued. First, while the four Low German Bibles were all approximately 8" × 12" for the printed text, the fourteen high German bibles varied from 5" × 8" to 8½" ×14", reflecting

---

22. Martin Brecht, *Martin Luther: His Road to Reformation, 1483–1521*, trans. James L. Schaaf (Minneapolis: Fortress Press, 1993), 16.

23. While the Low German Cologne Bible of 1478, in its introduction, encourages the laity to read the Bible in Germanic, this technical term may not mean only Low German. The word *duitschen*, which the Cologne Bible used, encompassed Low German, High German and Dutch according to Strand, *Early Low German Bibles*, n. 5, 28.

24. Hövelmann, *Kernstellen der Lutherbibel*, 20. See also Johann Dietrich Bellmann, "Scriptura semper est transferenda," in *Kanzelsprache und Sprachgemeinde*, J.D. Bellmann, hg. Schriften des Instituts für niederdeutsche Sprache (Bremen: Reihe Kirche 1, 1975), 32.

25. Strand, *German Bibles Before Luther*, 26–27. The first four high German bibles, and one or two of the later editions, were generally bound in one volume. When bound in two volumes, the first volume generally concluded with the Psalms and the second volume began with Proverbs.

26. Strand, *German Bibles Before Luther*, 26.

27. Strand, *German Bibles Before Luther*, 26. See also note 3, 26. Many of the books in these bibles had two or three different introductions.

their varied uses.[28] The smaller versions were more suitable for personal use, while the largest versions worked better for use in pulpits or libraries. Second, while the first two high German Bibles did not include any woodcuts, all of the later high German Bibles had woodcut illustrations. The printers had quickly learned that the inclusion of illustrations greatly increased the appeal of their Bibles, which in turn increased sales. Very quickly, illustrations became an "essential feature of the vernacular German Bible."[29] The earliest illustrated editions had pictures that fit into one of the two columns on each page and measured about 3" × 3" or 3" × 4", while later versions, beginning with the Koberger Bible of 1483, introduced woodcuts that spanned both columns, measuring around 7" wide and 4 to 4½" high. In the earlier editions, the illustrations were found only at the beginning of biblical books, but later editions had woodcuts scattered throughout the text. Two other changes were introduced in the first and second editions of the Schönsperger Bible printed in Augsburg in 1487 and 1490, respectively. The 1487 edition had the text broken into paragraphs for the first time, and the 1490 edition added a title page.[30] As each new edition of a German Bible was published, new features were found. The printing of Scripture as a book and as a work of art was in demand, and the printers did their best to meet the challenge. Printed Bibles were best sellers and were thus crucial for the stability of the printing industry. Luther built upon these innovations and incorporated them into his own translations and, as his later versions came out, he added further improvements of his own.

MYTHS ABOUT THE QUALITY
OF PRE-REFORMATION GERMAN BIBLES

The second myth associated with the Luther Bible claims that Luther's translation was qualitatively superior to all previous translations, thus setting the standard for modern high German language. This myth was perpetuated by none other than the linguist and Luther scholar Heinz Bluhm: "Of Luther's several great achievements, the German Bible is perhaps the greatest and probably the most enduring, . . . renowned for sheer readability, it has become under Luther's magic touch, a German book, indispensable to German literature," and "more than a mere specimen of

28. Strand, *Early Low German Bibles*, 23; and *German Bibles Before Luther*, 26–7.
29. Pettegree, "Publishing in Print," 167. See also Richard Muther, *Die deutsche Bücherillustration der Gothik und Frührenaissance (1460–1530)* (Munich: George Hirth, 1884).
30. Strand, *German Bibles Before Luther*, 28.

magnificent literary style."[31] Nor was Bluhm alone in giving credit to Luther. The nineteenth century philosopher Friedrich Nietzsche declared that the Luther Bible was "the best German book thus far." [32] But were they correct in making these claims? While Luther and the Reformers wanted a vibrant, lively translation of the Gospel, it is a great exaggeration to suggest that the previous versions were vastly inferior to Luther's work.[33] As Andrew Gow bluntly insists,

> Scholars who acknowledge the wide circulation of vernacular Bibles often argue that they were linguistically inferior, claiming that Luther relied exclusively on the "original Greek" text of the New Testament in his translation (which places more weight on Erasmus' faulty 1516 edition of the New Testament in Greek and on Luther's use of it than either can bear, ignores Luther's reliance on both earlier German translations and the Vulgate, and gives him more credit as a philologist than he deserves).[34]

William Lockwood made a similar assertion, noting that "It has been a common error of criticism to regard the Mentel Bible [1466] as typical of the pre-Luther stage of biblical translation. Recent researchers, however, have shown that the elements of Luther's style are already present in a large measure in the manuscript literature of the fourteenth and especially the fifteenth centuries."[35] Further, the claim that Luther's translation was superior to previous German Bibles only works when it is compared to the Mentel Bible, which was indeed an antiquated if not inferior translation. The Mentel Bible reflected the "language and translation technique of about the beginning of the fourteenth century."[36] However, it did not take long for freer, more idiomatic translations to appear on the scene.[37] These Bible translations were of much better quality, because they had to compete with other translations.

31. Heinz Bluhm, "Luther's German Bible," in *Seven-Headed Luther: Essays in Commemoration of a Quincentenary, 1483–1983*, ed. Peter Newman Brooks (Oxford: Clarendon Press, 1983), 178, 183, 184.
32. Friedrich Nietzsche, "Jenseits von Gut und Böse," in *Werke in drei Bänden*, 7th ed., ed. Karl Schlechta (Munich: Carl Hanser, 1973), 247, 715.
33. Cameron, "The Luther Bible," 217.
34. Andrew Colin Gow, "The Contested History of a Book: The German Bible of the Later Middle Ages and Reformation in Legend, Ideology, and Scholarship," *Analecta Gorgiana* (Piscataway, N.J.: Gorgias Press, 2012), 265–66.
35. William B. Lockwood, "Vernacular Scriptures in Germany and the Low Countries before 1500," in *The Cambridge History of the Bible. Volume 2: The West from the Fathers to the Reformation*. Three Volumes. Ed. G.H.W. Lampe (Cambridge: Cambridge University Press, 1969), 2:434.
36. Lockwood, "Vernacular Scriptures in Germany," 433.
37. Lockwood, "Vernacular Scriptures in Germany," 433.

The debate over the quality of Luther's translation also depends on how quality is measured. When compared to the two spheres where German was used, namely in humanism and in the courts of the nobility, Luther's translation left something to be desired. His translation satisfied the standards or expectations of neither the humanists nor the political, courtly circles. As Horst Beintker observed, "Luther's choice of words very rarely agrees with the artistic language of the humanists, and it rarely harmonizes with the style of the court."[38] Luther was not translating the Bible for the court or the humanists, however. He and his Wittenberg colleagues were aiming at the target audience of the common people in their translation.

THE MYTH THAT THE LUTHER BIBLE STANDARDIZED THE GERMAN LANGUAGE

In lockstep with the myth that Luther's Bible was a superior translation was the idea that because of the quality of this translation, Luther developed and set the standard for High German. Some nationalist Germans, for example, claimed that "couched as linguistic scholarship, . . . Luther's German Bible formed or even invented the standard form of early modern German."[39] The noted early twentieth century German philologist Adolf Bach stated that Luther's translation "unified the German language."[40] This third myth has some truth to it, but it gives Luther and his colleagues too much credit. Their Bible translation into high German was indeed significant, in part due to its wide circulation, but one cannot say that Luther and his colleagues *developed* or even *standardized* high German. This process took longer than Luther's lifetime. As Martin Brecht states,

> The formation of literary high German had begun before Luther and continued after him. In this process the language used at the court of the Wettiners in Meissen played a significant role. It was precisely in the area of Saxony where the dialects merged. With a certain accuracy, Luther later stated that he did not have a German of his own, but used a common German that could be understood in both southern and northern Germany. "I speak the language of the Saxon chancellery which all the princes of Germany imitate." . . . His usage was oriented toward chancellery language only for

38. Horst Beintker, "Luthers Anteil an der Sprachwendung des Neuhochdeutschen und dessen möglicher Ermittlung durch lexikalische Untersuchungen," *Muttersprache* 76 (1966), 233. See also Hövelmann, *Kernstellen der Lutherbibel*, 18.
39. Gow, "The Contested History of a Book," 265–66.
40. Adolf Bach, *Geschichte der deutschen Sprache*, 7th ed. (Heidelberg: Quelle und Meyer, 1961), 207.

the sake of common understanding, for it avoided particularly courtly and stilted expressions and refrained from using either foreign words or slang. Such a language should speak to people, and they should be able to understand it. At least some eighty or ninety percent of Luther's linguistic expressions, substantially more than in the earlier translation, could be understood in both southern and northern Germany.[41]

Luther and his colleagues did not create or develop high German, but they did make use of it to reach as wide an audience as possible. The language was to convey the gospel. Creating a new, high German language would not have served such a purpose. Even though Luther and his colleagues did not create or develop high German through their translation of the Bible, the appearance of the 1534 Luther Bible was, as Thomas Kaufmann stated, a "singular accomplishment nonetheless—as a theological and cultural, if not quite political breakthrough."[42] Its readability and popularity, however, helped high German become more familiar to people, even if it did not create high German. It was a symbiotic relationship.

THE MYTH OF BANNED BIBLES

A fourth myth associated with Luther's translation work claims that prior to the Reformation, the Roman Catholic Church banned the publication or reading of *all* Bibles. As Gow notes, "one of the most persistent inaccuracies regarding the European Middle Ages—both among the general public and even among scholars—is the notion that the Roman church forbade or banned the reading of the Bible in the vernacular."[43] By implication, vernacular German Bibles were also banned. Unfortunately, this myth of the Roman church banning vernacular Bibles has been commonly accepted. For example, one scholar wrote in 1980 that "the medieval church, fearing the social consequences of religious egalitarianism, *had always forbidden* the circulation of vernacular Bibles among the laity and vigorously suppressed the Gospel translations of groups like the Waldensians and the

41. Martin Brecht, *Martin Luther: Shaping and Defining the Reformation, 1521–1532*, trans. James L. Schaaf (Minneapolis: Fortress Press, 1994), 48. The quote from Luther is taken from "Table Talks (1532)," WA TR 2:639,17–18 (No. 2758).
42. Thomas Kaufmann, "Vorreformatorische Laienbibel und reformatorisches Evangelium," *Zeitschrift für Theologie und Kirche*, 101 (2004), 138–174.
43. Gow, "The Contested History of a Book," 263. See also Rudolf Bentzinger's dismissal of this old myth in his very useful paper "Zur spätmittelalterlichen deutschen Bibelübersetzung. Versuch eines Überblicks," Irmtraud Rösler (ed), *"Ik lerde kunst dor lust." Ältere Sprache und Literatur in Forschung und Lehre. FS Christa Baufeld*. Rostocker Beiträge zur Sprachwissenschaft 7; (Rostock: Universität Rostock, 1999), 29–41.

Wyclif Bible of the Lollards."[44] While banning specific bibles used by groups that had been condemned as heretical did indeed happen, it is not accurate to conclude that all vernacular bibles were banned.

Vernacular German bibles were not the problem; the main reason for banning certain vernacular bibles was their lack of proper licensing by the church's authorities.[45] Archbishop and Elector of Mainz, Berthold von Henneberg, did in fact ban two "*unlicensed* translations of the Bible and other religious writings" in 1485–86.[46] Generally, however, Bibles in the vernacular were not banned, only *unlicensed translations* of the Bible. The abundance of published scriptural excerpts, early catechetical material, and illustrated Bible stories in stained glass windows, statues, and paintings, make it clear that people could see—if not read—the biblical text with their own eyes.[47] As Kenneth Appold notes, "While most people, particularly those in rural areas, were unable to read bibles, they had other means of encountering its contents. These included pictorial representations, such as the illustrated bibles often called *Biblia pauperum* ('Bibles of the Poor'),[48] as well as paintings and sculptured reliefs in churches."[49] The stories of the Bible surrounded the people, even if they were not reading actual biblical texts. Thus, access to complete or partial texts of Bibles were easily available in the late medieval era. Moreover, in the last half of the fifteenth century ninety-four editions of the *licensed* Vulgate were published, "of

---

44. Steven Ozment, *The Age of Reform, 1250–1550: An Intellectual and Religious History of Late Medieval and Reformation Europe* (New Haven: Yale University Press, 1980), 202 (emphasis added). Ozment is correct in stating that in England there were general bans against making or owning Bibles in the vernacular, in large part due to an attempt to suppress the Lollards, but elsewhere such bans were either local, temporary, or directed against a specific vernacular translation such as the ban on the Waldensian Bible by the Archbishop of Metz in 1199 and later confirmed by Pope Innocent III as a means to squash this specific heresy. See Margaret Deanesly, *The Lollard Bible and other Medieval Versions* (Cambridge: Cambridge University Press, 1920), 18–130.

45. Gow, "Contested History of a Book," 271.

46. Cameron, "The Luther Bible," 218. Emphasis added.

47. R.L.P. Milburn called these illustrated versions the "People's Bible." For a detailed description, see idem., "The 'People's Bible:' Artists and Commentators," in *The Cambridge History of the Bible, Volume 2: The West from the Fathers to the Reformation*. Three Volumes. Ed. G.W.H. Lampe (Cambridge: Cambridge University Press, 1969). 2: 280–308.

48. For the texts, and a detailed study of these Pauper's Bibles (Bibles of the Poor), see Franz J. Luttor, *Biblia Pauperum: Studie zur Herstellung eines inneren Systems; mit dem Texte der in der Wiener k. k. Hofbibliothek aufbewahrten Handschrift und einem Lichtdruck.* Veszprém: Opitz, 1912. 14–18.

49. Kenneth G. Appold, The Importance of the Bible for Early Lutheran Theology," in *The New Cambridge History of the Bible. Volume 3: From 1450 to 1750.* Four Volumes. Ed. Euan Cameron (Cambridge. University of Cambridge Press, 2016). 3:440. See also Graham, *Beyond the Written Word*, 141–42. Graham argues that besides the visual transmission of biblical stories, the telling of these stories was also a robust tradition.

which 22 were closely modelled on the *Gutenberg Bible*."[50] Bibles were available to the reader.

So why does the myth persist that Bibles, and in particular vernacular Bibles, were banned by the Roman church? There are four basic reasons. First, the most obvious reason for banning unlicensed vernacular Bibles was that such translations might show sympathy toward what the Roman church had determined as heresy. The medieval church was concerned with misinterpretations of the biblical texts themselves.[51] Heresies could easily arise from poor translations that led to false interpretations. But the pure biblical text itself, as approved and translated by the Roman church, was not the problem.

Second, the reason for the Roman church banning unlicensed translations was not purely theological. There was also a financial element at play. Unlicensed vernacular versions could adversely affect the revenue of the printers who were licensed and protected by church authorities. If all vernacular Bibles—which made money for only the printers—were not banned, the "official" printers for the church might go out of business, and then the Roman church officials would have no one to print their worship material or their academic books.[52] Issuing printing licenses to printers who published only church-approved material served to protect the church printers' viability.

Third, the Roman church was concerned that the vernacular Bibles, unlike the Latin Vulgate, could not properly express the sublime depths of theological truths found in Scripture.[53] While this concern is different from the outright banning of Bibles in the vernacular, it shows how closely theological thought and discourse was tied to the Latin language in the Roman church. Using a vernacular language could inadvertently change the theological nuances so important to the church. Every language requires theology to fit into its particular linguistic framework, forcing the translator to re-examine theological constructs. German could not express theology in the same way as did Latin. Ironically, this same

50. Stephan Füssel, *Gutenberg and the Impact of Printing*, trans. Douglas Martin (Aldershot: Ashgate, 2005), 159.

51. Werner Schwarz, *Principles and Problems of Biblical Translation: Some Reformation Controversies and Their Background* (Cambridge: Cambridge University Press, 2009), 62–3. Hövelmann argues that "the church sought to limit the reading of the Bible in the language of the people only when conventional Scriptural interpretations against the church were given." Hövelmann notes, however, the partial bans of Scripture in *Kernstellen der Lutherbibel*, 29.

52. While vernacular Bibles could make a profit for printers, the market was more geographically restricted than the more popular Latin Bibles. Pettegree, "Publishing in Print," 167–68, 183.

53. Cameron, "The Luther Bible," 218.

debate later played out in North America in the debates over switching from German to English. Some Lutheran leaders "felt that English was simply not a suitable language for the complexities of Lutheran theology."[54] There was an assumption that translating theological ideas could be constrained by linguistic limitations.

Finally, Luther's own experiences justified his impression that vernacular Bibles were banned or that reading Bibles was highly discouraged. For example, Luther criticized the Roman church for placing its ultimate authority on the pope and its councils, rather than on Scripture: "it is an accursed lie that the pope is the arbiter of Scripture or that the church has authority over Scripture."[55] Anything that threatened, or was perceived as threatening, the authority of the pope or the councils to alone interpret Scripture would thus be banned. If everyone acquired access to Bibles, chaos might ensue, and a wall that the church had placed around its own authority would be torn down.[56] That would never do!

Luther also felt that the church discouraged Bible reading by making it inaccessible to people.[57] In 1527 he stated that in the Roman church, "Scriptures have been lying under the bench."[58] This bold statement prompted a quick response from Petrus Sylvius, who criticized Luther for making such an unfounded statement.[59] Nevertheless, a decade later he claimed that "Thirty years ago no one read the Bible."[60]

Luther's experience as a young monk and theologian also fueled his claims that the Bible was "out of reach" to most people. The student and biographer of Luther, Johannes Mathesius, reported, for example, that in Erfurt, the Augustinian monks "took the Bible away" from Luther when

---

54. Mark Granquist, *Lutherans in America: A New History* (Minneapolis: Fortress Press, 2015), 127–128.

55. "Lectures on Galatians (1535)," LW 26:57; WA 40:119,7–8.

56. Luther attempts to tear down this wall that protects the notion that only the pope and the "Romanists" are "masters of Scripture" in the first part of his 1520 treatise, "To the Christian Nobility of the German Nation (1520)," LW 44:133–36; WA 6:411–12.

57. For a detailed discussion on Luther's stories about the inaccessibility of the Bible in his time, see Rost, *Die Bibel im Mittelalter*, 37–66 and 314–16.

58. "*die schrifft under der banck gelegen ist.*" LW 20:279; WA 23:606,25; "German Commentary on Zechariah (1527)."

59. See LW 20:279, n. 5. Petrus Sylvius, *Von den vier Evangelion, szo eyn lange tzeit untter der banck seyn gelegen. Das ist von den irrigen Artickeln, der vier unchristlichen ketzereyen. Nemlich der Pickarden, der Muscouitern, des Wigkleffs, und des Husss. Auss welchen allen Lutther seyn funfft Euangelium, wie maas hie vor augen wirt sehn, tzusamen gelesen und tzuhauffen gesetzt, etc.* (Leypsick: V. Schumann, 1528).

60. "*Die Biblia war im Papstthum den Leuten unbekannt.*" WA TR 3:24, (No. 2844b) 1532; "*Nam ante 30 annos nullus legit bibliam.*" WA TR 3:598, (No. 3767) (1538.

he was ordained, with instructions that he should instead study the "soph-ists and scholastics." Luther's teacher Bärtholomäus Arnoldi of Usingen told him to not bother with reading Scripture because the ancient teachers had already "extracted the sap of the truth from the Bible."[61] These experi-ences caused Luther to believe that the church did not want people reading and interpreting Scripture. No wonder he stated that "under the papacy, the Bible was unknown by the people," or that Karlstadt did not possess a Bible for a long time[62] and only began reading the Bible eight years after earning his doctorate.[63] Observations such as these suggest that accessible Bibles were scarce, if not actually banned. When the French extended their ban on all of Luther's writings to include all vernacular translations of the Bible, it no doubt fueled his sense that the church was all too willing to ban the Scriptures.[64] From his perspective, the Bible was, in practice, on the church's scarce book list. It is easy to see how such reminiscences would foster the common misconception that the Bible was banned by the church until the time of the Reformation, with Luther being portrayed as a hero who tore down this wall and freed the Bible from the clutches of a Roman church that had locked away the Bible, finally giving the laity access to the Scriptures in their own language.[65] This image of Luther the hero and liberator of the Bible is consequently not far from the surface.

The myth of banned vernacular Bibles in the medieval era does not stand up to scrutiny. As Alister McGrath notes, "no *universal* or *absolute prohibition* of the translation of scriptures into the vernacular was ever issued by a medieval pope or council, nor was any similar prohibition directed against the use of such translations by the clergy or laity."[66] None of the German-language Bibles printed before Luther's New Testament of 1522 received an official license from an episcopal or other ecclesiastical

61. Robert Kolb, *Martin Luther and the Enduring Word of God: The Wittenberg School and Its Scripture-Centered Proclamation* (Grand Rapids: Baker Academic, 2016), 29. Mathesius's com-ment is found in *Historia Vnsers Lieben herren vnd Heylands Jesu Christi . . . auß den heilgen Euangelisten genommen* (Nuremberg: Gerlatz, 1568), V1a. The reference to Luther's recollec-tion of Usingen's comments is found in "Table Talks (1531)," WA TR 2:5–6,1–3, (No. 1240). See also Kolb, *Martin Luther as He Lived and Breathed: Recollections of the Reformer* (Eugene: Cascade, Books, 2018), 31.
62. "Table Talks (1532)," WA TR 2:129,9–12, (No. 1552); WA TR 1:80,9–12, (No. 174).
63. "Table Talks (1532)," WA TR 3:24,3–4, (No. 2844b).
64. Pettegree, "Publishing in Print," 178–79. See also Francis Higman, *Censorship and the Sorbonne; A Bibliographical Study of Books in French censored by the Faculty of Theology in the University of Paris, 1520–1551* (Geneva: Droz, 1979), 23–47.
65. Gow, "The Bible in Germanic," 211.
66. Emphasis added. Alister E. McGrath, *The Intellectual Origins of the European Reformation* (New York: Blackwell, 1987), 124. McGrath echoes Adolf Risch, *Luthers Bibelverdeutschung* (Leipzig: Heinsius, 1922), 10.

agency.[67] The failure to receive an official license did not mean that these vernacular German Bibles were banned: they were just not endorsed. The church had officially licensed many versions of lectionaries and *plenaria*[68] that were printed in the vernacular, for use by priests in the parishes, but generally the people who had access to these Bibles and books, such as priests and theologians, were under church control. This was not the case, however, for the general population.

The Roman church did not ban vernacular Bibles, as a matter of principle. However, vernacular Bibles did raise concerns for them. After all, if the laity had access to vernacular Bibles, they might interpret the Scripture in ways that were not aligned with the church-endorsed interpretations. This could lead to the laity seeing themselves as equal to the pope, in terms of having the right to interpret Scripture. The polemicist Johannes Colchaeus, one of Luther's Roman contemporaries, echoed this concern after Luther's 1522 New Testament was published. Colchaeus declared that "Luther's translation was read (as the source of all wisdom, no less) by tailors and shoemakers, even women and simpletons, many of whom carried it around and learned it by heart, and eventually became bold enough to dispute with priests, monks, even masters and doctors of Holy Scripture about faith and the gospels."[69] The fear that Colchaeus expresses was not about the actual *reading* of Scripture, but of its potentially erroneous *interpretations*. When the interpretations of the Bible by the laity contradicted the official inter-pretations of the church, or when translations that supported heretical teachings by known heretics or heretical groups surfaced, the church was not afraid to act. The Roman church had no qualms reading the Latin Scriptures aloud in worship or quoting the Bible in their liturgies, because the Vulgate and the Liturgy had been authorized by the church. Besides, few (if any) of the congregants would understand the Latin text, forcing the worshippers to depend on the church's interpretation of the passages. But the Roman church was not antagonistic, in prin-ciple, toward printed vernacular Bibles. Their Latin Vulgate, after all,

---

67. Gow, "The Contested History of a Book," 271.

68. Plenaria were similar to lectionaries: "renderings of selected Biblical passages, chiefly the litur-gical lessons appointed to be read in the vernacular, the so-called pericopes." Bluhm, *Martin Luther: Creative Translator*, 5.

69. Johannes Cochlaeus, *Historia Martini Lutheri: das ist, kurtze Beschreibung seiner Handlungen und Geschrifften, der Zeit nach, vom M.D. XVII biss auff das XLVI. Jar seines Ableibens, ordentlich vnnd getrewlich den Nachkommenen zü gütem: erstlich in Latein durch Weiland den ehrwürdigen vnd hochgelehrten Herrn Ioannem Cochlaeum . . . beschrieben vnd jetzo auss dem Latein ins Teutsch gebracht . . .* (Ingolstadt: David Sartorium, 1582), 120.

was the primary example of a vernacular Bible. They were, however, cautious about licensing such Bibles.

In contrast with the caution exhibited toward vernacular Bibles by the Roman church, both Luther and Melanchthon advocated in the early years of the reformation that all should have access to the Bible. In the "Preface to Romans," Luther suggested "it is worthy not only that every Christian should know [Romans] word for word, by heart, but also that he should occupy himself with it every day, as the daily bread of the soul. We can never read it or ponder over it too much; for the more we deal with it, the more precious it becomes and the better it tastes."[70] Likewise, he stated,

> Above all, the foremost reading for everybody, both in the universities and in the schools, should be Holy Scripture—and for the younger boys, the Gospels. And would to God that every town had a girls' school as well, where the girls would be taught the Gospel for an hour every day either in German or in Latin . . . Is it not only right that every Christian man know the entire holy Gospel by the age of nine or ten?[71]

This rise of other evangelical groups such as those led by Ulrich Zwingli or even Luther's former colleague Andreas Bodenstein von Karlstadt—whom he labeled "*Schwärmer*" (enthusiasts)—caused both Luther and Melanchthon to rethink their approach, however. Zwingli and Karlstadt's interpretation of John 6:63 ("the flesh is useless") or Matthew 26:26 ("This is my body") caused them to reject the real, bodily presence of Christ in the Lord's Supper. Luther commented that Karlstadt, Zwingli, and other "enthusiasts" who "swarmed about the biblical text" in fact "distorted each word singly and collectively, putting the last things first, rather than accept the true meaning of the text, as we have observed."[72] The multitude of interpretations of prophetic visions and apocalyptic books, such as Daniel and the Revelation of John, also influenced Thomas Muntzer's call for a theocratic rule and support for the peasants' revolt in 1525, "based on his prophetic visions and interpretations of Scripture."[73] Such actions caused the Wittenberg reformers to be more cautious about encouraging everyone to read the Bible—at least without some prior grounding in the basics of Lutheran theology. Luther later concluded

---

70. "Preface to the Epistle of St. Paul to the Romans (1522)," LW 35:365; WA DB 7:2,4–16.
71. "To the Christian Nobility of the German Nation (1520)," LW 44:205–6; WA 6:461,11–15.
72. "About the Jews and Their Lies," in *Christian Life in the World*, eds. Hans J. Hillerbrand, Kirsi I. Stjerna, and Timothy J. Wengert., Vol. 5, TAL, 504.
73. H. Ashley Hall, Introduction to "To the Councilmen of All Cities in Germany That They Establish and Maintain Christian Schools," in *Christian Life in the World*, eds. Hans J. Hillerbrand, Kirsi I. Stjerna, and Timothy J. Wengert, Vol. 5, TAL, 238.

that "the text of the canonical Bible presented material perplexing to the simple reader."[74] The Lutherans therefore reluctantly concluded that guidance was needed to read the Bible in order to prevent the rise of heresies.[75] Thus, by the time of the publication of the 1546 edition of the Bible, most references to the reading of Scripture by the common people had been dropped from the original 1522 preface.[76] Luther's early ideal of having the Bible in the hands of everyone and freeing Scripture from the tyranny of the pope was thus tempered by his realization that doing so might produce unintended consequences. Reading the Bible out of context could cause problems, both in terms of theology and politics. Caution in handling Scripture was needed. The solution Luther came up with was to write his catechisms, which both he and the authors of the Epitome of the Formula of Concord called "the Bible for the laity."[77] These would serve to provide an overview of the main themes of the Bible so that it wouldn't be misinterpreted.

The Lutherans, as with the Roman authorities, had legitimate concerns associated with laity reading the Bible without proper interpretation. While the Roman church authorities felt that they alone provided the official, proper interpretation, the reformers felt that reading the text through the lens of the gospel led to the proper interpretation. In both cases,

---

74. Ruth B. Bottigheimer, "Bible Reading, 'Bibles' and the Bible for Children in Early Modern Germany," *Past and Present* 139 (May 1993), 72. See also Hermann Gelhaus, *Der Streit um Luthers Bibelverdeutschung im 16. und 17. Jahrhundert* (Tübingen: Max Niemeyer, 1989).

75. Richard Gawthrup and Gerald Strauss, "Protestantism and Literacy in Early Modern Germany," *Past and Present* 104 (August 1984), 34 n. 14, 35. As they note, 'Confronting an increasingly pluralistic and unstable religious scene, Lutheran authorities were too frightened of heterodoxy to encourage people to meet the Bible on their own terms' (p. 42).

76. Luther's colleague Philip Melanchthon (1497–1560) also became more cautious about placing the Scriptures in the hands of the common folk without proper guidance because of the way enthusiasts and political opportunists used the Bible for their own gain. At first he encouraged everyone to read the Bible as the only true source of Christianity: "There is nothing I should desire more, if possible, than that all Christians be occupied in greatest freedom with the divine Scriptures alone and be thoroughly transformed into their nature . . . Anyone is mistaken who seeks to ascertain the nature of Christianity from any source except canonical Scripture," "Dedicatory Letter," *Loci communes theologici*, 1521, trans. Lowell J. Satre. *Melanchthon and Bucer*, Ed. Wilhelm Pauck (Philadelphia: Westminster Press, 1969), 19. Three decades later he emphasized that "rightly oriented teachers are needed . . . to clarify and preserve the proper meaning of the words of the prophets and apostles . . . This should be the purpose of a catechism," "Dedication by Philip Melanchthon to Anna, Wife of Joachim Camerarius, September 21, 1553 (Matthew the Apostle)," *Loci communes theologici*, 1555, trans. And ed. Clyde L. Manschreck (New York: Oxford University Press, 1965), xliii.

77. Luther refers to the catechism as the "the laymen's Bible" in one of his "Table Talks," WA TR 5:581,30–32, (No. 6288). This same term is found in the *Epitome, Formula of Concord*, "Concerning the Binding Summary," 5, BC 487; BSELK 1218,6.

however, reading the Bible was controlled neither by the Roman church nor by Lutherans. Both, however, recognized the dangers that could arise from laity reading the Bible without guidance.

SUMMARY

There are many myths surrounding the availability and quality of Bibles in the late fifteenth and early sixteenth centuries. Many of these myths have been passed on in popular lore to the present time. History tells a different story, however. Luther was not the first to translate the Bible into German. There were eighteen bibles translated into German and published between the years 1466 and 1522, when the first translation of Luther's New Testament was printed in Wittenberg. While some of these earlier translations were indeed "wooden" or "stilted," other versions were more idiomatic and eminently more readable. Nor were vernacular versions of the Bible banned by the Roman church. The plethora of biblical images in churches, telling the story of the faith, along with the popularity of published Bibles, biblical devotional readings, *plenaria*, lectionaries and individually published books of the Bible speak otherwise. Nor would publishers keep printing these materials if there was no demand for them. As a result, the Word was proclaimed in the language of the people. That was its function, and that was the legacy for which Luther the translator wanted to be known.

4.

From the September Testament of 1522 to the Luther Bible of 1534

"There has been much talk about the translation of the Old and New Testaments. The enemies of the truth charge that in many places the text has been modified or even falsified, whereby many simple Christians, even among the learned who do not know the Hebrew and Greek languages, have been startled and shocked."[1]

"I have also undertaken to translate the Bible into German. That was necessary for me; otherwise I might have died someday imagining that I was a learned man."[2]

INTRODUCTION

Luther had been translating passages of the Bible long before his New Testament appeared at a book fair in September of 1522.[3] After learning Hebrew, and then Greek, he began relying on his own

---

1. "On Translating (1530)," LW 35:181; WA 30.II:632,11–15.
2. "A Letter of Consolation to All Who Suffer Persecution (1522)," LW 43:70; WA 10.II:60,13–15.
3. There are different accounts about whether the 1522 New Testament was first exhibited in Frankfurt or Leipzig. Andrew Pettegree argues for the Frankfurt book fair, in *Brand Luther: How an Unheralded Monk Turned His Small Town Into a Center of Publishing, Made Himself the Most Famous Man in Europe—and Started the Protestant Reformation* (New York: Penguin Books, 2015), 186. Euan Cameron, however, states that it was first shown at the Leipzig Book Fair, thus irritating Luther's nemesis, Duke Georg of Saxony, "in whose lands Leipzig lay." Cameron, "The Luther Bible," in *The New Cambridge History of the Bible. Volume 3: From 1450 to 1750,* ed. Euan Cameron (Cambridge. University of Cambridge Press, 2016), 220. For details on the Frankfurt Book Fair, see James Westphal Thompson, *The Frankfurt Book Fair. The Francofordiense Emporium of Henri Estienne* (New York: Burt Franklin, 1911).

translations of biblical passages, rather than those of earlier versions of the German Bibles or *Plenaria* (Lectionaries). As he "studied, wrote, lectured and preached," his own "spontaneous partial translations of Scripture into German"[4] conveyed a better sense of immediacy in his preaching and teaching. This is clear even in his very first publication—a translation of the seven Penitential Psalms in 1517.[5] But this work was only the beginning, as Bluhm has noted. Luther felt that some of the earlier German Bibles and *Plenaria* lacked a sense of immediacy and were not very readable.[6] The Word needed to be spoken in a "language common to his beloved sixteenth-century Germans," usable in worship.[7] Thus, he turned to the task himself, and it occupied him for the next twenty-five years. This task was made possible because of the development of the printing industry, particularly in Wittenberg. Printing was crucial for the dissemination and, thus, proclamation of the gospel.

THE DEVELOPING PRINTING INDUSTRY

The time, effort, high overhead, and carrying costs required to print a Bible were immense. The returns on their investment for a publisher could be substantial—albeit not as profitable as publishing a Latin Bible.[8] Unknown in 1515, four years later Luther was Europe's most published author.[9] Thus, when rumors surfaced that Luther was translating a New Testament, printers began lining up for the job, since his short books and pamphlets, easily typeset and printed in a few days, had already led to big profits.

The University of Wittenberg, founded in 1502, got its first printing press when Johann Rhau-Grunenberg set up shop in 1508 in the

---

4. Cameron, "The Luther Bible," 219.
5. Heinz Bluhm, "Luther's German Bible," in *Seven-Headed Luther: Essays in Commemoration of a Quincentenary 1483–1983*, ed. Peter Newman Brooks (Oxford: Clarendon Press, 1983), 179. See LW 14:137-205; WA 18:479-530.
6. Heinz Bluhm, *Martin Luther: Creative Translator* (St. Louis: Concordia, 1965).
7. Timothy J. Wengert, "Martin Luther's September Testament: The Untold Story," *The Report: A Journal of German-American History* 47 (2017), 52.
8. Bibles took about two years to print. Andrew Pettegree, "Publishing in Print: Technology and Trade," in *The New Cambridge History of the Bible. Volume 3: From 1450 to 1750*, ed. Euan Cameron (Cambridge. University of Cambridge Press, 2016), 163–67.
9. In 1515, Luther was not even in a list of the top one hundred professors at three minor German universities. In the next four years, however, he published forty-five titles, which turned into 291 editions by the time the printers had moved on to other projects. Pettegree, *Brand Luther*, 104–5.

Augustinian monastery, close to the teaching hall.[10] For Luther's bibli-cal lectures, Rhau-Grunenberg printed the Vulgate text with generous space between the lines of text and wide margins. This allowed Luther to make corrections to the text as he encountered other translations and commentaries.[11] Luther quickly realized, however, that the local printer left something to be desired. He used poor quality type, and his text proofing was substandard.[12] Luther often expressed his dissatisfaction with the printing quality in his letters, when he was out of town and unable to personally supervise the process.[13] For example, while in the Coburg Castle in the summer of 1530, he asked his spouse, Katharina, to oversee the printer's work.[14] Despite his complaints about the quality of Rhau-Grunenberg's work, he still appreciated the printer's moral character.[15] The printer was honest and pious, and not interested in making a profit at the expense of others. Luther also defended the Wittenberg printers when other printers, who had access to bigger markets, threatened the Wittenberg printers' ability to survive.[16] Yet Luther, like most authors of the time, received not a penny for his work.[17] This made the inflationary profits of the printers even more intolerable for the reformer—especially when the authors had to spend so much time correcting the sloppy work of some printers. Once, when Luther was still in the Wartburg castle, he vented his frustrations with the printer after seeing a copy of his treatise "On Confession."[18] He wrote:

> I cannot say how unhappy and disgusted I am with the printing. I wish I had sent nothing in German! It is printed so poorly, so carelessly and

10. Pettegree, "Publishing in Print," 172. For the first decade, only a few books were published. See also Hans Volz, *Martin Luthers deutsche Bibel: Entstehung and Geschichte der Lutherbibel* (Hamburg: Friedrich Wittig, 1978), 94–97.

11. Hilton C. Oswald, "Introduction," LW 25:ix-x. See also Robert Kolb, *Martin Luther and the Enduring Word of God: The Wittenberg School and Its Scripture-Centered Proclamation* (Grand Rapids: Baker Academic, 2016), 133.

12. Rhau-Grunenberg had set up his printing press in 1508. Besides poor quality (likely second-hand) metal type, he used many abbreviations, as was the practice of the early printers.

13. Pettegree, *Brand Luther*, 141–42.

14. "Letter to Katharina von Bora (August 15, 1530)," LW 49:403; WA BR 5:546,18–26 and "Letter to Katharina von Bora (September 8, 1530)," LW 49:417–18; WA BR 5:608,14–19.

15. Lotter Jr., however, eventually left town after allegedly attacking an apprentice with an awl. Robert Kolb, *Luther's Wittenberg World: The Reformer's Family, Friends, Followers and Foes* (Minneapolis: Fortress Press, 2018), 41.

16. "Letter to Elector John Frederick (July 8, 1539)," LW 50:186–87; WA BR 8:491,6–23. (No. 286). See also "Letter from Publishers Goltz, Schramm and Vogel to Luther (November 1539)," WA BR 12:285,1–286,49, (No. 4273).

17. "On Translating (1530)," LW 35:193; WA 30.II:640,1–3.

18. "Von der Beichte (1521)," WA 8:138–85.

confusedly, to say nothing of the bad type faces and paper. John [Johann Rhau-Grunenberg] the printer is always the same old John and does not improve. For goodness' sake, under no circumstances let him print any of the German *Postils!* What I have sent of them should be stored away, or rather returned to me so that I may send it somewhere else. What good does it do to work hard if such sloppiness and confusion causes other printers [who may reprint from this first edition] to make more mistakes that are worse? I do not want the Gospels and Epistles to be sinned against in this way; it is better to hide them than to bring them out in such a form. . . . I shall send nothing more until I have seen that these sordid money-grubbers, in printing books, care less for their profits than for the benefit of the reader.[19]

Luther's frustration with Rhau-Grunenberg's printshop was lessened when a new printer arrived, thanks to Lucas Cranach the Elder and Christian Döring. They convinced Melchior Lotter the Elder, a printer in Leipzig, to send his son Melchior Lotter Jr. to set up shop in Cranach's workshop.[20] Initially, Luther was impressed with the new printer. Lotter had access to better quality type and a wider selection of font sizes, useful for printing marginal notes. As a result, the choice of font used by the printers also helped identify whether the publication was supportive of the reformation. There were three basic fonts used at the time. Gutenberg's "Gothic" font imitated the appearance of liturgical manuscripts; the academy used the Antiqua (Roman or Textur) font; and the reformers used the Schwabacher/ Fraktur family of fonts, developed in Germany. Rhau-Grunenberg used the Antiqua font and a poor-quality Schwabacher typeface, while Lotter had access to the Schwabacher and the newly developed Fraktur fonts. The Fraktur font immediately became identified as font of the Reformation,[21] setting it apart from the Gothic, Roman fonts.

Cranach also soon realized that a successful printing business needed a secure access to paper—which could often represent a major portion of

---

19. "Letter to Spalatin (August 15, 1521)," LW 48:292–93; WA BR 2:379–81. Luther had also complained about Rhau-Grunenberg's work to Spalatin in 1518; LW 48:73–76; WA BR 1:190–91; and LW 48:80–83; WA BR 1:195–96.
20. Cranach set Lotter up at #1 Schloßstrasse in Wittenberg. Pettegree, *Brand Luther*, 157.
21. See LW 48:19, n. 8; WA BR 1:56, n.3; and Hartmut Hövelmann, *Kernstellen der Lutherbibel: Eine Anleitung zum Schriftverständnis*. Texte und Arbeiten zur Bibel, Deutschen Bibelgesellschaft, Band 5 (Bielefeld: Luther Verlag, 1989), 45–46. The selection of fonts to make a political statement surfaced again in the 1940s. Nazis banned the use of Schwabacher and Fraktur type fonts, claiming they were Jewish creations (Anordnung 2/41), Yannis Haralambous, "Typesetting in Old German: Fraktur, Schwabacher, Gotisch and Initials," *TEX 90 Conference Proceedings* (Providence: TEX Users Group, 1991), 131, and Appendix D, 137–38. For printing mills, see Heinrich Kühne, "Der Wittenberger Buch- und Papierhandel im 16. Jahrhundert," *Vierhundertfünfzig Jahre Reformation*, eds. Leo Stern und Max Steinmetz (Berlin: Deutscher Verlag der Wissenschaften, 1967), 318.

printing costs. When Lotter Jr. arrived in Wittenberg, Cranach bought the Rühelsche paper mill to support his printing business.[22] Not long afterward, Cranach sold his shares of the printing business to the goldsmith Döring. Then, shortly before Döring died in 1533, he sold the business to three others, who financed the printing of the 1534 Luther Bible.

While the printers recognized the financial benefits of publishing a New Testament or Bible, Luther and his colleagues wanted a translation so that God's Word would be proclaimed whenever Scripture was read aloud. Thus, Luther and his team kept the parish pastors and preachers in mind, since they were the ones publicly proclaiming the gospel.[23] The translations were meant for them. The Bible Project was for breathing the gospel into the community, not profit. Thus, Luther complained that:

> God blesses a moderate and just profit, but a wicked and intolerable profit is cursed. It was so with Melchior Lotter, who got a very large return from his books; every penny earned a penny. At first the profits were so very large that Hans Grünenberg had conscientious scruples and said, "Dear Doctor, the yield is too great; I don't like to have such books." He was a godly man and was blessed. But Lotter is now cursed for a second time on account of his unspeakable profit.[24]

THE 1522 NEW TESTAMENT

Luther's desire that biblical translations capture a sense of the living, breathing Word did not immediately lead to his deciding to translate the Bible himself. He first looked to others who he felt were more skilled for the task.[25] In mid-1521, Luther's colleague Johann Lang produced a very literal translation of the Gospel of Matthew. Even though Luther preferred a more inspired style of translation, he applauded Lang's efforts

22. Pettegree, *Brand Luther*, 108, 157. See also Pettegree, "Publishing in Print," 172–73; and Hövelmann, *Kernstellen der Lutherbibel*, 46.

23. See Robert Kolb, "The Enduring Word of God, in Wittenberg," *Lutheran Quarterly* 30 No. 2 (Summer 2016), 197; and Wengert, "Martin Luther's September Testament," 55. In the Augsburg Confession, Article V, "Concerning the Office of Preaching" follows the article on justification. The preaching office is to proclaim justification by grace through faith, that is, the gospel, which brings the church to life. AC Articles IV and V, BC 38 & 40; BSELK 98 & 100 (German Text).

24. "Table Talks (1532)," LW 54:141; WA TR 2:58,15–22, (No. 1343).

25. This was also the case for the *Small Catechism*. Luther initially thought John Agricola and Justus Jonas would lead this project. BC 345–6.

and encouraged him to continue with this project.[26] But soon he began to consider the benefits of doing his own translation of the Bible. He first floated the idea to colleagues when, disguised as Knight George in the Wartburg,[27] he secretly visited Wittenberg in early December of 1521. This group of Luther's peers—clearly led by Melanchthon—convinced Luther to begin translating the Bible, marking "the fateful hour for Luther's Bible translation."[28] The monk, who had learned Hebrew and Greek by doing comparative readings of Scripture and who received lessons from the biblical scholars at the University of Wittenberg, began his daunting task. Initially, he thought translating the New Testament would take him at least until Easter (April 20, 1522). He soon realized, however, that translating the Old Testament was too much for one person to take on, and so while still working on the New Testament, he wrote to Amsdorf, suggesting that his friend find a secret room in Wittenberg in which he and his team could translate the Old Testament.[29] Meanwhile, he would work on the New Testament. Luther later wrote to Lang, saying that he expected he would be at the Wartburg until Easter,[30] working on his translation.

Luther had few resources at hand when he translated the New Testament.[31] He likely had only a copy of Erasmus's 1519 Greek New Testament, a copy of the Vulgate,[32] and perhaps a German Bible, such as the Zainer Bible of 1475.[33] He may also have had some *Plenaria* (the Lectionary texts for the Gospels) in German, since he was also working on his *Advent Postils*[34] at the time—sermons to be read in congregations or in the home. Luther's language skills were also under debate. Those who argue that his Greek skills were not sufficient for the task[35] insist that he relied only

---

26. Martin Brecht, *Martin Luther: Shaping and Defining the Reformation, 1521–1532*, trans. James L. Schaaf (Minneapolis: Fortress Press, 1994), 46. "Letter to Lang (December 18, 1521)," LW 48:356; WA BR 2:413.

27. St. George was the patron saint of Saxony.

28. Otto Albrecht, "Historical and Theological Introduction to Luther's Translation of the New Testament," WA DB 6:lxx–lxxi.

29. "Letter to Amsdorf (January 13, 1522)," LW 48:363; WA BR 2:423,51–55.

30. "Letter to Lang (December 18, 1521)," LW 48:356–57; WA BR 2:413,5–7. See also Scott Hendrix, *Martin Luther: Visionary Reformer* (New Haven: Yale University Press, 2015.), 26.

31. Andrew C. Gow, "The Contested History of a Book: The German Bible of the Later Middle Ages and Reformation in Legend, Ideology, and Scholarship," *Analecta Gorgiana* (Piscataway, NJ: Gorgias Press, 2012), 286–89.

32. Brecht, *Shaping and Defining the Reformation*, 47.

33. Albrecht, "Introduction," WA DB 6:lxxi. Brecht, however, doubts Luther had a Zainer Bible with him. Brecht: *Shaping and Defining the Reformation*, 47.

34. These *Advent Postils* are found in LW 75; WA 10.I.2:1–208.

35. Gow doubts that "Luther relied exclusively on the 'original Greek' text of the New Testament," since that "ignores Luther's reliance on both earlier German translations and the Vulgate, and

on earlier German Bibles and his own translations of the Vulgate.[36] Others suggest that Luther completed his translation so quickly because the *Plenaria* were already translated into German, so a large portion of the work was already done for him.[37] Moreover, there are many similarities between Luther's translations of the Gospels and those in the *Plenaria*, most likely because he heavily relied upon them in his daily preaching and teaching.[38] In the final analysis, however, while discussions of Luther's sources are fascinating, what set his translation apart from others was the unifying message of the gospel that flowed through the oral nature of his translation.[39] The translated New Testament was to be an auditory event. Scripture was meant to be preached and heard.

Luther completed his draft translation of the New Testament by March of 1522. He then headed to Wittenberg, armed with a preacher's two most powerful tools: the Scriptures and a collection of sermons in the language of the people. Willem Jan Kooiman compares Luther's return to Wittenberg as a Moses coming down from the Wartburg [mountain], not with the law but with the gospel,[40] even though Luther would have preferred the focus to be only on Christ coming down from Mt. Golgatha with the gospel. He did not want attention placed on himself.

By leaving the Wartburg castle, Luther defied the wishes of his elector, Frederick the Wise, who had wanted to keep him safely hidden. Luther informed him in a letter that like Paul (Gal 1:8), he [Luther] had received the gospel from Christ alone, and he was called to be a minister and evangelist. Luther further stated that if he were captured, he would not blame the elector for failing to protect him.[41] The Gospel had to be preached and

---

gives him more credit as a philologist than he deserves." Gow, "The Contested History of a Book," 265–66.

36. Wilhelm L. Krafft, *Ueber die deutsche Bibel vor Luther und dessen Verdienste um die Bibelübersetzung,* Dissertation (Bonn: Formis Caroli Georgi University, 1883), claimed that Luther borrowed extensively from the Koberger Bible, while Erwin Mühhaupt, "Bibel und Buchdruckerkunst vor Luther," *Die Bibel in der Welt* 6 (1955), 14, argued that Luther relied on the Zainer Bible. See also Hövelmann, *Kernstellen der Lutherbibel,* 21.

37. Krafft, *Ueber die deutsche Bibel,* 12–15. See also Hövelmann, *Kernstellen der Lutherbibel,* 21.

38. Heinrich Bornkamm, "Die Vorlagen zu Luthers Übersetzungen des Neuen Testaments," *Theologische Literaturzeitung* 72 (1947), 28. See also Willem Jan Kooiman, *Luther and the Bible* (Philadelphia: Muhlenberg Press, 1961), 94; and Heinz Bluhm, *Martin Luther: Creative Translator* (St. Louis: Concordia, 1965), 5.

39. "The central contribution of Luther's September Testament comes from its surprisingly oral nature," most suited for the Christian assembly. Wengert, "Martin Luther's September Testament," 52.

40. Kooiman, *Luther and the Bible,* 118.

41. "Letter to Elector Frederick (March 5, 1522)," LW 48:390, 392; WA BR 2:455,39–43; 456,95–96.

taught. Heading to Wittenberg, Luther carried with him the Scriptures and a collection of sermons to preach, both in the language of the people.

Upon arriving in Wittenberg, Luther immediately turned to his close friend and colleague Philip Melanchthon for help with editing and improving his translation.[42] Editing the draft translation kept them busy for a month. By the beginning of May, it was given to the printer. Three presses were used to print the work. Luther closely supervised the printing process, proofing the pages as they were ready. This task took almost as much time as the actual translating work.[43] By early June, Luther had sent the complete Gospel of Matthew to Spalatin, as a gift to Elector Frederick. On September 25, "Luther sent the first complete copy to Hans von Berlepsch, the guardian of the Wartburg, under whose protection the work had been done."[44] It was a momentous day for Luther. Luther later stated that "This German Bible (this is not praise for myself but the work praises itself) is so good and precious that it's better than all other versions, Greek and Latin, and one can find more in it than in all commentaries, for we are removing impediments and difficulties so that other people may read in it without hindrance."[45] He also stated, "I'd like all my books to be destroyed so that only the sacred writings in the Bible would be diligently read."[46] That required, however, the rest of the Bible to be translated.

THE PUBLICATION OF THE SEPTEMBER TESTAMENT

Lotter printed 3,000 to 5,000 copies of the New Testament in an affordable format, which hit the press by September 25, 1522. While the translators were not named, the place of publication was given as Wittenberg, revealing who was behind this project.[47] It was illustrated with woodcuts from the Cranach workshop.[48] It was designed for easy reading, with a single

42. When Melanchthon received the manuscript, he immediately passed on the news in a letter to Caspar Cruciger. "Letter to Cruciger (March 6, 1522)," MBWT 1:458 (No. 219). See also Hendrix, *Martin Luther: Visionary Reformer*, 126.
43. Pettegree, "Publishing in Print," 172. See also Volz, *Martin Luthers deutsche Bibel*.
44. Kooiman, *Luther and the Bible,* 120–21. LW 49:14–15; WA BR 2:596, 23–24; "Letter to Spalatin, September 21, 1522," reports that only the Preface to Romans was left, and that was finished the next day. Luther asked that the first copy be sent to Berlepsch in his "Letter to Spalatin (September 25, 1522)," WA BR 2:604,1–8.
45. "Table Talk (1540)," LW 54: 408. WA TR 5:59,4–8, (No. 5324).
46. "Table Talk (March 29, 1539)," LW 54:274; WA TR 3:623,2–3, (No.3797).
47. Brecht, *Shaping and Defining the Reformation*, 53; Kooiman, *Luther and The Bible*, 121.
48. Pettegree, "Publishing in Print," 172–73. See also Volz, *Martin Luthers deutsche Bibel*, 8; and Cameron, "The Luther Bible," 220.

column of text (unlike the double columns of the earlier German Bibles), and marginal notes were used "to explain particular words or points."[49] It was set in Schwabacher font, reflecting the "down to earth" incarnational theology of the reformers, unlike the "heavenly" Gothic font of the Vulgate and the liturgical missals of the Roman church.[50] Thus, both the translation and the font used served to highlight the gospel.

The 1522 New Testament also contained twenty-one full-page illustrations in the book of Revelation, produced in the Cranach workshop in Wittenberg, which housed Lotter's press. The only other illustrations were ornamental initials at the beginning of all but two of the books of the New Testament.[51] The illustrated initials were replaced by a woodcut in Acts, showing the outpouring of the Holy Spirit, and Revelation had the woodcut series instead of an ornamental initial at the beginning of the book.

Luther's New Testament continued the tradition of including prefaces for each of its individual books. He also added marginal notes. The inside margins contained references to similar passages in the Bible, as the Vulgate had done. The outer margins contained historical, chronological, or archeological explanations, although Luther occasionally added some contemporary context.[52] He also rearranged the order of the New Testament. Hebrews, James, Jude, and Revelation were placed at the end of the New Testament and, unlike the Gospels and other letters, were not numbered in the table of contents—suggesting their lesser value.[53] The apocryphal Letter to the Laodiceans, which had followed Galatians in the earlier German and Vulgate versions, was removed. Finally, Acts was moved from after Hebrews to after the Gospels.[54] The arrangement was

49. Cameron, "The Luther Bible," 221.
50. Leopold Nettelhorst, *Schrift muss passen: Schriftwahl und Schriftausdruck in der Werbung, Handbuch für die Gestaltungsarbeit an Werbenmitteln* (Essen: Wirtschaft & Werbung Verlagsgesellschaft, 1959), 122. See also Hövelmann, *Kernstellen der Lutherbibel*, 46; and Horst Heiderhoff, *Antiqua oder Fraktur? Zur Problemgeschichte eines Streits* (Frankfurt: Polygraph Verlag, 1971), 17. The more "down to earth" Fraktur and Schwabacher fonts may also have better reflected Luther's own "down to earth" theology, as outlined by Gerhard O. Forde, *Where God meets Man: Luther's Down-to-Earth Approach to the Gospel* (Minneapolis: Augsburg Publishing House, 1972).
51. Kooiman, *Luther and the Bible,* 121.
52. Kooiman, *Luther and the Bible,* 123.
53. Brecht, *Shaping and Defining the Reformation,* 50–51. For an image of the title page of the *Septembertestament* and the index numbering the books, see Volz, *Martin Luthers deutsche Bibel,* 114.
54. Hans Volz, "Continental Versions to c 1600: German Versions," in *The Cambridge History of the Bible: The West from the Reformation to the Present Day,* ed. S.L. Greenslade (Cambridge: Cambridge University Press, 1963), 100; Kenneth A. Strand, *German Bibles Before Luther: The Story of 14 High-German Editions* (Grand Rapids: Eerdmans, 1966), 26.

consistent with Luther's evaluation of the books based on what pushed Christ (*was Christum treibet*).

The cost of this New Testament ranged from "a half gulden, one gulden, to one and a half gulden," depending on whether it was bound or decorated with initial letters.[55] This would be about one-fifth of the price of the complete Luther Bible that would later come out in 1534.[56] The publication sold out in a couple of months, and a second edition of 3,000 copies was published, gaining the nickname "The December Testament."

Despite its popularity, the September Testament had its critics. Hans von Dolzig, a member of Elector Frederick's court, suggested that Luther shorten some phrases to make the translation sound better.[57] Paul Bachmann, the Cistercian Abbott at Mulde, Saxony, criticized it for the five hundred errors it contained.[58] Johannes Colcheaus, another opponent, complained that with its Lutheran gospel, it made "tailors and shoemakers, women and simple-minded idiots" think they were theologians, leading them to argue with their priests or even masters of Holy Scripture about interpretations of the Bible.[59] They felt that this flawed translation corrupted the minds of simple folk with its Lutheran heresies.

The strongest criticisms came from Jerome (Hieronymus) Emser, the secretary and chaplain for Duke George of Saxony, Luther's perennial foe. Duke George had banned Luther's work in his territories. Emser's scathing review of Luther's translation noted about fourteen hundred errors, while the prefaces and glosses contained heresy.[60] He admitted that Luther had "translated 'somewhat more gracefully and sweet-soundingly' than his predecessors, but it was precisely this that made his work dangerous."[61]

---

55. Brecht, *Shaping and Defining the Reformation*, 53.

56. An unbound 1534 Luther Bible cost two gulden, eight groschen. Martin Brecht, *Martin Luther: The Preservation of the Church, 1532–1546*, trans. James L. Schaaf (Minneapolis: Fortress Press, 1993), 100.

57. "Letter to Spalatin (January 1, 1527)," WA BR 4:150,19–32. See also Kolb, *Luther's Wittenberg World*, 34; Brecht, *The Preservation of the Church*, 107–8.

58. Paul Bachmann, "Response to Luther's Open Letter to Albert of Mainz (1530)," *Luther as Heretic: Ten Catholic Responses to Martin Luther, 1518–1541*, eds. M. Patrick Graham and David Bagchi (Eugene: Pickwick, 2019), 191.

59. Hövelmann, *Kernstellen der Lutherbibel*, 27–28.

60. Hieronymus Emser, *Auß was gründ ‖ vnnd vrsach ‖ Luthers dolmatschung/ vber das ‖ nawe testament/dem gemeinẽ man ‖ billich vorbotten worden sey.‖ Mit scheynbarlicher anzeygung/wie/ wo/vnd ‖ an wölchen stellen/Luther den text vorkert/vnd ‖ vngetrewlich gehandelt . . . ‖ hab.‖ . . . ‖* (Leipzig: Wolfgang Stöckel, 1523). See also Brecht, *The Preservation of the Church*, 107–8.

61. Brecht, *Shaping and Defining the Reformation*, 53. See also Kenneth A. Strand, *"Reformation Bibles in the Crossfire: The Story of Jerome Emser, His Anti-Lutheran Critique and His Catholic Bible Version* (Ann Arbor: Ann Arbor Publishers, 1961).

Emser also preferred a more literal translation and thus took exception to Luther's addition of the "alone" (*allein*) in Romans 3:28, since it ruled out justification by faith and works.[62] Luther responded by stating that a good German translation implied, if not required, the addition of the *allein*.[63] Later, in 1527, Emser published his own translation (under the name of Duke George) of the New Testament, which was basically Luther's translation of the New Testament, changing the prefaces and removing the "*allein*" that had so offended him. Upon seeing Emser's version, Luther dared anyone to place his version next to the "scribbler's" (Emser) edition, for they would quickly discover who did the real work of translating.[64] Ironically, Luther's forbidden translation, plagiarized by Emser, was now being read by Duke George's own subjects!

THE 1534 LUTHER BIBLE

Luther's ultimate goal had been to translate the complete Bible.[65] He began translating the Old Testament right after the New Testament was in print.[66] Originally he wanted the Old Testament published in three parts, to make the task more manageable and to make it more affordable.[67] In November of 1522, Luther told Spalatin that he was translating Leviticus, and that he hoped to get the Pentateuch to the printer by January; by December, a draft was ready for editing by Melanchthon and Matthew Aurogallus, Wittenberg's Old Testament scholar.[68] The completed Pentateuch came out in mid-1523.

Luther began work on the historical books (Joshua–Esther) at the beginning of 1524. He soon realized, however, that other printers throughout the land were flagrantly copying his translations and publishing them

62. "On Translating (1530)," LW 35:182; WA 30.II:632,28–30; WA DB 7:38.
63. "On Translating (1530)," LW 35:187–89; WA30.II:636,11–637,22. See also Cameron, "The Luther Bible," 221; Brecht, *Shaping and Defining the Reformation*, 53.
64. "On Translating (1530)," LW 35:185; WA 30.II:634,25–635,7.
65. "Letter to Amsdorf (January 13, 1522)," LW 48:363 and 372; WA BR 2:423,48–56; and 427,128–30, (No. 111).
66. For a detailed description of the chronology and problems faced by Luther and his colleagues in translating the Old Testament and Apocrypha, see Brecht, *The Preservation of the Church*, 95–113.
67. Brecht, *Shaping and Defining the Reformation*, 55.
68. "Letter to Spalatin (November 3, 1522)," WA BR 2:614,15–19, (No. 546). See note 7. See also Brecht, *Shaping and Defining the Reformation*, 55.

without his permission.[69] He became very irate because these printers did not give credit either to the author or to the original publisher, and the original publisher would suffer a loss of sales, making its printing less viable. Even worse, these printers changed the text, obliterating and falsifying what he had wanted to emphasize. This "thievery" led to the first prototype of a copyright symbol, which Luther included in the second part of his translation of the Old Testament (Joshua–Esther), printed in 1524. On the last page, the printer placed two emblems, designed by Cranach and Luther. On the left was a Lamb carrying a flag with a cross on it, and on the right was the "Luther rose." Underneath the two emblems Luther had written, "This mark bears witness / that such books have gone through my hands / for the printing of false and distorted books / has now become quite common."[70] From that point on, while other printers still reprinted his works without authorization, they did not copy the two emblems. Eventually, the name "Luther" began appearing on the title page, which often guaranteed a sale.

Luther then translated Job, Proverbs, Ecclesiastes, and the Song of Solomon. These were published together, in the Fall of 1524.[71] Job was especially hard to translate. Its descriptive language meant that he had to translate the ideas rather than the words.[72] Luther then turned his attention to the Prophets. This ought to have gone quickly, since Luther had already

69. In 1524, a portion of Luther's Lenten Postil manuscript was stolen from the printer and published in Regensberg, even though Wittenberg was given as the place of publication. This made Luther hesitant to continue his translation of the Prophets. Luther commented:

> "... a rogue, the typesetter, who lives off our sweat, came along and stole my manuscript before I was even done with it, carried it out, and had it printed elsewhere, thus using up our effort and labor. . . . You are a thief, obliged before God to make restitution. . . . Nevertheless, this could have been endured if only they did not treat my books so falsely and shamefully. . . . I do not recognize my own books. Here something is left out; there something is transposed; here something is falsified; there something was uncorrected. They have also learned the art of printing "Wittenberg" on top of certain books which were never produced or [even] present in Wittenberg . . . to deceive the people with our name and to ruin our [friends]." "Preface to the Lent Postil (1525)," LW 76:453; WA 17.II:3,9–4,4.

The theft of manuscripts led Luther and others to request that elector John the Steadfast issue a "text of privilege" (*Wortlaut des Privilegs*) to the publishers Cranach and Döring, forbidding anyone else in Saxony from publishing Luther's biblical translations. WA DB 8:xlix–l, and n. 14.
70. WA DB 9.II:392. See also Stephan Füssel, *The Bible in Pictures: Illustrations from the Workshop of Lucas Cranach (1534)*, (Cologne: Taschen, 2009), 25; and Steven Ozment, *The Serpent and the Lamb: Cranach, Luther, and the Making of the Reformation* (New Haven: Yale University Press, 2011), 3–5.
71. WA DB 9.II:xviii–xix. The Pentateuch is found in WA DB 8; the historical books in WA DB 9:I and 9.II, and the poetic books in WA DB 10.I and 10.II.
72. As Luther states in the 1545 Preface, "for example, when he says something like this, 'The thirsty will pant after his wealth' [Job 5:5], that means 'robbers shall take it from him'; or when he says, 'The children of pride have never trodden it' [Job 28:8], that means 'the young lions

translated the Prophets for his lectures.[73] But he wanted to revise them before he published them. Thus, Jonah was published in 1526, Isaiah and Zechariah in 1528, and Ezekiel and Daniel in 1530.[74] His translation work often had to be put aside because of various demands on his time and the many absences from Wittenberg by him or members of his translating team. The work was also difficult, with Luther comparing it to trying to get a nightingale to teach its song to a cuckoo.[75] To his chagrin, the Anabaptists Ludwig Härtzer and Hans Denck published their own translation of the Prophets in Worms before Luther's translation was complete. While he appreciated parts of the Härtzer-Denck translation, he felt its language was confusing.[76] He also questioned the theology implicit in that translation, suggesting it rejected the Trinity and the divinity of Christ. Thus, Luther consulted the Worms translation, but he did not rely on it.[77] With all these delays and challenges, the Wittenberg translation of the Prophets was not ready until 1532.[78] In the end, Luther was pleased with his revised translations of the Prophets and Psalter.[79] They pointed to a Living God who cared for and understood people.

Luther next began translating the Apocrypha. He linked the Apocrypha to the Old Testament, but felt it had no canonical authority. Thus, in his index of the Old Testament, the canonical books were numbered, but the apocryphal books were not.[80] When Melanchthon was at the Diet of Speyer in 1529, Luther had a cold that prevented him from preaching and lecturing, so he turned to translating the Wisdom of Solomon. He appreciated this book because of its focus on the Word and because it was easy to apply to the contemporary context. He also translated part of the book of Sirach but apparently left the translation of the other books of the Apocrypha to Melanchthon and Jonas.[81] His task was now to work

---

that stalk proudly'; and many similar cases." "Preface to the Book of Job (1545)," LW 35:252; WA DB 10,I:6,1–8.

73. Brecht, *Shaping and Defining the Reformation*, 55.

74. Hövelmann, *Kernstellen der Lutherbibel*, 17.

75. "Letter to Link (June 14, 1528)," WA BR 4:484,21–23, (No. 1285). See also "Preface to the Prophet Isaiah (1528/1545)," LW 35:277–78; WA DB 11.I:22,14–19, where Luther notes the difficulties of translating Hebrew into a German that is not stiff or wooden.

76. "Letter to Link (May 4, 1527)," LW 49:165; WA BR 4:198,6–8, (No. 172). See also "On Translating (1530)," LW 35:194–95, and 194, n. 59; WA 30.II:640,28–32.

77. George Witzel levelled this charge against Luther in 1536. Brecht, *The Preservation of the Church*, 95.

78. Brecht, *The Preservation of the Church*, 95.

79. "Table Talks (1532)." LW 54:135–36; WA TR 2:40,19–22, (No. 1317), and WA TR 2:439,11–13, (No. 2381).

80. WA DB 8:34.

81. Brecht, *The Preservation of the Church*, 96.

on revisions of the previous translations and to write the prefaces for each of the books and sections of the Bible.

While Luther did the bulk of the translation of the Bible, it was by no means his work alone. Beginning in 1531, a Bible "Revision Committee" met to review the translations. Luther nicknamed his group the "Sanhedrin," and they met fifteen times between mid-January and mid-March in 1531. It was composed of Luther, Matthew Aurogallus, Johannes Bugenhagen, Caspar Cruciger, Justus Jonas, and Philip Melanchthon. After reviewing Luther's new translation of the Psalms and the Prophets prior to their publication in 1532, the group began gathering together all the parts of the Old Testament in 1533. When they were not translating, they were revising. The New Testament, for example, was revised six times before the complete Bible was published.[82] Once the Bible was published in 1534, they immediately began revising and correcting their work.

COMPLEMENTING THE TRANSLATION OF THE GOSPEL

To help the preacher make full use of the first "Lutheran Study Bible,"[83] the Wittenberg team prepared prefaces to accompany the text, while also working with the publisher to include appropriate illustrations. The addition of these "study aids" had begun with Jerome, who added prefaces and marginal notes to his early-fifth century translation of the Vulgate. Erasmus had followed suit in his New Testaments. The prefaces in the Luther Bible, however, differed significantly from those of Jerome and Erasmus. In Luther's view, previous prefaces had obscured the distinction between the Law and Gospel, thus misleading people.[84] Luther stated:

> Erasmus has indeed put out very disgraceful prefaces, even if he did soften them, because he makes no distinction between Christ and Solon. Moreover, as the prefaces to Romans and to the canonical First Epistle of John show, he obscures the authority of Paul and John, as if these writings were of no moment, as if the Epistle to the Romans had no relevance for our time, as

82. Hendrix, *Martin Luther: Visionary Reformer*, 227–28.
83. Kolb, "The Enduring Word of God," 197.
84. Brecht, *Shaping and Defining the Reformation,* 51. Wengert states that some prefaces in the Vulgate were written by Pelagius, not Jerome, including the Preface to Romans. Pelagius emphasized human cooperation with God for one's salvation. Wengert, "Martin Luther's September Testament, 57.

if the difficulty in this epistle outweighed its value, etc. Is this praise for the book's author? For shame![85]

Likewise, in the 1522 preface to James and Jude, Luther called James a "book of straw," since it did not "push Christ." The gospel was lacking. On the other hand, the preface to Romans, prepared for the 1522 New Testament but reused in the 1534 Bible, declared that it contained the heart of the gospel, since law and gospel were at the "very center of Scripture."[86] These prefaces provided the lenses through which the preachers were to read the texts in preparing their sermons. Luther's prefaces, first prepared for earlier publications of various parts of the Bible, did not simply give an outline of each biblical book along with moral injunctions for living as upright Christians. Instead, the Wittenberg prefaces guided the reader about what to look for in the text. They were Luther's "personal testimony to the living and abiding dynamic of the Scriptures.

The inclusion of glosses and marginal notes to aid in the interpretation of Scripture was also not a Lutheran innovation. They appeared in the fourteenth-century commentaries of Nicholas of Lyra, which Luther often consulted. However, advances in printing led to a significant visual change in the sixteenth-century publications. No longer was a small amount of biblical text placed in a small box in the middle of the page and surrounded by comments. Instead, the biblical text was now front and center, with the marginal notes in smaller print in the margins. The inner margins (closest to the binding) now provided cross-references to other biblical passages, while explanations of words or phrases and specific interpretations of a verse were in the outer margins.[87] This practice is most obvious in Romans, where Luther uses the outer marginal notes to help clarify law and gospel, thus pointing the reader to Christ. Yet it is striking that almost all the marginal notes are found in the New Testament.[88] This may be because preachers would most often focus on either the Gospel text or the Epistles, as Luther's Postils did. These Postils did not contain

85. "Table Talks (April 1, 1533)," LW 54, 189; WA TR 3:149,7–13, (No. 3033b). Solon was a famous classical Greek lawmaker.
86. Timothy J. Wengert, *Word of Life: Introducing Lutheran Hermeneutics* (Minneapolis: Fortress Press, 2019), 32.
87. Wengert, "Martin Luther's September Testament," 58–59; Hövelmann, *Kernstellen der Luther-bibel*, 48.
88. In the 1534 Luther Bible, marginal notes in the first two parts (Pentateuch and Joshua-Esther) are very rare, while in Part 3 (Job–Malachi) there are outer margin notes, giving information, but no inner notes. However, in the Psalter of Part 3, there is information in both inner and outer margins. The Apocrypha contains a combination, with the inner and outer marginal notes sometimes providing references, while other times information.

sermons on the Old Testament lectionary texts. This focus on the use of the translated Bible in public worship and preaching also led to a 1530 edition of the New Testament that included an index for the liturgical Epistles and Gospels.[89] The marginal notes and prefaces directed the preacher's attention to the gospel.

The 1534 Bible also used illustrations to point to the gospel. As with the earlier German Bibles and Luther's New Testament of 1522, it was adorned with woodcuts, in defiance of the iconoclasts who considered pictures idolatrous. The "Wittenberg Unrest" that had brought Luther back from his hiding in the Wartburg had attempted to cleanse the churches of their "idolatrous" artwork, but Luther thought that people created idols in their minds all the time. He challenged the assumption that artwork was idolatrous in the eight sermons he preached upon returning to Wittenberg in March of 1522. Six months later, his *Septembertestament* was published, richly illustrated with woodcuts from the Cranach workshop, challenging his iconoclastic despisers.[90] The *Septembertestament* illustrations were in the same places as those found in the 1478 and 1480 Cologne Bibles, with all twenty-one illustrations found in the book of Revelation.[91] Surprisingly, there were no illustrations in the Gospels, perhaps because "Luther may have discouraged the inclusion of Gospel woodcuts on the grounds that they were incapable of communicating the one central fact about Christ, that is, the significance of his death and resurrection for human salvation. Compared to this, Jesus' earthly deeds may have been regarded as of lesser import."[92] This theory fit with Luther's insistence on emphasizing what is at the heart of the gospel but is only speculation. Nevertheless, the Bibles printed in Wittenberg did move away from the earlier "speculative" images of the pre-Lutheran Bibles to Christ-related images.[93] Others, however, have proposed that there were sufficient illustrations in the *Plenaria*, and

---

89. Cameron, "The Luther Bible," 221.

90. "Third Invocavit Sermon (March 11, 1522)," LW 51:81–83; WA 10.III:26,3–30,5. Luther also addressed the question of "images" in "Against the Heavenly Prophets (1525)," LW 40:99–100; WA 18:82,21–83,15.

91. Cranach's workshop based these illustrations on the 1498 series, *Die heimliche Offenbarung Johannis* by Albrecht Dürer, with one major change—adding a triple (papal) tiara to the beast in Revelation 10. See Wengert, "Martin Luther's September Testament," 55–56, and W. Gordon Campbell, "The 'Last Word' in Pictures: Enhanced Visual Interpretation of Revelation in Luther's High German Bible (1534)," *Postscripts* 11 no. 1 (2020), 5–9.

92. Carl C. Christensen, "Luther and the Woodcuts to the 1534 Bible," *Lutheran Quarterly* 19 no. 4 (Winter 2005), 395–96.

93. Hövelmann, *Kernstellen der Lutherbibel*, 48. See also Philipp Schmidt, *Die Illustration der Lutherbibel 1522–1700: ein Stuck abendlandische Kultur-und Kirchengeschiclite mit Verzeichenissen der Bibeln, Bilder und Kunstler, 400 Abbildungen* (Basel: Friedrich, 1962), 20–21, 180ff.

so more were not needed.[94] If that were the case, though, why did the editors of the *Plenaria* keep the illustrations for Revelation? Illustrations were also very popular in various publications of the New Testament, the Bible, or other religious pamphlets.

The 1530 New Testament expanded the number of illustrations from twenty-one to twenty-six, with the additions done by an artist known only by the initials "AW." The 1534 Bible included 117 total woodcuts, five of which occur twice.[95] When the illustrations depicted specific people, they most often portrayed God the Father (19 times), followed by Christ (11 times). Also, unlike the earlier bibles, the depictions of God the Father are scattered throughout the Old Testament, rather than being restricted to the Pentateuch. In the Luther Bible, God is almost always seated on a throne and always appearing with somebody.[96] This is a God who speaks the Word throughout all of Scripture, bringing people into community by engaging with others. This was the gospel to be preached to the eyes and to the ears.

THE PUBLICATION OF THE LUTHER BIBLE

The popularity of Luther's writings meant that the Wittenberg printing presses were busy. But Luther's primary printers were now gone. The Lotter family had been forced out of the Cranach printshop in 1523 and out of Wittenberg by 1528, while Rhau-Grunenberg had died around 1529. New printers arrived, and each of them wanted the contract to print the 1534 Luther Bible. Joseph Klug had taken Lotter's spot in the Cranach workshop, and in 1524 he printed Wittenberg's first work in Hebrew making him a strong candidate. Yet it was Hans Lufft who secured the coveted contract. He, like Klug, had moved from Leipzig in 1523 and was soon printing almost everything connected with the translation

---

94. Jan Kooiman, *Luther and the Bible*, 121–22.
95. Campbell, "The Last Word in Pictures," 79; Füssel, *The Bible in Pictures,* 33. Kooiman, however, counts 124 illustrations, of which seven are used twice. Kooiman, *Luther and the Bible*, 177. Christensen reports that "The distribution of the 117 woodcuts among the various segments of the 1534 Luther Bible is quite uneven. Revelation contains by far the most, with twenty-six. Next in order of frequency come: Genesis (10 woodcuts), Exodus (10), 1 Samuel (8), 1 Kings (8), Judges (6), 2 Kings (6), Daniel (4), Joshua (3), 2 Samuel (2), Jeremiah (2), and Ezekiel (2). Thirty biblical books contain one woodcut each. Twenty-eight books contain no textual illustrations at all, while an additional six books otherwise lacking woodcuts repeat one or another of the original 117 compositions that already had appeared in the text." Christensen, "Luther and the Woodcuts," 395.
96. Christensen, "Luther and the Woodcuts," 396–97.

project.[97] Döring, who was granted the exclusive right to print the Luther Bible in 1533 by Elector John Frederick, hired Lufft to do the printing. However, Döring then sold his publishing interests and material assets to three Wittenberg booksellers: Moritz Golrz(e), Christoph Schramm, and Bartholomäus Vogel. After negotiations with the Elector, Lufft took over the printing privilege for the complete Bible on August 6, 1534.[98] He spent the summer of 1534 printing the Bible in the Schwabacher font, completing the job in late September, just in time for the huge fall book fair in Leipzig.[99] Sales were so good that the three booksellers became the richest men in Wittenberg.[100] Yet Luther and his colleagues received not a cent. But now they had a Bible that "spoke German," and which could be used by preachers to do the one thing that Luther and his colleagues had wanted when they began this project: to proclaim God's grace in Christ in a way that people would experience the gospel.

SUMMARY

The translation of the Old Testament and Apocrypha took twelve years. Despite the length of time taken and the ongoing supervision by the translating team, there were many errors in its publication, which left the impression that it was a rushed job, done without proper editing.[101] It also lacked a consistent layout. For example, the page numbers start over for each section of the Bible, making it hard to locate specific passages. The divisions between the Old Testament, Apocrypha, and New Testaments were not prominent. Almost identical title pages were used for both the prophetic books and the New Testament, while a picture of Joshua in armor was used for the Historical books. A simple "marker" page distinguished the beginning of the Poetic books, and an unillustrated title page with a table of contents was used for the Apocrypha.[102] This would gradually change as the editorial revision committee continued its work.

97. Kolb, *Luther's Wittenberg World*, 41–43; Volz, *Martin Luthers deutsche Bibel*, 104–8.

98. WA DB 4:xxiv. It is not clear whether Döring and Lufft each received a printing privilege (for the publisher and printer, respectively), or whether the references are to one single privilege that applied to both.

99. Volz, *Martin Luthers deutsche Bibel*, 154–55; Hövelmann, *Kernstellen der Lutherbibel*, 46.

100. Brecht, *The Preservation of the Church*, 100–101. See also WA DB 8:6–9. The first person to purchase the 1534 Bible was Levin Metzsch of Mylau, who paid two gulden (florens) and eight groschen for an unbound copy on October 17, 1534. WA DB 4:xxiv–xxv.

101. Füssel, *The Bible in Pictures*, 26.

102. Luther also "inaugurated the Protestant practice of separating the Apocrypha into a distinct location between the two canonical testaments." Cameron, "The Luther Bible," 223.

Yet the lack of clear delineation between the sections reflected Luther's understanding that all of Scripture was both law and gospel, thus tying the Bible together.[103] "The books of Moses and the Prophets are also Gospel," said Luther, "since they proclaimed and described in advance what the apostles preached or wrote later about Christ."[104] Also, "the chronological distinction between the two books was nullified."[105] They were a unified witness to God breaking sin's hold over people through the law, driving them to Christ (*was Christum treibet*) and, thus, the gospel.

Despite the flaws, and the relatively expensive price of the 1534 Luther Bible, the first printing of 3,000 copies quickly sold out, and it was reprinted in 1535, 1536, and again in 1539.[106] Its popularity lay in the fact that it was not simply a translation of a sacred text, but a textbook for experiencing the Living Word who proclaims gospel.

103. "Advent Postils (1522)," LW 75:146; WA 10.I.2:159,7–10.
104. "Sermon on 1 Peter (1523)," LW 30:19; WA 12:275,5–7.
105. Heinrich Bornkamm, *Luther and the Old Testament*, trans. Eric W. Gritsch and Ruth C. Gritsch (Philadelphia: Fortress Press, 1969), 81.
106. Füssel, *The Bible in Pictures*, 27.

5.

Luther's Emphasis on "Word"

"God created everything through the Word.
Therefore the Word of God makes and brings everything."[1]

"God's Word remains forever."[2]

INTRODUCTION

The 1534 Luther Bible introduced two innovations that deliberately highlighted the Gospel in the Biblical texts: first, the use of punctuation to direct the reading of the text, and second, the use of capitalization to highlight certain words and phrases. In his study of Luther's use of punctuation, Helmar Junghans stated that "Luther himself attested that he paid attention to the 'marking of sensory breaks and breathing spaces . . . far more honorably than do many of my contemporaries.' Punctuation was the best way of breaking up speech into sections."[3] The same was also true of paragraph breaks. Likewise, Luther sometimes capitalized the first letter of a word to draw attention to a particular point,[4] or to highlight what he considered the most important points in the text itself.

---

1. "Commentary on Genesis (1539–1540)," LW 4:386; WA 43:413,29–30.
2. "*Ve[rbum D[omini M[anet I[n E[ternum*." "Lectures on Isaiah (1528/1529)," LW 17:12; WA 31.II:269,22–34; and "Lectures on 1 Peter (1522)," LW 30:59–60; WA 12:299,8–23. This verse, represented with the initials from the Latin text (VĐME) became the motto of Elector John the Steadfast of Saxony, and then the motto for the Schmalkald League.
3. Helmar Junghans, "Interpunktion und Großschreibung in Texten der Lutherzeit." *Lutherjahrbuch* 74 (2007), 161. See also Herbert Wolf, *Martin Luther: eine Einführung in germanistische Luther-Studien* (Stuttgart: Metzler, 1980), 32; and Otto Albrecht, "Luthers Übersetzung des Neuen Testaments. Historisch-theologische Einleitung," WA DB 6:xc-xci.
4. Junghans, "Interpunktion," 165–66.

Second, Luther's use of capitalizing the first letter in a word for emphasis eventually evolved into capitalizing every letter in certain words or phrases. In the 1534 Bible, Luther deliberately highlighted his theology by using capital letters (majuscules) for every single letter in seven specific words or phrases.[5] This practice was first used by Luther in his 1529 translation of Wisdom of Solomon 16:12, and every Luther Bible from 1534 onward used this same form of emphasis.[6] Hövelmann called these instances of highlighting a word or phrase with majuscules for every letter "*Kernstellen* (core places)."[7] The 2017 edition of the Luther Bible continues a variation of this long tradition by placing certain key verses in bold font.[8] The reader was meant to pay attention to these words or phrases.

These original highlighted phrases were not due to printer's errors or sloppy typesetting. They were deliberate. One might assume that the printer Hans Lufft added the highlighting to put his mark on the Bible. However, three things indicate that Luther himself authorized this highlighting. First, he was closely involved in determining which biblical passages would be illustrated in the 1534 Bible and where these woodcuts were placed. Moreover, his concern over punctuation, capitalization of certain words, and even where to place the paragraph breaks indicates that he was a very "hands on" author. Christoph Walther, a corrector in Lufft's printshop, reported that Luther basically determined which illustrations would be included in the Wittenberger's Bible, including "how they should be sketched or painted, and ordered to sketch and copy the text in the simplest manner, and would not tolerate that a superfluous and unnecessary thing be added that would not serve the text."[9] Luther's concern to select the textually appropriate illustrations suggests he would

5. This does not include all instances where the translators regularly capitalized every letter in the Word *HERR* (Lord) when it refers to the Hebrew translation of the Tetragammaton *YHWH*. See the discussion that follows in the text.

6. Luther carried this practice over into the Large Catechism in his explanation of the Sacrament of the Altar. At one point, he capitalizes every letter of the words, "FOR YOU," to emphasize their importance. See "Sacrament of the Altar," LC 64; BC, 473. See here: On the Sacrament of the Altar. LXXXV. Deudsch | | Catechis = | | mus. | | Mart. Luther. | | Rhau, Georg; Wittenberg, 1529, [1], XCII Bl.: Title version; 4, VD16 L 4339 RFB: 4 ° PTh218b. Reformation Historical Research Library Wittenberg - Ev. Preacher's seminar, 4 ° PTh218b

7. Harmut Hövelmann, *Kernstellen der Lutherbibel: Eine Anleitung zum Schriftverständnis*. Texte und Arbeiten zur Bibel, Deutschen Bibelgesellshaft, eds., Bd. 5 (Bielefeld: Luther-Verlag, 1989), 49–74.

8. *Die Bibel: Nach Martin Luthers Übersetzung. Lutherbibel Revidiert 2017* (Stuttgart: Deutsche Bibelgesellschaft, 2017).

9. WA DB 6:lxxxvii. The English translation is from Stephan Füssel, *The Bible in Pictures: From the Workshop of Lucas Cranach (1534)* (Cologne: Taschen, 2009), 31.

also want to oversee what are also, in effect, a visual emphasis of certain, carefully chosen highlighted words or phrases.

Second, Luther was heavily involved in every aspect of the printing business. He regularly proof texted every page of a book to ensure an accurate rendering of his work.[10] For example, in his preface to a book written by Caspar Huberinus, Luther began by saying, "I have gladly seen this little book into print, as I have done before with several others."[11] A second example of this attention to detail in the printing process was his consistent use of *HERR* (LORD) to indicate a translation of the Tetragammaton, *YHWH,* and the capitalization of only the first two letters of "LOrd" (HErr) to translate another common name for God (*Adonai*) in his Old Testament and in the 1534 Bible. As Luther stated, "Whoever reads this Bible should also know that I have been careful to write the name of God which the Jews call "Tetragrammaton" [YHWH] in capital letters thus, LORD [HERR], and the other name which they call Adonai only half in capital letters thus, LOrd [HErr]."[12] His attention to this detail, insisting upon the different versions of capitalization as a tool to denote different names for God in the original text, suggests that he was also the instigator of the capitalization of every letter in the words or phrases in specific passages in the 1534 Bible.

The most telling argument for Luther being responsible for the highlighted text is his own emphasis of these particular words or phrases throughout his writings. These highlighted words proclaim the gospel, and the primary audience for his German Bible was evangelical preachers, to help them prepare their sermons. His lectures and biblical commentaries served the same function. This explains why his lectures sound very similar to his sermons; both helped pastors in their preaching. That was also the main reason for doing exegesis.[13] The cost of a Bible, combined with various church ordinances in Germany requiring congregations and pastors to have access to a Bible, also dictated who would be using German Bibles. Such Bibles were "bought by governments, by parish churches with revenues set aside for this purpose, and by ministerial candidates who were required by seminary regulations

10. Pettegree, *Brand Luther*, 110, 269–70. See also WA DB 6:lxxxvii.
11. "Luther's Preface, *On the Wrath and Mercy of God,* (1534)," LW 60: 69; WA 38:325,2–3.
12. "Prefaces to the Old Testament (1545/1523)," LW 35:248–49; WA DB 8:30,19–22. Although this explanation does not appear in the 1534 Luther Bible's Preface to the Old Testament, the practice is still followed.
13. Robert Kolb, *Martin Luther and the Enduring Word of God: The Wittenberg School and Its Scripture-Centered Proclamation* (Grand Rapids: Baker Academic, 2016), 135.

to own them."[14] Using majuscules to highlight specific words or phrases was Luther's way of using a yellow highlighter to draw attention to a specific text, drawing the preachers' attention to the gospel in these words of Scripture. Proclaiming the gospel was the preachers' responsibility and, to do that, they had to find the gospel in the text. Luther simply facilitated this task with his highlighting of these texts. These *Kernstellen* drew the reader's eye to the text that Luther wanted the pastors and readers to read as they prepared their sermons or meditated on Holy Scripture.

WORD IN WISDOM OF SOLOMON

In reading through the 1534 Luther Bible from beginning to end, the first instance that one encounters the highlighting of a word or phrase is not in the Old Testament but in the Apocrypha.[15] All the other instances are found in the New Testament. The decision to highlight WORD in Wisdom of Solomon rather than in some other canonical Old Testament book, however, seems at first glance somewhat puzzling. After all, the Old Testament is replete with phrases such as "The Word of the Lord" and "God's Word."[16] Since Luther himself stated in the 1534 title page for the Apocrypha in the Luther Bible that "these books are not held equal to the Scriptures but are useful and good to read,"[17] it seems strange to use Wisdom of Solomon to identify one of the "core places" (*Kernstellen*) for his biblical theology, even if he observed that "there are many good

14. Richard Gawthrup and Gerald Strauss, "Protestantism and Literacy in Early Modern Germany," *Past and Present,* no. 104 (August 1984), 40. Their claim that seminaries required the purchase of a Bible, however, are under dispute. It is not clear if the Wittenberg Faculty regulations required the purchase of a Bible. "This assertion rests on a reading of two kinds of sources: firstly, church constitutions (*Kirchenordnungen*) which mandated Bibles in churches and in the private libraries of pastors, published in *Die evangelischen Kirchenordnungen des XVI. Jahrhunderts*, ed. Emil Sehling, 5 Volumes (Leipzig, 1902–11)"; and "secondly, the protocols of Lutheran visitations throughout the sixteenth century, which, among other concerns, investigated the contents of pastors' libraries." Thus, they argued that these translations, with prefaces and glosses, were primarily for use by the pastors in the pulpits, and not by the laity.

15. Luther had taken the apocryphal books—which were scattered throughout the canonical books of the Old Testament in the Vulgate and earlier pre-Lutheran German Bibles—out of the Old Testament and placed them in a separate section, with its own title page, in his 1534 Bible. His collecting of all the apocryphal books together is still the common practice today for Protestants.

16. In the NRSV as well as the Luther Bibles from 1534–1546, the phrase, "Word of the Lord" ("*wort des Herrn,*" "*Herrn wort*" and "*Wort Gottes*" in the Luther Bible) is used over 250 times, of which only eight are in the Apocrypha.

17. "Prefaces to the Apocrypha (1534)," LB Apoc., IA; LW 35:337, n. 1; WA DB 12:2,2–4; 547.

things in this book and it is well worth reading."[18] Yet there are three basic reasons that the choice of Wisdom of Solomon as a location for a "core place" is perfectly logical. First, Luther had a deep appreciation for the book. Based on the length of the apocryphal prefaces, "Luther gave first place to Wisdom of Solomon."[19] One of the main reasons for his high regard for this book is the prominent theme of God's righteousness and grace toward the sinner. Wisdom, like justification by grace through faith, is something given by God alone; it cannot be earned. In the "Preface to Wisdom of Solomon," written in 1529, Luther stated,

> Mark well that whatever praise and glory you hear ascribed herein to wisdom is said of nothing other than the Word of God. For even [the author] himself says, in chapter 16[:12], that the children of Israel were not sustained by manna, nor saved by the bronze serpent, but by the Word of God. . . . This is why [the author] teaches that wisdom comes from nowhere else than from God, and brings many illustrations from Scripture. So he ascribes to wisdom what Scripture ascribes to the Word of God.[20]

This echoes Luther's comments in the "Freedom of a Christian," when he wrote, "For the person is justified and saved, not by works or laws, but by the Word of God, that is, by the promise of his grace, and by faith, that the glory may remain God's, who saved us not by works of righteousness which we have done [Titus 3:5], but by virtue of his mercy by the word of his grace when we believed [1 Cor. 1:21]."[21] Wisdom, like grace, comes from the Word of God alone, and the human response can only be to praise and honor God.

The apocryphal book, the Wisdom of Solomon, is very similar to Paul's letter to the Romans, in that it highlights the theme of the righteousness of God as defined by the Exodus event. In fact, Romans 2:6–8, claims Jonathan Linebaugh, is actually "a somewhat crude but accurate precis of Wisdom's soteriology: crude because it captures none of the qualifying nuances of the so-called 'Mercy Dialogue' (Wis. 11:17–12:27); accurate because for all its subtlety Wisdom, [echoes] Romans 2:6–8."[22] Salvation is a matter of God's grace, and the author of Wisdom of Solomon

18. "Preface to the Wisdom of Solomon (1529)," LB Apoc., XIB; LW 35:343: WA 12:53,13–14.
19. Roy A. Harrisville, "Apocrypha and Pseudepigrapha," *Dictionary of Luther and the Lutheran Traditions*, ed. Timothy J. Wengert (Grand Rapids: Baker Academic, 2017), 35.
20. "Preface to Wisdom of Solomon (1529)," LW 35:344; WA DB 12:53,33–54,7.
21. "Freedom of a Christian (1520)," LW 31:362–363; WA 7:63,3–7.
22. Jonathan A. Linebaugh, *Grace, and Righteousness in Wisdom of Solomon and Paul's Letter to the Romans*. Texts in Conversation, Novum Testamentum, Supplements, 152. M.M. Mitchell and D.P. Moessner, gen. ed. (Leiden: Brill, 2013), 126.

recognized this. God's grace, as found in Wisdom of Solomon, was central to Luther's theology. It is a book about God's decision to grant salvation apart from works, knowledge, logic, or reasoning. Wisdom and justification proclaimed the gospel. Yet Luther also saw the place of the law at work in Wisdom of Solomon. For example, in a lecture on the Psalms, he commented that "Here [in Wis 15:2] the Law, revealing sin, pushes (*treibet*) the person to Christ, where the Gospel is experienced."[23]

Second, Luther's decision to locate a "core place" in Wisdom of Solomon reflected his understanding of the first commandment. The subtitle of this book in the original 1529 translation, and which was also included in the 1534 Bible, was "To the Tyrants."[24] Luther saw this book as a portrayal of the struggle between those tyrants who tried to be gods in God's place and the community of the faithful. This struggle could be between the Roman Emperor Caligula and the Jewish community represented by Philo, who some early church theologians thought authored the book. Or it could also be applicable to the Emperor Charles V and his brother Ferdinand, who, at the second Diet of Speyer, was trying to force the evangelical princes and territories to "return to Rome," since Luther translated the book and wrote the preface for it, while Melanchthon was representing the Wittenberg theologians at the Diet that year. Regardless of who the tyrants might be, the message of Wisdom of Solomon was clear in echoing Luther's explanation of the first commandment in the Large Catechism, which was written around the same time. Luther stated this clearly in the preface to Wisdom of Solomon, when he declared,

> Finally, this book is a proper exposition and illustration of the first commandment. For here you see that the author throughout is teaching you to fear and trust God; he terrifies with examples of divine wrath those who are not afraid and who despise God, and he comforts with examples of divine grace those who believe and trust him. All of this is simply a correct understanding of the first commandment.
>
> From this one can also see that all wisdom wells up and flows forth from the first commandment, as from a central spring.[25]

In the Large Catechism, Luther pointed out that "to have a god is nothing else than to trust and believe in that one with your whole heart," and "If your faith and trust are right, then your God is the true one."[26]

23. "Psalm Lectures (1519–1521)," WA 5:280.11–15.
24. "Preface to the Wisdom of Solomon (1529)," LB Apoc., XIIB; LW 35:340; WA DB 12:xxvii.
25. "Preface to the Wisdom of Solomon (1529)," LB Apoc., XII; LW 35:344; WA DB 12:54,19–25.
26. LC, First Commandment, 2–3; BC 386; BSELK 930.

To understand the first commandment properly is to exhibit wisdom from God. The epic story of the Exodus from slavery in Egypt to a land promised by God, to which Wisdom of Solomon often points, is also an illustration of the first commandment, describing the story of rulers trying to place themselves above God. Yet as the Exodus story unfolds and is commented upon in Wisdom of Solomon, it becomes clear that there is only one God. This God alone saves, delivers from wrath, and heals (Wis 16:12 and 18:22). Thus, in Wisdom of Solomon 6, the author reminds the tyrants that they are not above God, but rather, they are subject to God who created and rules over all creation.

The third and most important reason for locating one of the seven "core points" or *Kernstellen* of the 1534 Luther Bible in Wisdom of Solomon is found in the very word that Luther chose to highlight: WORD. The capitalization of WORD in Wisdom of Solomon 16:12 in the 1529 translation marked the first time that Luther used this visual device to emphasize a specific word or text. His 1529 translation of Wisdom of Solomon 16:12 read, "For neither herb nor poultice cured them but it was your WORD, O LORD that heals all people."[27] As well as being the very first time that Luther capitalized every letter in a word or phrase in any of his translations (other than *HERR*, denoting *YHWH*, the Lord), Wisdom of Solomon 16:12 is also the only time in Luther's Bible translations that the words *WORT HERR* are found together in this specific order, and not separated by punctuation or the article *des* or placing the word *HERR* in the genitive (possessive) case. Elsewhere, he translated it as "*HERRN wort*," "*wort des HERRN*," or "*wort Gottes*." It was yet another way that Luther drew attention to this text, since *WORT HERR* is only used in this one verse.

When Luther revisited his translation of Wisdom of Solomon in preparation for including it in the 1534 Bible, he decided to also capitalize "WORD" in Wisdom of Solomon 18:22: "He conquered the wrath not by strength of body, not by force of arms, but by his WORD he subdued the avenger, appealing to the oaths and covenants given to our ancestors."[28] With this capitalization, Luther stressed that the Word heals and gives life, but it also conquers God's wrath. He also made clear that in these passages, the WORD does not refer to Scripture but to the Living Word. In

27. LB Apoc, XX; WA DB 12: 96; See also Hövelmann, *Kernstellen der Lutherbibel*, 49. Verse numbering was not used by Luther. This practice is first introduced five years after Luther's death by Robert Estienne (Stephanus), in his Greek New Testament, published in Geneva; see John Brown, *The History of the English Bible* (Cambridge: Cambridge University Press, 1912), 75. The numbering of verses was given only to assist in identifying where to find the citation in the relevant chapter.
28. LB Apoc. XXII; WA DB 12:104.

der Weisheit.   XX.

warnung/Denn sie hatten ein heilsam zeichen/auff das sie gedechten
an das gebot inn deinem Gesetze/Denn welche sich zu dem selbigen
zeichen kereten/die wurden gesund/nicht durch das/so sie anschawe-
ten/sondern durch dich/aller Deiland/Vnd daselbst mit beweisestu
vnsern feinden/das du bist der helffer aus allem vbel

(Numeri.rvi.)
Die eherne schlan-
ge war dis zeichen
widder die feuri-
ge schlangen.

Aber jhene wurden durch hewschrecken vnd fliegen zu tod gebis-
sen / vnd kundten kein hülffe jres lebens finden / Denn sie warens
werd/das sie damit geplagt wurden. Aber deinen kindern kundten
auch der gifftigen Drachen zene nicht schaden/Denn deine barmhertzigkeit war dafur/vnd machte sie gesund/Denn sie wurden darumb
also gestrafft vnd flugs widder geheilet/auff das sie lerneten an deine
wort gedencken/vnd nicht zu tieff ins vergessen fielen/sondern blieben
vnabgewendet von deinen wolthaten/Denn es heilete sie weder
kraut noch pflaster/sondern dein WORT HERR/welchs alles hei-
let/Denn du hast gewalt/beide vber leben vnd vber tod / Vnd du furest hinuntern zur Dellen pforten / vnd furest widder heraus. Ein
mensch aber/so er jemand tödtet durch seine bosheit/so kan er den aus
gefaren geist nicht widder bringen/noch die verschiedene seele widder
holen.

(wolthaten)
Das sie nicht ver-
gessen der wunder
zeichen/ so jne ge-
schehen waren.

Aber vnmüglich ists/deiner hand zu entfliehen/Denn die Gott-
losen/so dich nicht kennen wolten/sind durch deinen mechtigen arm
gesteupt/da sie durch vngewönliche regen / hagel / gewesser/ den sie
nicht entgehen kundten/verfolget /vnd durchs fewer auffgefressen
worden/Vnd das war das aller wünderlichst/das fewer am meisten
im wasser brand/welchs doch alles auslesschet /Denn die welt streit
fur die gerechten/Zu weilen thet die flamme gemach/das sie ia nicht
verbrennete die thier/so vnter die Gottlosen geschickt waren / Sondern das sie selbs sehen musten/wie sie durch Gottes gerichte also zu
plagt worden/Zu weilen aber brennete die flamme im wasser/vber die
macht des fewers/auff das es die vngerechten vmbbrechte.

(wasser)
Im plagtregen.

Da gegen neretestu dein volck mit Engel speise/vnd sandtest jnen
brod bereit vom himel /on erbeit/welchs vermocht allerley lust zu ge-
ben/vnd war einem jglichem nach seinem schmack eben (Denn so
man auff dich harret/das macht deinen kindern offenbar / wie süsse
du seiest) Denn ein jglicher machte daraus/was er wolt/nach dem jn
lust an kam/so odder so zu schmecken/Dort aber bleib auch der schnee
vnd schlossen im fewer/vnd verschmoltzen nicht / Auff das sie jnne
würden/wie das fewer/so auch im hagel brennete vnd im regen bli-
tzete/der feinde früchte verderbet/ Das selbige fewer/auff das sich
die gerechten bekereten/must es seiner eigen krafft vergessen/Denn die
Creatur/so dir/als dem Schepffer/dienet / ist hefftig zur plage vber
die vngerechten/vnd thut gemach zur wolthat vber die/so dir trawen/
Darumb lies sie sich auch dazumal jnn allerley wandeln / vnd dienete
jnn der gabe/welche alle nerete nach eines jglichen willen / wie ers
bedurfft/Auff das deine kinder lerneten/die du HERR liebhast/das
nicht die gewachsen früchte den menschen erneren / Sondern dein
Wort erhelt die/so an dich glewben/Denn das/so vom fewer nicht
verzeret ward/das ward schlecht von eim geringen glantz der Sonnen
warm vnd verschmeltzt/Auff das kund wurde/das man/ehe die
Sonne auffgehet/dir dancken solle/Vnd fur dich tretten/wenn das

(allerley lust)
Das ist/Er kundte
machen wo zu er
wolt/ backen/bra-
ten/ sieden/ koch-
en/dörren etc.

(dein wort)
Matthei.iiij. Der
mensch lebt nicht
allein vom brod
etc.
Exo.rvi.Da das
himel brod von
der Sonnen zu-
schmalg.

Dij   liecht

both verses from Wisdom of Solomon, the emphasis on "Word" proclaims this Living Word as a Word of life, a Word that speaks gospel and thus transforms its hearers. When God speaks this Word, creation happens. Life happens. Timothy Wengert explains, "Understanding the Bible as the Word of God does not have to do so much with what a text is or means or with its relative position in the canon of Scripture as with what it *does* to its hearers."[29] In these two passages from Wisdom of Solomon, that is exactly what happens. The Word gives life and destroys wrath. The living voice of the gospel (*viva vox evangelii*) is breathed onto people and all creation, bringing healing and life while also destroying wrath. At the heart of this Bible translation by the Wittenberg theologians, therefore, is Luther's theology of the Word.

LUTHER'S THEOLOGY OF THE WORD

The emphasis on the "Word" in these passages from Wisdom of Solomon identifies the starting point for Luther's theology. By Word, Luther often means Christ, the Living Word, and not just, or only, Scripture. The power of this Word is that it is active, creating life. Here, Luther obviously had in mind both the Word spoken to bring about creation (Gen 1) and the Word that is God become flesh (John 1:1 and 1:14). By highlighting "Word" in Wisdom of Solomon, then, Luther immediately set the tone for the gospel message of the relational and actively creating nature of the Word, especially as it relates to all the other "core places" that he chose to highlight in his first complete edition of the German Bible. This approach would inform his understanding of authority residing in God as Word, rather than in Scripture itself, and related directly to the other instances of highlighting in the 1534 Bible.

Luther's emphasis on the Word is not surprising. There is a reason that theologians have said that his theology is a "theology of the Word" and, even more specifically, a preached or oral Word.[30] What is surprising is that

29. Timothy J. Wengert, *Reading the Bible with Martin Luther: An Introductory Guide* (Grand Rapids: Baker Academic, 2013), 30–31.
30. Thus, for example: Oswald Bayer, *Martin Luther's Theology: A Contemporary Interpretation*, trans. Thomas H. Trapp (Grand Rapids: Eerdmans, 2008), 8, 82–83, and *Promissio. Geschichte der reformatorischen Wende in Luthers Theologie,* 2nd ed. (Darmstadt: Wissenschaftliche Buchgesellschaft, 1989; Christine Helmer, *The Trinity and Martin Luther*, rev. ed. (Bellingham: Lexham Press, 2017), 210; Paul R. Hinlicky, *Luther and the Beloved Community: A Path for Christian Theology after Christendom* (Grand Rapids: Eerdmans, 2010), 130; Kolb, *Martin Luther and the Enduring Word of God*, 46; Steven D. Paulson, *Lutheran Theology*. Doing Theology Series (London: T & T Clark, 2011), 225; Jaroslav Pelikan, *Reformation of Church and Dogma*

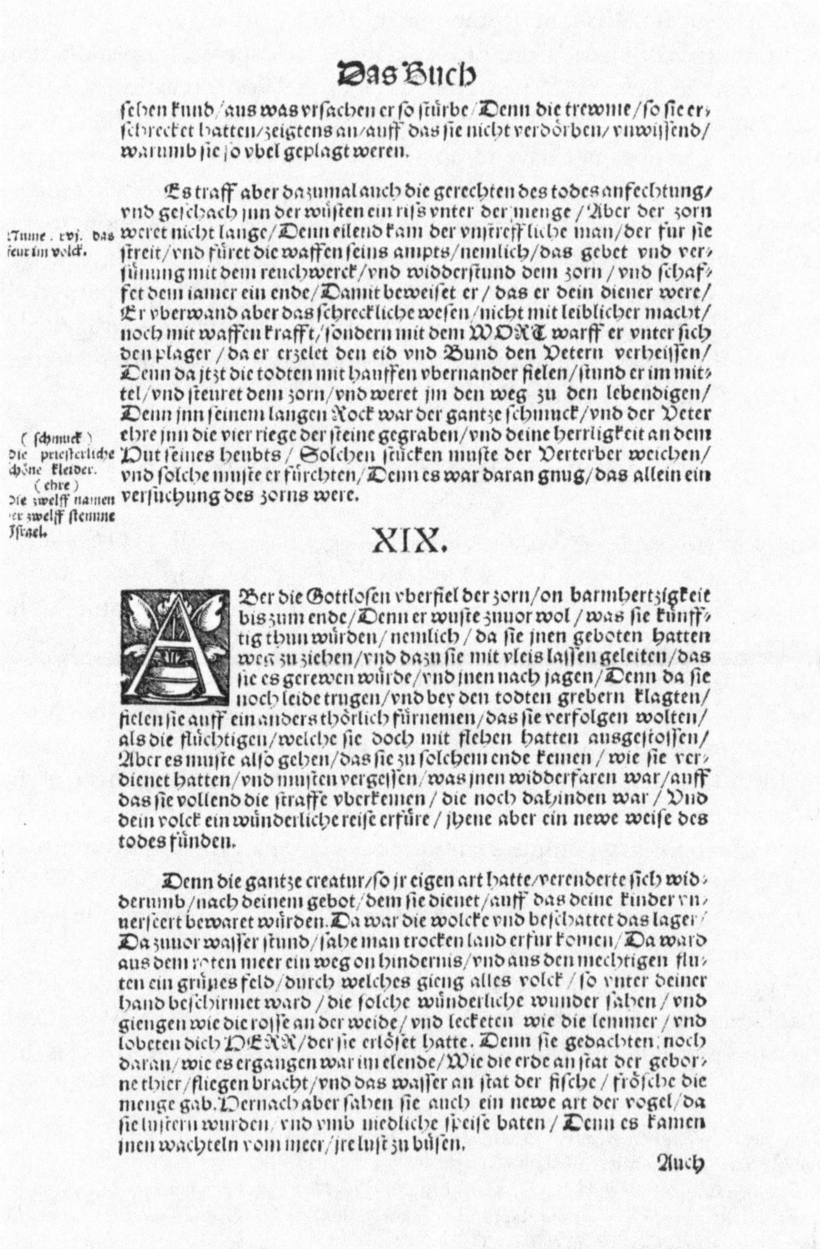

Das Buch

sehen kund/aus was vrsachen er so stürbe/Denn die trewme/so sie er-
schrecket hatten/zeigtens an/auff das sie nicht verdörben/vnwissend/
warumb sie so vbel geplagt weren.

Es traff aber dazumal auch die gerechten des todes anfechtung/
vnd geschach jnn der wüsten ein riß vnter der menge / Aber der zorn
weret nicht lange/Denn eilend kam der vntreffliche man/der fur sie
streit/vnd füret die waffen seins ampts/nemlich/das gebet vnd ver-
sünung mit dem reuchwerck/vnd widderstund dem zorn / vnd schaf-
fet dem iamer ein ende/Dannt beweiset er / das er dein diener were/
Er vberwand aber das schreckliche wesen/nicht mit leiblicher macht/
noch mit waffen krafft/sondern mit dem WORT warff er vnter sich
den plager / da er erzelet den eid vnd Bund den Vetern verheissen/
Denn da jtzt die todten mit hauffen vbernander fielen/stund er im mit-
tel/vnd steuret dem zorn/vnd weret jm den weg zu den lebendigen/
Denn jnn seinem langen Rock war der gantze schmuck/vnd der Veter
ehre jnn die vier riege der steine gegraben/vnd deine herrligkeit an dem
Hut seines heubts / Solchen stücken muste der Verterber weichen/
vnd solche muste er fürchten/Denn es war daran gnug/das allein ein
versuchung des zorns were.

Side notes left margin:
:Nume. rvj. das
feur im volck.

(schmuck)
die priesterliche
schöne kleider.
(ehre)
die zwelff namen
er zwelff steinne
Israel.

XIX.

Ber die Gottlosen vberfiel der zorn/on barmhertzigkeit
bis zum ende/Denn er wuste zuuor wol / was sie künff-
tig thun würden/nemlich / da sie jnen geboten hatten
weg zu ziehen/vnd dazu sie mit vleis lassen geleiten/das
sie es gerewen würde/vnd jnen nach jagen/Denn da sie
noch leide trugen/vnd bey den todten grebern klagten/
fielen sie auff ein anders thörlich fürnemen/das sie verfolgen wolten/
als die flüchtigen/welche sie doch mit sleben hatten ausgestossen/
Aber es muste also gehen/das sie zu solchem ende kamen / wie sie ver-
dienet hatten/vnd musten vergessen/was jnen widderfaren war/auff
das sie vollend die straffe vberkemen / die noch dahinden war / Vnd
dein volck ein wünderliche reise erfüre / jhene aber ein newe weise des
todes fünden.

Denn die gantze creatur/so jr eigen art hatte/verenderte sich wid-
derumb/nach deinem gebot/dem sie dienet/auff das deine kinder vn-
erseert bewaret würden. Da war die wolcke vnd beschattet das lager/
Da zuuor wasser stund/sahe man trocken land erfur komen/Da ward
aus dem roten meer ein weg on hindernis/vnd aus den mechtigen flu-
ten ein grünes feld/durch welches gieng alles volck / so vnter deiner
hand beschirmet ward / die solche wünderliche wunder sahen / vnd
giengen wie die rosse an der weide/vnd leckten wie die lemmer / vnd
lobeten dich HERR/der sie erlöset hatte. Denn sie gedachten noch
daran/wie es ergangen war im elende/Wie die erde an stat der gebor-
ne thier/fliegen bracht/vnd das wasser an stat der fische / frösche die
menge gab.Dernach aber sahen sie auch ein newe art der vogel/da
sie lüstern wurden/vnd vmb niedliche speise baten / Denn es kamen
jnen wachteln vom meer/jre lust zu büsen.

Auch

"WORT" in Wisdom of Solomon 18:22, 1534 Luther Bible.
(Reformation Historical Research Library Wittenberg—
Stiftung Luthergedenkstätten, LH, Ag 2 ° 86)

in both the American and Weimar editions of Luther's collected works, there are only two references to one of these verses, even though Luther liberally cites from Wisdom of Solomon, especially prior to the mid-1530s. The first citation is found in the preface to Wisdom of Solomon, written specifically to accompany Luther's translation of the text, and the second is in his Psalms lectures.[31] Regarding the first citation, Luther's preface for Wisdom of Solomon gives an insight into his reason for highlighting "Word" in his translation of 16:12 and 18:22. He stated:

> It pleases me beyond measure that the author here extols the Word of God so highly, and ascribes to the Word all the wonders God has performed, both on enemies and in his saints. . . .
> Mark well that whatever praise and glory you hear ascribed herein to wisdom is said of nothing other than the Word of God. For even [the author] himself says, in chapter 16[:12], that the children of Israel were not sustained by manna, nor saved by the bronze serpent, but by the Word of God. just as in Matthew 4[:4] Christ says, "Man shall not live by bread alone," etc. This is why [the author] teaches that wisdom comes from nowhere else than from God, and brings many illustrations from Scripture. So he ascribes to wisdom what Scripture ascribes to the Word of God. . . .
> To refer to this book as Wisdom of Solomon is as much as to call it: A Book of Solomon about the Word of God. So the spirit of wisdom is nothing other than faith, our understanding of that same Word.[32]

The Word is a communicative word. The Word creates and conveys faith to believers, and in this Word, the faithful find wisdom in this Living Word that acts upon them. One *experiences*, and not just reads, the Word. As a result, these two passages from Wisdom of Solomon spell out the message (*die Botschaft*) that the Living Word proclaims. This Word, claimed Luther, becomes flesh and proclaims a God who is acting in the world and, in the process, bestowing wisdom. The Word is the source of life, a theme consistently highlighted in Luther's understanding of the gospel. This is precisely what Oswald Bayer meant when he claimed

(1300–1700), The Christian Tradition: A History of the Development of Doctrine, Volume 4, ed. Jaroslav Pelikan (Chicago: University of Chicago, 1983), 181–82; Carl R. Trueman, *Luther on the Christian Life: Cross and Freedom*, ed. Stephen J. Nichols and Justin Taylor, Theologians on the Christian Life (Wheaton: Crossway, 2015), 97; Vilmos Vajta, *Luther on Worship: An Interpretation* (Philadelphia: Fortress Press, 1958), 68; and Timothy J. Wengert, *Martin Luther's Catechisms: Forming the Faith* (Minneapolis: Fortress Press, 2009), 108.
31. "Preface to the Wisdom of Solomon (1529)," LW 35:344; WA DB 12:54,1–7, and "Operationes in Psalmos (1519–1521)," WA 5:381,5–7.
32. "Preface to the Wisdom of Solomon (1529)," LW 35:343, 344; WA DB 10.II:3.

that Luther's theology is a theology of a "promising Word."[33] Theology "takes place in prayer, in the *oratio*: in praise and in lament—in the speaking of the heart with God in petition and intercession, with thanks and adoration."[34] It is about God addressing humanity with promises of life. Therefore, this Word—a term that refers to the life-giving Word as found in Christ, and not only in Holy Scripture—is the foundational theology by which Luther approached the other highlighted phrases in the Luther Bible. As Kolb notes,

> Although Luther's theology can be summarized in any number of single phrases—theology of the cross, theology of justification, theology of Christ—his concept of God's Word permeates his thinking, both reflection and giving form to other parts of his body of doctrine. Luther viewed human life as the product of God's Word. This Word continually engages his people in their daily life. . . . Luther's thought can rightly be designated a theology of the Word of God.[35]

It is this engaging and life-giving Word that Luther was thinking about as he translated Wisdom of Solomon and then wrote the preface for it in 1529, while his colleague Melanchthon was away at the Second Diet of Speyer, fighting for the evangelical cause.

THE WORD: EXPERIENCING CHRIST

Jaroslav Pelikan has argued that Luther's theology of the Word "manifests a striking lack of specificity."[36] Yet Luther was very specific in identifying the Word as Scripture and, even more significantly, as Christ the Living Word. The Word cannot be separated from the person of Jesus Christ or the gospel. Seeing the Word in action is to see Christ in action, as described in Scripture. Furthermore, God is also described in Scripture as the Word made flesh. The Word is also "made flesh, full of grace and

---

33. Bayer, *Martin Luther's Theology*, 81–82. See also Johannes von Lüpke, "Luther's Use of Language," in *The Oxford Handbook of Martin Luther's Theology*, eds. Robert Kolb, Irene Dingel, and L'ubomír Batka (Oxford: Oxford University Press, 2014), 147; and Kolb, *Martin Luther and the Enduring Word of God*, 46, 74.

34. Bayer, *Martin Luther's Theology*, 16.

35. Kolb, *Martin Luther and the Enduring Word of God*, 74.

36. Pelikan, *Reformation of Church and Dogma (1300–1700)*, 183. See also Mark D. Thompson, *A Sure Ground on Which to Stand: The Relation of Authority and Interpretive Method in Luther's Approach to Scripture*, Studies in Christian History and Thought (Eugene: Wipf & Stock, 2006), 47.

truth" (John 1:14), and is, as Luther described it, "God's only begotten Son."[37] In his commentary on John 1:14, Luther explained, "the Word, the true and natural Son of God, became man, with flesh and blood like that of any other human."[38] This Word is made incarnate in the body of Christ, the church, written on the heart (Rom 2:15), to be "known and read by all" (2 Cor 3:2), which in turn brings the Word alive. The Christ, the tangible Word, also becomes human in flesh and blood in the sacraments. There, the gathered people, the church (*Gemeinde*), as the body of Christ, receive and experience Christ and the Gospel in the flesh. The church experiences the Word in the Christ who brings life.

The Word—both Living and written, audible and visible—cannot be separated from its target audience, the church. Luther thus described the church as a "mouth-house,"[39] called to proclaim the gospel so that people could experience Christ and Christ's life-giving Word. In his 1539 treatise, "On the Councils and the Church," he called the Word the first marker, or identifier, of the holy Christian people, the church. As Luther observed, "the holy Christian people are recognized by their possession of the holy word of God."[40] This Word, like John the Baptist, points to the Living Word (Christ). Thus, the church is found wherever the Word, as the person of Christ revealed in Scripture, engages the *ecclesia* (churchly community). The resulting union that results is like that of a marriage: "Christ and the church are one body, as husband and wife are."[41] Luther thus insisted that "God's word cannot be without God's people and, conversely, God's people cannot be without God's word. Otherwise, who would preach or hear it preached, if there were no people of God? And what could or would God's people believe, if there were no word of God?"[42] Without Christ the Word being proclaimed and experienced, the church—and faith—cannot exist. Luther identifies this external word as a confession of faith (Matt 10:32) by a people experiencing the gospel, rather than a text.[43] This "external word, preached orally," in order to be experienced, is therefore how the church is recognized.[44] L'ubomír Batka, paraphrasing Luther, summarizes it thus: "Where there is Christ,

37. *"das wort ist der eigeborne Son Gottes."* "Sermons on John (1537)," LW 22:8; WA 46:543,12
38. "Sermons on John (1537)," LW 22:110; WA 46:631,28–29.
39. "Advent Postils (1522)," LW 75:51, note 72; WA 10.I.2:48.5. See also LW 25:xi.
40. "On the Councils and the Church (1539)," LW 41:148; WA 50:628,29–30.
41. "On the Councils and the Church (1539)," LW 41:163; WA 50:641,8–9.
42. "On the Councils and the Church (1539)," LW 41:150; WA 50:629,34–630,2.
43. "On the Councils and the Church (1539)," LW 41:149; WA 50:629,20–23.
44. "On the Councils and the Church (1539)," LW 41:149; WA 50:629,17–18.

there the Gospel is being preached to the people."[45] The Word, therefore, cannot be separated from Christ proclaiming the Word to people and creating the life-giving Gospel in people. This is the Word that "became flesh, full of grace and truth" (John 1:14), and this Word, this Christ, *does* something "for us human beings and for our salvation," as the Nicene-Constantinopolitan Creed states.[46] So the Word, as Luther used the term, is both a *noun*, referring to Christ, the person, and a *verb*, denoting how God creates life in people.

Luther insisted on putting emphasis on Christ as the Living Word. As Wengert observes, "Luther was far more interested in God's Word *proclaimed* and not merely shut up in a book."[47] Proclaiming the Word makes Christ present and God's grace public. Gospel is experienced. Thus, everything revolves around this Living Word, proclaimed, preached, and heard. As such, the Word is a litmus test. Luther noted, "Scriptures must be understood in favor of Christ, not against him. For that reason, they must either refer to him or must not be held to be true Scriptures."[48] Christ the Living Word becomes the measuring tool of Scripture. Applying Christ as the "standard" could be dangerous, however, apart from Luther's understanding of law and gospel as a starting point. The reformer thought that if the Word of law and gospel—this Word of life and death—is ignored, then the truth of Scripture is ignored, no matter how committed a person is to an inerrant view of Scripture. Theology begins and ends with the Living Word, as witnessed to in Scripture.

Luther also placed great emphasis on the oral nature of the proclaimed Word, as compared to the written word of the Bible.[49] Emmanuel Hirsch commented that for Luther, the Bible was not so much a "reading book [*Lesebuch*]," as a "listening book [*Hörebuch*]."[50] This distinction is best seen in the emphasis Luther placed on preaching. Preaching is an oral event, where one experiences the Word of gospel. In his commentary on Romans 10:15, "How blessed are the feet of those who proclaim good news," Luther thus declared:

---

45. L'ubomír Batka, "Luther's Theology of the Word in the Exposition of Psalms 1–25 at Coburg (1530)," *Canon & Culture*, 11 No. 2 (2017), 55.

46. Creeds, Second Confession, 4. BC 23; BSELK 49.

47. Wengert, *Reading the Bible with Martin Luther*, vii–viii.

48. Thesis 41, "Theses Concerning Faith and Law (1535)," LW 34:112; WA 39.I:47,3–4.

49. For a detailed study of the importance of orality in Luther's understanding of the Word, Scripture, and preaching, see Simon Kuntze, *Die Mündlichkeit der Schrift: Eine Rekonstruktion des lutherischen Schriftprinzips* (Leipzig: Evangelische Verlagsanstalt, 2020), and Graham, *Beyond the Written Word*.

50. Emmanuel Hirsch, *Luthers Deutsche Bibel: ein Betrage zur Frage ihrer Durchsist* (Munich: Raiser, 1928), 70.

In the expression "of those who preach the gospel" the Spirit expresses something more than we have indicated in the gloss, and that is the fact that "peace" and "good things" are not the kind of things which are visible according to the world, for they are so hidden that they are not proclaimed except through the Word and are not grasped except through faith. For these good things and this peace are not exhibited to the senses but announced by the Word and can be perceived only by faith, that is, without personal experience until the future life comes.[51]

Those who preach are "breathing Christ"—and thus, breathing the Gospel—into the ears and hearts of the hearers of the Word: the preachers' "voices are like feet or vehicles or wheels by which the Word is carried or rolled or it walks to the ears of the hearers." Luther thus concludes, with some interesting logic, "Whatever runs has feet: the Word runs, therefore the Word has feet."[52] The preached Word, the sermon, grows feet so that it can "run" into a person's heart. And the path into a person's heart goes through the ears. In his commentary on Hebrews, Luther stated that the "ears alone are the organs of a Christian, for [a person] is justified and declared to be a Christian not because of the works of any other member of the body but because of faith."[53] It is not in the use of one's hands, feet, or mouth that a person finds the righteousness of God. Salvation is not something done or accomplished by humans, it is something God *does* to humanity.

After arriving in the small town of Schmalkalden in February 1537 for a meeting of the Schmalkald League of Protestant rulers, Luther preached a sermon on the articles of the Creed in the home of the town treasurer. In his sermon, he emphasized the target of the orally proclaimed Gospel is, in the end, not actually the ear but the heart of the person:

> This, then, is the chief point of this sermon: we ought to know and believe that we are Christians and are redeemed from eternal death and sin. If someone asks us: "How do you know this?" we answer: I know this because I hear this in the Word and in the Sacrament and in the Absolution, and because the Holy Spirit likewise tells me this in my heart, just as I hear it with my ears.[54]

51. "Commentary on Romans (1516)," LW 25:416; WA 56:424,27–425, 5.
52. "Commentary on Romans (1515–1516)," LW 25:417; WA 56:425,18–19, 21–22. In the Latin text, Luther uses the word, *sermo* (sermon), rather than *verbum* (word). The ET in LW nevertheless translates *sermo* as "word," although the idea of "sermon" fits better with the preacher's task, which Luther is here describing.
53. "Lectures on Hebrews (1517–1518)," LW 29:224; WA 57.III:222,7–9. See also Kolb, *Martin Luther and the Enduring Word of God*, 28.
54. "House Sermon on the Articles of the Creed (1537)," LW 57:251; WA 45:24,3–7. See also Kuntze, *Die Mündlichkeit der Schrift*, 106.

It is through the Holy Spirit that this orally proclaimed Word of life enters the ears and penetrates the heart. Preaching publicly airs the Word so that the Gospel reaches and transforms hearts.

Words written in ink were, in Luther's mind, as-yet-unrealized proclamations. When a person read a text, it was usually read aloud. As Richard Losch observes, "it was considered a most unusual talent to be able to read silently; most people read aloud."[55] Reading a written text aloud brought the words to life. The Augsburg Confession, for example, was read aloud before Charles V and not simply handed over to him."[56] If the document were to be handed over only in written form, it would be akin to the document being stillborn. The Word needed to be spoken, in the same way that God spoke to bring about creation (Gen 1). Thus, when the attempt failed to have the Augsburg Confession received only in writing, the emperor moved the reading to "the episcopal court so that there would be no room for a public audience," because he knew the power of a spoken word.[57] To emphasize this point, Elector John's chancellor, Christian Beyer, read the Augsburg Confession with a very loud voice before the emperor, making it a "living" document.[58] But there was a secondary reason for reading it aloud: it was so that the people gathered outside the episcopal court could hear the Lutheran confession of their faith. The act of reading it aloud effectively made the written document a public testimony, a "confession before kings" (Mark 13:9). Reading a document aloud also moved the words on a page into speech to be heard with the ears and, thus, experienced with the heart. This was especially

55. Richard R. Losch, *All the People in the Bible: An A–Z Guide to the Saints, Scoundrels, and Other Characters in Scripture* (Grand Rapids: Eerdmans, 2008), 344–345. Losch makes this statement about practices in the first century CE, but it was also applicable to the late medieval era. See also Robert Kolb and Charles P. Arand, *The Genius of Luther's Theology: A Wittenberg Way of Thinking for the Contemporary Church* (Grand Rapids: Baker Academic, 2008), 188–90; and Philip Ruge–Jones, *Cross in Tensions: Luther's Theology of the Cross as Theologico–Social Critique,* Princeton Theological Monograph Series, eds. K. C. Hanson, Charles M. Collier, and D. Christopher Spinks (Eugene: Pickwick Publications, 2008), 66. Brett Muhlhan reports that Luther defined "meditation as outward and vocal, as the age old practice of reading aloud—which implies listening to and holding our inner words accountable." Brett Muhlhan, *Being Shaped by Freedom: An Examination of Luther's Development of Christian Liberty, 1520–1525* (Eugene: Pickwick, 2012), 126. Stephen Dempster notes that the Bible was first experienced as oral proclamation, which was then made permanent through writing, pointing to the Hebrew word for proclamation, which literally means "to call out and read aloud (*qārā'*)." Stephen G. Dempster, "Canon and Old Testament Interpretation," in *Hearing the Old Testament: Listening for God's Address,* eds. Craig G. Bartholomew and David J. H. Beldman (Grand Rapids: Eerdmans, 2012), 162.
56. Julius Köstlin, *Life of Luther,* 2nd ed. (London: Longmans, Green, and Co., 1895), 352.
57. LW CV: 239, n. 55. See also "Letter from Jonas to Luther (ca. June 30, 1530)," WA BR 5:427–28.
58. "Editor's Introduction to the *Augsburg Confession,*" BC 28.

important for the reading of Scripture in the gathered congregation. Richard Muller notes that the term *viva vox* (Living Word) "was used by the Reformers and by the Protestant orthodox to indicate the reading aloud of vernacular Scriptures during worship."[59] The written words of the Bible come alive as the living, breathing Word when orally proclaimed. The written Word is meant to be words proclaimed, so the ear could hear and the heart understand, allowing one to experience the gospel.

SUMMARY

Based on Luther's understanding of the "Word," it comes as no surprise that the first "core place" highlighted in reading through the Bible from beginning to end is WORD, as found in the two places in Wisdom of Solomon. Designating WORD as a "core place" (*Kernstellen*) intentionally emphasized the theological themes of the Wittenberg reformers. These first two "core places" in Luther's translation of Wisdom of Solomon drive home the fact that this evangelical theology of the reformation begins—and ends—with the Word. This Word is not bound within the covers of a written text that could collect dust on a bookshelf, but it is the sacred text where one encounters and experiences the Living Word, namely, Jesus the Christ and the gospel promises. This Word is whom the crucified and risen One proclaims. In Christ, the Living Word, one finds the life and the light of all people (John 1:4). This Living Word, moreover, makes life happen. As God speaks the Word, the breath (Spirit) goes forth and life is created (Gen 1). As this Word goes forth, resurrections happen (Ezek 37). When this Living Word is preached, it enters human ears and hearts, and faith is created and nourished. In other words, the WORD is something that is to be experienced, and not just read. And when such a WORD is spoken, one would be wise to listen to it and experience this Word in its fulness, just as Luther had intended.

---

59. Richard A. Muller, *Dictionary of Latin and Greek Theological Terms: Drawn Principally from Protestant Scholastic Theology* (Grand Rapids: Baker Book House, 1985), 328.

6.

Luther's Emphasis on "Listen to Him"

"God says to you: 'Behold, you have My Son. Listen to Him, and receive Him. If you do this, you are already sure about your faith and salvation'."[1]

"You must judge everything solely in the light of the words of Christ the Lord; for it is written: 'Listen to Him' (Matt 17:5). And if you give ear only to Him, then I want you to know that everything you say and do in faith in the Son will also have My approval."[2]

INTRODUCTION

In his 1534 Bible translation, Martin Luther's emphasis on "WORD" in the apocryphal book, the Wisdom of Solomon, emphasized Christ, the Living Word, rather than the written text of Scripture. This Word is the Living God who speaks and gives life. He and his colleagues wanted to translate the Bible into a language spoken and understood by the people so that they could experience for themselves the Word who gives life, this Word cradled in the manger of Scripture. But this was only the first step in his attempt to translate not just the Scripture but also the gospel into the language of the people. By focusing on the Word as Christ, Luther shifted attention from the Word as a Biblical text to the Word as the Living God, the Word in relationship. The Word becomes flesh and enters into relationship with humanity. A relationship initiated by God, through

---

1. "Lectures on Genesis (1535–1545)," LW 5:46; WA 43:460,23–24.
2. "Sermons on John (1537)," LW 22:260; WA 46:774,9–13.

Christ, involves God inviting humanity to experience what God is doing and what God desires for those brought into this relationship.

The story of the transfiguration of Jesus is a specific account of the God in heaven communicating directly to some of the disciples. Peter, James, and John, upon seeing Moses and Elijah appear alongside of a radiant Jesus, had spontaneously decided to build three dwellings for Moses, Elijah, and Jesus. Before they can get any further with their plans, however, a voice from heaven interrupts them, saying, "This is my Son, the Beloved: LISTEN TO HIM" (*DEN SOLT IR HOREN*).[3] It was a "Pay attention!" moment for the disciples. Nevertheless, the capitalization of every letter in this particular phrase in every one of the Synoptic Gospels appears, at first glance, quite puzzling. The capitalization of "LISTEN TO HIM" first appeared in the 1530 revision of the New Testament and was kept in the 1534 Bible.[4] But why emphasize these particular words, among all the options that Luther could have chosen? After all, these transfiguration accounts are likely not the first texts from the Gospels that come to mind when thinking about "core places" (*Kernstellen*) in the the New Testament. It makes more sense, perhaps, to emphasize Jesus's mission declaration at the beginning of his ministry (Luke 4:18–19), or in his last words—either on the cross (Matt 27:46 or Luke 23:46), or in the Great Commission (Matt 28:19–20), given immediately before he ascends into heaven, since society likes to emphasize an important person's last words. Or, with Luther's preference for the Gospel of John, the "chief gospel,"[5] why not highlight John 3:16? After all, Luther considered this verse "one of the best and most glorious Gospel readings, . . . worthy of being written in golden letters, not on paper but on the heart, if it could be." [6] Instead, Luther chose the phrase "Listen to Him," from the transfiguration accounts, to be a "core place" in his translations of the gospels. Equally puzzling is why Luther did not emphasize the phrase, "This is my beloved Son"—which immediately precedes the chosen highlighted words, since the voice from heaven also spoke

---

3. Matthew 17:5; Mark 9:7, and Luke 9:35. In the 1534 Luther Bible itself, the highlighting can be seen at LB NT 12b, XXVIIIb, and XLVa. In the Weimar edition, since it focuses on the 1522 and 1546 New Testament translations, the capitalized text is in the footnotes, at WA DB 6:78,170, and 254.

4. Hartmut Hövelmann, *Kernstellen der Lutherbibel: Eine Anleitung zum Schriftverständnis*. Texte und Arbeiten zur Bibel, Deutschen Bibelgesellschaft, Bd 5. (Bielefeld: Luther Verlag, 1989), 49.

5. "Prefaces to the New Testament (1546/1522)," LW 35:362; WA DB 6:10,26.

6. "Summer Postils (1544)," LW 77:365; WA 21:479,19–22.

Euangelion

bewme sehe.Darnach legte er abermal die hende auff seine augen/
vnd machet jn sehend.Vnd er ward widder zu rechte bracht/das er al=
les scharff sehen kunde. Vnd er schicket jn heim / vnd sprach/Gehe
nicht hinein jnn den Flecken/vnd sage es auch niemand drinnen.

Vnd Jhesus gieng aus vnd seine Jünger jnn die merckte der stad   Matth.
Cesaree Philippi/ vnd auff dem wege fraget er seine Jünger/ vnd   xvj.
sprach zu jnen/Wer sagen die leute/das ich sey? Sie antworten/Sie   Luce. ix
sagen/du seiest Johannes der Teuffer/Etliche sagen/ du seiest Eli=
as/Etliche/du seiest der Propheten einer.Vnd er sprach zu jnen/Jr
aber/wer saget jr/das ich sey? Da antwortet Petrus vnd sprach zu
jm/Du bist Christus.Vnd er bedrawet sie/das sie niemands von jm
sagen solten/Vnd hub an sie zu leren/des menschen Son mus viel lei=
den/vnd verworffen werden von den Eltesten vnd Hohen priestern
vnd Schrifftgelerten/vnd getödtet werden/vnd vber drey tage auff=
ersteben.Vnd er redet das wort frey offenbar. Vnd Petrus nam jn zu
sich/fieng an jm zu weren. Er aber wand sich vmb/ vnd sahe seine
Jünger an / vnd bedrawet Petron / vnd sprach / Gehe hinder mich
du Satan/denn du meinest nicht das Göttlich/sondern das mensch=
lich ist.

Vnd er rieff zu sich dem volck sampt seinen Jüngern/vnd sprach   Mat. x
zu jnen/Wer mir wil nachfolgen/der verleugne sich selbs/vnd neme Luce.ix.
sein creutz auff sich/vnd folge mir nach/Denn wer sein leben wil be=
halten/der wirds verlieren/Vnd wer sein leben verleuret vmb meinen
vnd des Euangelj willen/der wirds behalten. Was hülffs den men=
schen / wenn er die gantze welt gewünne/vnd neme an seiner seelen
schaden? Odder was kan der mensch geben/damit er seine seele löse?
Wer sich aber mein vnd meiner Wort schemet/vnter diesem ehebre=
cherschen vnd sundigen geschlecht/des wird sich auch des menschen
Son schemen/ wenn er komen wird jnn der Herrligkeit seines Va=
ters/mit den heiligen Engeln. Vnd er sprach zu jnen/Warlich ich sa=
ge euch/Es stehen etliche hie/die werden den tod nicht schmecken/
bis das sie sehen das Reich Gottes mit krafft komen.

IX.

NO nach sechs tagen/nam Jhesus zu sich Petron/Ja=   Matth.
coben vnd Johannen/vnd füret sie auff einen hohen   xvij.
berg besonders alleine/vnd verkleret sich fur jnen/vnd Luce.ix.
seine kleider wurden helle vnd seer weis/wie der schnee/
das sie kein ferber auff erden kan so weis machen. Vnd
es erschein jnen Elias mit Mose/vnd hatten eine rede
mit Jhesu/Vnd Petrus antwortet/vnd sprach zu Jhesu/Rabbi/Hie
ist gut sein / lasset vns drey hütten machen/dir eine/Mosi eine/vnd
Elias eine.Er wuste aber nicht was er redet/denn sie waren verstörtzt.
Vnd es kam eine wolcken/die vberschattet sie/vnd eine stimme fiel aus
der wolcken/vnd sprach/Das ist mein lieber Son/DEN SOLT
JR HOREN. Vnd bald darnach sahen sie vmb sich/vnd sahen
niemand mehr/denn allein Jhesum bey jnen.

Da sie aber vom berge erab giengen/verpot jnen Jhesus/ das sie
niemand sagen solten / was sie gesehen hatten / bis des menschen
Son aufferstünde von den todten. Vnd sie behielten das wort bey
sich/vnd befragten sich vnternander/Was ist doch das aufferstehen
von den

"DEN SOLT IR HOREN" in Mark 9:7, 1534 Luther Bible.
(Reformation Historical Research Library Wittenberg—
Stiftung Luthergedenkstätten, LH, Kn D 254)

these words at the baptism of Jesus (Matt 3:17, Mark 1:11 and Luke 3:22).[7] In fact, Luther sometimes conflates the two events. While the baptismal accounts do not say, "Listen to Him," Luther mistakenly adds it in some places.[8] This phrase is important for Luther because it reveals the identity of Jesus the Messiah. However, Luther's focus in the transfiguration accounts is not on God's relationship to Christ, as crucial as that is, but on God's relationship, through Christ, with humanity. Knowing that Jesus is the Son of God reveals that what Christ does "for us and our salvation" is commissioned by God, so people need to pay attention to what Christ says and *does*. What this Word *does* is to transform people when this voice is heard.[9] Christ's authority has been confirmed by God's voice, and so people ought to pay attention. Something is going to happen, as God works through Christ.[10] It is thus not just words that humanity are to listen to; people are called to listen to the Living Word that transfigures all creation.

Luther liked to quote the voice from heaven that told the disciples to "Listen to Him." This phrase played a significant role in his theology. Although he referenced the highlighted "Word" verses in the Wisdom of Solomon only twice, Luther quotes "Listen to Him" (Matt 17:5, Mark 9:7 or Luke 9:35) hundreds of times. But the importance of "Listen to Him" cannot be assessed solely through his frequent use of the phrase. What is important is *how* the phrase is used. The phrase points to a foundation of his theological thought. Luther's emphasis on "Listen to Him" also cannot be separated from "Word." People are called to "listen to Christ" because Christ is the Living Word that gives life. As the crucified and risen one, Christ the Living Word reveals the gospel.

Luther's emphasis on the words "Listen to Him," is fourfold, best understood as a series of concentric circles. First, in the innermost circle, this injunction revealed his trinitarian approach to theology, as revealed through the Word. In the second circle going outward, Luther insisted that God's command to listen to Christ is central to the faith because

7. The 1537 New Testament, however, does capitalize "This is my Beloved Son" in both the baptism and transfiguration accounts, and the increasing use of "core places" in later editions of the Luther Bible also include a great number more "core places" that are highlighted with the use of all capital letters. See Hövelmann, *Kernstellen der Lutherbibel*, 49.
8. An example of Luther's conflation of the texts is found in "Sermons on John (1537)," LW 22:77; WA 46:602,32–36, and again in LW 22:172; WA 46:685,19–23.
9. "Understanding the Bible as the Word of God does not have to do so much with what a text is or means or with its relative position in the canon of Scripture as with what it *does* to its hearers." Timothy J. Wengert, *Reading the Bible with Martin Luther: An Introductory Guide* (Grand Rapids: Baker Academic, 2013), 30–31.
10. Hövelmann, *Kernstellen der Lutherbibel*, 52.

Christ proclaims the gospel, and the distinction between law and gospel is clarified. Third, the proclaimed Word of gospel shapes and defines the church. Finally, in the fourth, and outer, circle, Luther explored how listening to the voice from heaven, commanding the disciples to listen to Christ, informed the evangelical understanding of pastoral care and the role of the church engaged in society.

THE TRIUNE GOD DEFINES THEOLOGY

Based on the transfiguration story, Luther insisted that Jesus had the authority to speak the Word on behalf of the triune God. In a sermon on John's Gospel, Luther has Jesus saying, "The only right method is to hear My Word, to listen to Me, to let yourself be persuaded that My Words are also My Father's Word. For the Father has His Word proclaimed from My lips, and He enlightens your heart that you may realize that it is His Word. Thus the Father draws him whom He wishes to bring to Me." He then summarized this, with an obvious reference to the transfiguration account, by saying, "We must let the Son proclaim the Word, and we must listen to Him."[11] He also alluded to the transfiguration story when he commented that "Three persons and one God—they appeared as distinguishable. The figures are different from one another: there is the Father who speaks, the Son about whom the Father speaks and the Holy Spirit . . . in the shining cloud. . . . True faith is that the Father, Son and Holy Spirit are the one God."[12] He also noted that "God by His command sends us back to the Son and wants us to worship and adore the Son. Therefore the thought agrees with these expressions of the gospel: 'This is My beloved Son, listen to Him' (Matt 17:5)."[13] In his Genesis commentary, Luther again has Jesus speaking: "For 'He who sees Me,' says Christ, 'also sees the Father Himself' (cf. John 14:9)."[14] The transfiguration of Jesus is a trinitarian event. The voice from heaven calls Christ the beloved Son. In the theophany at the baptism of Jesus, the Holy Spirit, in the form of a dove, also is present. To listen to Christ is to listen to the triune God.

11. "Sermons on John (1530–1532)." LW 23:96; WA 33:146,39–147,8.
12. "Sermon on Trinity Sunday (1538)," WA 46:433,10–13, 19–20.
13. "Commentary on the Psalms (1532)," LW 12:84; WA 40.II:300.25–28. Luther also states, "these expressions . . . refer to each other, the Father to the Son and the Son to the Father, so that no one can doubt that this King is true, proper, and natural God. And if you do not worship and embrace this King, you cannot worship God, for the Father and the Son are one (John 10:30)." "Commentary on the Psalms (1532)," LW 12:84; WA 40.II:300.33–36.
14. "Lectures on Genesis (1535–1545)," LW 5:45; WA 43:459.29–31.

The highlighted words from the transfiguration account reflect what Philip Watson called Luther's "Copernican Revolution" of theology.[15] Copernicus, a contemporary of Luther, argued that contrary to popular thought, the earth revolved around the sun, while Luther insisted that theology revolved around what God says through Christ. The human being is not at the center of theology. This was most clearly, and consistently, revealed in Luther's understanding of justification. Justification is all about God's actions alone, rather than about what humans do for God. Luther criticized any approach that suggested people could obtain God's grace by "doing what is within themselves." His response was that when a person is "doing what is in him, he sins and seeks himself in everything," thus "adding sin to sin."[16] The theocentric approach is also used in Luther's translating. His first principle for translating was to remember that Scripture was, first and foremost, about the works of God.[17] No wonder Luther reinforced the presence of the Trinity in the transfiguration account, stressing that "the entire Trinity appears here to strengthen all believers: Christ the Son in His glorious form, the Father in the voice declaring that the Son is Lord and Heir, the Holy Spirit in the bright cloud covering them or infusing faith."[18] Everything revolves around God's voice, revealed in Christ, yet it is also most definitely Trinitarian.

Luther was also able to insist that the First Commandment was important in the transfiguration emphasis on a Trinitarian understanding of God. The first commandment left no middle ground. A person listened either to the Lord God or to other gods. Paul Hinlicky rightly observes that "Luther takes his theological point of departure *von oben*, as in the heavenly command in the transfiguration story, the Father's *Hunc audite*."[19] Thus, when any voice other than God speaks, the Christian should flee as far as they could from this other voice, because "it has been determined by God that Christ wants to speak in His church and does not want to tolerate any other teacher, as the voice of the Father resounds from heaven: 'Listen to Him' (Mt. 17:5)."[20] Luther further suggested that true worship

15. Philip S. Watson, *Let God Be God! An Interpretation of the Theology of Martin Luther* (London: Epworth Press, 1954), 33–38. Watson picks up this idea from Heinrich Boehmer, *Luther and the Reformation in the Light of Modern Research,* trans. Eva Suzette Gertrude Potter (London: George Bell and Sons, 1930), 80; and Anders Nygren, *Agape and Eros: A Study of the Christian Idea of Love,* trans. Philip Watson (Philadelphia: Westminster Press, 1953), 681–91.

16. "Heidelberg Disputation (1518)," LW 31:50; WA 1:360,25–26.

17. "Table Talks (Winter 1542–1543)," LW 54:445–46; WA TR 5:218,8–29, (No. 5533).

18. "Annotations on Matthew (1535/1538)," LW 67:312; WA 38:660,17–661,1.

19. Paul R. Hinlicky, *Luther and the Beloved Community: A Path for Christian Theology after Christendom* (Grand Rapids: Eerdmans, 2010), 130.

20. "Lectures on Genesis (1535–1545)," LW 8:271. WA 44:778,23–25.

of God involved hearing this voice: "Therefore, when we preach faith, that we should worship nothing but God alone, the Father of our Lord Jesus Christ, as we say in the Creed: 'I believe in God the Father almighty and in Jesus Christ,' then we are remaining in the temple at Jerusalem. Again, 'This is my beloved Son; listen to him' [Matt 17:5]. 'You will find him in a manger' [cf. Luke 2:12]. He alone does it."[21] Thus, to "Listen to Him" is to put one's trust in this God of heaven and earth, and to worship this God alone.

While Luther understood the transfiguration in Trinitarian terms, he insisted that the triune God was revealed most clearly through Jesus the Christ. In his Lectures on John, Luther bluntly stated, "His only message is (Mt. 17:5): 'This is My beloved Son; listen to Him.' And the Son distinctly proclaims: 'I am the Way.' He who sees, knows, accepts, and finds Me accepts and finds, sees and knows, the Father."[22] God has chosen to be revealed in the incarnate Christ, and in that self-revelation God appoints Christ as "Teacher, Master, and Doctor of the whole world, as the Father's voice speaks from heaven: 'This is My beloved Son, with whom I am well pleased; listen to Him' [Matt 17:5]. Whoever receives this beloved Son of God and believes in Him has and finds the real, true God."[23] However, those who scorn this self-revelation of God, especially when found in the infant Jesus, will not hear the Living Word. Luther stated:

> Indeed no God will avail for you except the God of Him who sucked the virgin's breasts. On Him fix your eyes. For you cannot grasp God in Himself, unless perchance you want a consuming fire. But in Christ you see nothing but all sweetness, humanity, gentleness, clemency—in short, the forgiveness of sins and every mercy, etc. When you have Him, then good for you; you are a tower of defense with God the Father. Cling to Christ, otherwise you will hear the Father Himself speaking against you when He says (Mt. 17:5): "Listen to Him."[24]

While Luther was concerned that people would scorn the idea of the divinity of Jesus if they were not willing to listen to Christ's voice as the voice of God, he was also concerned that they would disregard the Living Word and "separate and tear Christ from God."[25] Christ's voice was God's

---

21. "Last Sermon in Wittenberg (January 17, 1546)," LW 51:375; WA 51:128,19–24.
22. "Sermons John (1537)," LW 24:63; WA 45:518,21–24.
23. "Sermon on the Divinity of Christ (November 21, 1537)," LW 57:291; WA 45:281,18–22.
24. "Lectures on Isaiah (1527)," LW 16:55; WA 31.II:38,33–39,3.
25. "Sermons on John (1537)," LW 24:65; WA 45:520,29–30. Luther makes the same point in "Sermons on John (1530–1532)," LW 23:229; WA 33:362,1–29.

Euangelion

erſchienen jnen Moſes vnd Elias/die redten mit jm.Petrus aber ant-
wortet/vnd ſprach zu Jheſu/Herr/Die iſt gut ſein/wiltu/ſo wöllen
wir drey hütten machen/dir eine / Moſi eine/vnd Elias eine. Da er
noch alſo redete/ſihe/da vberſchattet ſie eine liechte wolcken. Vnd
ſihe/eine ſtimme aus der wolcken ſprach/Dis iſt mein lieber Son/an
welchem ich wolgefallen habe / DEN SOLT IR HOREN.
Da das die Jünger höreten / fielen ſie auff jre angeſichte / vnd er-
ſchracken ſeer. Jheſus aber trat zu jnen/rüret ſie an/vnd ſprach/Ste-
het auff/vnd fürchtet euch nicht. Da ſie aber jre augen auff huben/
ſahen ſie niemand/denn Jheſum alleine.

Vnd da ſie vom berge herab giengen / gebot jnen Jheſus / vnd
ſprach/Jr ſolt dis geſicht niemand ſagen/bis des menſchen Son von
den todten aufferſtanden iſt.Vnd ſeine Jünger frageten jn/vnd ſpra-
chen/Was ſagen denn die Schrifftgelerten/Elias müſſe zuuor komen? Jheſus antwortet vnd ſprach zu jnen/Elias ſol ia zuuor komen / vnd alles zu recht bringen/Doch ich ſage euch/es iſt Elias
ſchon komen/vnd ſie haben jn nicht erkand/ſondern haben an jm ge-
than/was ſie wolten/Alſo wird auch des menſchen Son leiden müſ-
ſen von jnen. Da verſtunden die Jünger / das er von Johanne dem
Teuffer zu jnen geredt hatte.

Vnd da ſie zu dem volck kamen/trat zu jm ein menſch/vnd fiel jm zu
fuſſen/vnd ſprach/Herr/erbarm dich vber meinen ſon / denn er iſt
monſüchtig/vnd hat ein ſchweres leiden/Er fellet offt jns fewr/vnd
offt jns waſſer / vnd ich hab jn zu deinen Jüngern bracht / vnd ſie
kunden jm nicht helffen. Jheſus aber antwortet/vnd ſprach / O du
vngleubige vnd verkerte art/wie lange ſol ich bey euch ſein? wie lange
ſol ich euch dulden? bringet mir jn hieher. Vnd Jheſus bedrawete
jn/vnd der teuffel fur aus von jm/Vnd der knabe ward geſund zu der
ſelbigen ſtunde.

Da tratten zu jm ſeine Jünger beſonders/vnd ſprachen/Warumb
kundten wir jn nicht austreiben? Jheſus aber antwortet/vnd ſprach
zu jnen/Vmb ewers vnglaubens willen / Denn ich ſage euch war- Lu.rvij.
lich/ſo jr glauben habt als ein ſenff korn/ſo müget jr ſagen zu dieſem
berge/heb dich von hinnen dort hin/ſo wird er ſich heben/Vnd euch
wird nichts vnmüglich ſein.Aber dieſe art feret nicht aus/denn durch
beten vnd faſten.

Da ſie aber jr weſen hatten jnn Galilea/ſprach Jheſus zu jnen/Es
iſt zukünfftig/das des menſchen Son vberantwortet werde jnn der Mar.ix.
menſchen hende/vnd ſie werden jn tödten/vnd am dritten tage wird Luce.ix.
er aufferſtehen. Vnd ſie wurden ſeer betrübt.

(frey) Wie wol
Chriſtus frey war/
gab er doch den
zins ſeinem nehesten
zu willen / Alſo iſt
ein Chriſten ſeiner
halben alles dings
frey/vnd gibt ſich
doch ſeinem nehe-
ſten willig zu dienſt

(Stater) Iſt ein
lot/wenn es ſilber
iſt/ſo macht es ein
halben gülden.

Da ſie nu gen Capernaum kamen / giengen zu Petro die den zins
groſſchen einnamen/ vnd ſprachen/ Pflegt ewer Meiſter nicht den
zins groſſchen zu geben? Er ſprach/Ja. Vnd als er heim kam / kam
jm Jheſus zuuor/vnd ſprach / Was dünckt dich Simon? von wem
nemen die Könige auff erden den zol odder zinſe? von jren kindern/
odder von frembden? Da ſprach zu jm Petrus / Von den frembden.
Jheſus ſprach zu jm/So ſind die kinder a frey/Auff das aber wir ſie
nicht ergern/ſo gehe hin an das meer/vnd wirff den angel/vnd den
erſten fiſch/der auffer feret/den nim/vnd wenn du ſeinen mund auff-
thuſt/wirſtu einen b Stater finden/den ſelbigen nim/vnd gib jn fur
mich vnd dich.

Zu der

"DEN SOLT IR HOREN" in Matthew 17:5, 1534 Luther Bible.
(Reformation Historical Research Library Wittenberg—
Stiftung Luthergedenkstätten, LH, Kn D 254)

voice. To separate these voices was as dangerous as trying to separate the Word and the Promise from the bread and the wine in the Lord's Supper.[26]

The voice of Christ was also the starting point in determining the doctrine. All teachings and doctrines must be found in Christ, witness to Christ, or be related to what Christ does to make forgiveness of sins, life, and salvation possible for all.[27] Luther commented, "These things should be taught, and they should also be transmitted to our descendants, in order that they may shun and abhor the revelation of new doctrines and may observe the heavenly command (Matt 17:5), 'Listen to Him,' that is, to the evangelists and the apostles. Let them read and listen to these, likewise to the Old Testament, which bears faithful testimony concerning all these things."[28] In his commentary on the Sermon on the Mount, he is even more specific:

> . . . the rule is this: Regardless of their size and number, no wonders or signs are to be accepted contrary to established teaching. We have God's commandment; He has commanded from heaven (Mt. 17:5): "Listen to Him, Christ is the only one to whom you should listen." In addition we have this warning, that false prophets will come and do great signs, but that they are all on the wrong track, away from Christ and toward something different. The only preventive is to have a good grasp of the doctrine and to keep it before your eyes continually. You can evaluate everything on this basis: Is this what the Gospel and the Creed teaches, which you pray every day, saying: "I believe in Christ alone, who died for me," or is it something different?[29]

On the basis of this rule Luther claimed to judge the teachings of the pope or even the early church theologians: "The Word must rule in the church. In this instance we have the clear command from heaven (Matt

---

26. For a discussion of separations in the Lord's Supper, see Gordon A. Jensen, "Luther and the Lord's Supper," *The Oxford Handbook of Martin Luther's Theology*, eds. Robert Kolb, Irene Dingel, and L'ubomír Batka (Oxford: Oxford University Press, 2014), 322–32.

27. "God sent us his Son to be our teacher and savior. Not satisfied with that, he himself preaches from his high, heavenly throne to us all, saying, *"Hunc audite,"* "Listen to him" [Matt 17:5]. Thus we should drop to our knees with the apostles and believe that we hear nothing else in the whole world." "On the Councils and the Church (1539)," LW 41:129–130; WA 50:613,3–7.

28. "Lectures on Genesis (1535–1545)," LW 4:126; WA 43:226,3–7.

29. "The Sermon on the Mount (1521)," LW 21:280 WA 32:531,36–532,5. In his sermons on John, Luther states: "You must judge everything solely in the light of the words of Christ the Lord; for it is written: 'Listen to Him (Mt. 17:5). And if you give ear only to Him, then I want you to know that everything you say and do in faith in the Son will also have My approval. If not, then all your actions and words will be displeasing to Me.' We know from experience what will happen if the opinions of men become all-important." "Sermons on John (1537)," LW 22:260; WA 46:774,8–15.

17:5): 'Listen to Him.'"[30] Anything not voiced by Christ or Scripture should be discarded, even if it was said by the pope, the early theologians of the church, or even Luther himself.

LISTENING TO THE GOSPEL

The injunction to "Listen to Him" is also key to understanding the gospel. The voice of Christ, as the voice from heaven had instructed, speaks gospel. Luther stated it clearly:

> The Father's voice agrees with and confirms this, as it resounds from heaven above: "This is My *beloved Son*, with whom I am well pleased." It is as if He said: "I have here a Son, whom I love dearly and with whom I am well pleased, and everything He does is well-pleasing to Me. That He is born and baptized, suffers and dies for your sake, etc., is exceedingly pleasing to Me. The Son can do no wrong in My sight, etc. If you receive Him and listen to Him, then you, too, are most pleasing to Me and beloved to Me. Believe in Him: that He is the Lamb of God, who took your sin upon Himself, who was born for you, has suffered for you, and was crucified and died for the sake of your sin. If you thus accept Him and believe in Him, then you are freed from all your sins, for then you, too, are beloved to Me, and I am well pleased with you, just as I am well pleased with My beloved Son."[31]

Luther read the gospel into the transfiguration accounts. Christ the beloved Son proclaims and makes possible the gospel for all humanity. Christ's voice proclaims and creates life. Listening to ourselves, however, only drowns out the voice of Christ and the gospel. The gospel "always and only puts God as the subject of the theological sentence. God acts. God suffers and dies. God raises Jesus from the dead. Jesus heals, forgives, blesses, and all the rest. So, when reading or listening to the Bible, one hears all that God does, and, when it comes time to preach and teach, one simply lets the Gospel out of the bag and surrounds it with baptism, absolution, and the Lord's Supper."[32] Moreover, while God's will was revealed to Moses on Mount Sinai through the law, the will of God is now

---

30. "Lectures on Genesis (1535–1545)," LW 2:274; WA 42:457,28–29. In his sermons on John, Luther states: "Therefore we should place no reliance in any of the fathers or in their writings, but we should crawl under the wings of our Brood Hen, the Lord Jesus, and depend solely on Him. For of Him God the heavenly Father Himself said: 'This is My beloved Son, with whom I am well pleased; listen to Him' (Mt. 17:5). God insists that we give ear to Christ alone, for He said neither too little nor too much." "Sermons on John (1537)," LW 22:257; WA 46:770,20–771,15.
31. "Epiphany Sermon (1546)," LW 58:364–365: WA 51:113,38–114,10.
32. Wengert, *Reading the Bible with Martin Luther*, 45.

revealed on Mount Tabor through the hearing and experiencing of the gospel. Luther reinforced this idea when discussing the works and words of Christ in relationship to the gospel: "To know [Christ's] works and the things that happened to him is not yet to know the true gospel, for you do not yet thereby know that he has overcome sin, death, and the devil."[33] Experiencing the gospel thus occurs by listening to Christ, who "drives home the gospel" (was Christum treibet) into people's hearts.[34] Knowing the actions and words of Christ imparts only information, leaving the heart unchanged. Thus, Luther claimed, "If I had to do without one or the other—either the works or the preaching of Christ—I would rather do without the works than without his preaching. For the works do not help me, but his words give life, as he himself says [John 6:63]."[35] Since Christ's words both create and sustain life, the injunction to "Listen to Him" is crucial. People hear the gospel when listening to the life-giving Word, for when they hear Christ's voice, they experience the forgiveness of sin and eternal life.[36] Through this voice, the Spirit of God is breathing life into creation.

The proper distinction between law and gospel is also much easier to understand if a person first listens to the voice of Christ. Luther observed:

> Moses commands, but where do we get [the power to do it]? [He says,] "Believe, love," but where [do we get the power to do it]? "Do this, or you are of Satan," but will you only open your mouth and tell me how? I cannot, because I am under the head [of Satan]. What am I to do? Moses says, "I will show you one who is coming. Listen to Him, and He will tell you how to stand before Him." Therefore, Christ preached the sermon which brought with it what Moses commands, because the Gospel says, "Here is Christ who conquered everything for you and gives it all to you." These words do not demand but only give. That is a much better sermon. Moses says, "Believe." Christ says, "Here you have it."[37]

---

33. "Preface to the New Testament (1546/1522)," LW 35:361; WA DB 6:9,14–16. This preface first appeared in the 1533 edition of Luther's New Testament and was retained in editions of Bible from 1534 onward. Compare LW 35:363, note 13.

34. "Preface to the Epistles of St. James and St. Jude (1546/1522)," LW 35:396; WA DB 7:384,27. Wengert notes: "Only when Scripture is approached as the inexhaustible resource that it truly is—as God's Word that kills and makes alive (2 Cor. 3:6) and thus as something that will not succumb to our categories, principles, or proof texting—will it *drive us away from itself and toward faith in Christ* under the cross." Italics added. Wengert, *Reading the Bible with Martin Luther*, 21.

35. "Prefaces to the New Testament (1546/1522)," LW 35:362; WA DB 6:10,20–23.

36. "Sermon on the Divinity of Christ (November 21, 1537)," LW 57:291; WA 45:281,15–22.

37. "Sermon on Easter Monday (April 2, 1526)," LW 56:171; WA 20:338,22–29.

"Hear you have it." Listening to Christ, the Living Word, a person hears God proclaiming the gospel—a gospel freely given. This gospel is also experienced in many ways, including through the "forgiveness of sin, life and salvation."[38] Encountering Christ, one experiences the gospel, because the Word, Christ, and the gospel cannot be separated.

A LISTENING CHURCH

Luther and his fellow reformers were often accused of "disrupting" the church. Their translation of the Bible into a vernacular German threatened the unity of the church, according to the Roman Curia. These church-disrupting claims were taken seriously by the reformers. Melanchthon even addressed this matter in a sermon preached at Luther's funeral. He declared, ". . . many cry out that the Church has been disturbed and that insoluble controversies have been spread." However, continued Melanchthon, these "divisions arise on account of the impudence of the godless. The fault lies with those who refuse to hear the Son of God, of whom the heavenly Father says, "Listen to Him" [Matt 17:5]. Luther brought to light the true and needful doctrine."[39] The church was where the believers had possession of, and listened to, the Word, the Living Christ.[40] Anyone refusing to listen to Christ broke the first commandment and separated themselves from the church, the body of Christ (1 Cor 12:27). Thus, in response to his critics who blamed the Wittenberg reformers for disrupting the church, they insisted that the church must be founded on listening to the Word. Caspar Cruciger, one of Luther's colleagues, stated, "The voice from heaven teaches the same thing, 'This is my beloved Son, in whom I am delighted, listen to him.' Therefore, he testifies that this Son is first loved, and because of him the church, which listens to this Son, is also elected and loved."[41] The church is only the church as it listens to the Word of God, the voice of the Good Shepherd recognized by the believers (John 10:5).[42] When the church listens to the voice of the Word, it will

38. SC, Sacrament of the Altar, 5–6. BC 362; BSELK 890.
39. "Funeral Oration of Dr. Martin Luther (February 22, 1546)," LW CV 43; CR 11:728. Melanchthon astutely noted that while political leaders hated upheaval or change (*mutationes*), that should not prevent them from listening to Christ, as the transfiguration accounts tell them. "Preface to the Second Volume of the Complete Edition of Luther's Latin Writings (June 1, 1546)," LW CV 71; CR 6:164.
40. "On the Councils and the Church (1539)," LW 41:148; WA 50:628,29–30.
41. Caspar Cruciger, *In Evangelivm Iohannis*, 42–46; found in: Craig S. Farmer et al., eds., *John 1–12: New Testament*, vol. IV, Reformation Commentary on Scripture (Downers Grove, IL: IVP Academic, 2014), 33.
42. "Lectures on Genesis (1535–1545)," LW 8:272; WA 44:778,37–42.

not break the first commandment of having gods other than the Lord God, the Living Word.[43] Luther concluded:

> The same thing should happen here in the Christian church; none other should be preached or taught except the Son of God alone. Of him alone is it said, "This is my beloved Son; listen to him" [Matt 17:5]—and of no other, be he emperor, pope, or cardinal.
>
> Therefore this is what we say: I grant that emperor, pope, cardinals, princes, and nobles are wise and understanding, but I shall believe in Christ; he is my Lord, he is the one God bids me to listen to, from him he bids me to learn what real, divine wisdom and understanding is.[44]

Because the church is founded on listening to Christ, the church's mission is also to be based on listening to this voice. In a Table Talk in 1533, Luther explained that when the voice from heaven said, "This is my Son, listen to him," it also meant that when Christ later ascended to heaven, "he sent apostles and instituted sacraments (baptism and the Lord's Supper), so that when these are present and are heard and received we can truly say, 'God says this.' . . . For God says that we should listen to Christ, but Christ says that we should listen to the apostles."[45] The apostles and the church can speak with authority only when they proclaim what they received from christ. As Cruciger asserted, God has promised to preserve the church when it proclaims this gospel message spoken by Christ and is passed on to the disciples.[46] If the church wants to survive, it must listen to Christ alone.

In the Augsburg Confession, the article on the Office of Preaching comes right after the article on justification, the very heart of the gospel. Likewise, Luther's emphasis on "Listen to Him" means that the preacher, like John the Baptist, is to point to the One who is the gospel made flesh. Luther stated:

> It was Christ's exclusive prerogative to proclaim: "If anyone thirst, let him come to Me and drink." No other person is entitled to say this. For any other preacher it is befitting to do no more than point others to Christ, leading them to hear His words; he must leave himself out of account and proclaim only Christ. None but Christ can declare: "I have been sent that you hear Me." Thus, the heavenly Father says of Him (Mt. 17:5): "This is My beloved Son; listen to Him." And in Ps. 2:7: "Thou art My Son; today I have begotten

43. "On the Councils and the Church (1539)," LW 41:173; WA 50:649,2–3.
44. "Last Sermon in Eisleben (February 15, 1546)," LW 51:388; WA 51:191,31–38.
45. "Table Talks (Spring 1533)," LW 54:89; WA TR 1:229,14–17, 20.
46. Cruciger, "Dedication to the Church Postils (1544)," LW 77:5, WA 21:199,17–27.

Thee." You must not rivet your attention on us preachers. No, look to Him, and hear Him; for I am unable to accomplish what He has accomplished.[47]

While Luther enjoined people to not focus on the preacher, he did acknowledge that when preachers are actually preaching what they heard from Christ, they are the equal to Christ—not in divinity or purity or holiness, but because they preach the same message.[48] It is in this sense that Luther called the church a "mouth-house" (*mundhaus*)[49] who proclaims gospel, or as Luther stated it in the *Small Catechism*, the "forgiveness of sins, life and salvation."[50] On the other hand, false teachers reveal they have not heard the voice that speaks life: "Anyone who confuses these two causes the people to go astray and misleads both himself and those who listen to him."[51] Luther's advice, then, was to dispose of those erroneous papal decrees down the toilet so no one can hear them.[52] It is a matter of life and death. One listens either to the Living Voice of Gospel, speaking forgiveness of sins, life, and salvation[53] or to the false "apple god" (*Apfelgott*).[54] People follow the voice they hear. Only the *sola vox viva*, the living voice alone, comes from the mouth of God in Christ. The task of the preaching office is to proclaim this Word that is heard and experienced in Christ.

In the Augsburg Confession, two things are considered essential in the foundation of the church and its unity: the Word and Sacrament.[55] Luther also insisted that the injunction of "Listen to Him" was central to both preaching and the sacraments. The sacraments were efficacious because they were connected with the Word and with faith. For example, when Luther discussed baptism in the Small Catechism, he stated that "Baptism is not simply plain water. Instead it is water enclosed in God's command and connected with God's Word."[56] He later added, "Clearly the water does not do it, but the Word of God, which is with and alongside the water, and faith, which trusts this Word of God in the water. For without

47. "Sermons on John (1530–1532)," LW 23:280–281; WA 33:447,16–39.
48. "Annotations on Matthew (1534/1535)," LW 67:120; WA 38:515.8–11.
49. "Advent Postils (1522)," LW 75:51, note 72; WA 10.I.2:48,5.
50. SC, Sacrament of the Altar, 5–6. BC 362; BSELK 888, 890.
51. "Sermon on the Mount, Postscript (1522)," LW 21:285; WA 32:536.13–14.
52. "But we shall relegate the decretals of the pope to the privy." "Lectures on Genesis (1535–1545)," LW 8:271; WA 44:778,26.
53. "Indeed, lest you tempt God, you should rather listen to Him when He promises. Cling to him in firm faith." "Lectures on Genesis (1535–1545)," LW 7:308; WA 44:538,10.
54. Luther uses this term in the LC, Commandments, 23; BC 389; BSELK 938:5. See also BC 389, note 40; BSELK 938 note 126.
55. AC VII, 1–3; BC 42; BSELK 102.
56. SC Baptism, 1–2. BC 359; BSELK 882.

the Word of God the water is plain water and not a baptism, but with the Word of God it is a baptism, that is, a grace-filled water of life and a 'bath of the new birth in the Holy Spirit.'"[57] When God speaks the Word through the Water, one should listen, for God is speaking and acting. Luther made this clear in his last sermon preached in Wittenberg:

> The Father did not speak of Gabriel or any others when he cried from heaven, "Listen to him" [Matt 17:5]. Therefore I should stick to the catechism; then I can defend myself against reason when the Anabaptists say, "Baptism is water; how can water do such great things? Pigs and cows drink it. The Spirit must do it." Don't you hear, you mangy, leprous whore, you holy reason, what the Scripture says, "Listen to him," who says, "Go and baptize all nations" [Matt 28:19], and "He who believes and is baptized [will be saved]"? [Mark 16:16]. It is not merely water, but baptism given in the name of the holy Trinity.[58]

When God speaks the Word of life, whether through preaching or through baptism, believers should sit up and listen, for God's voice is breathing the forgiveness of sin, life, and salvation into their hearts.

Luther made the same point with the sacrament of the altar. He insisted that his opponents simply listen to what Christ said at the very first supper, when he told the disciples to take, eat, and drink both the bread and the cup. To do otherwise would be to disobey the voice from heaven telling them to "Listen to Him."[59] One should not despise this Word of the Lord.

Luther also relied upon the command from heaven, "Listen to Him," in his debates with Ulrich Zwingli, Johann Oecolampadius, and Andreas Karlstadt over the real, bodily presence of Christ in the Lord's Supper.[60] At the Marburg Colloquy, Luther kept pointing to the words of institution spoken by Christ: "This is my Body," which he had previously written on the table for them to read.[61] He challenged them to listen to what Christ actually said, rather than to what they wanted the text to say to suit their theology. Christ did not say, insisted Luther, that "this is a sign of my body," or "this (pointing to himself) is my body," but he said, as he held the bread, "This is my body." Listening to Christ, one would know the truth of the Lord's Supper: "When you hear a fanatical antisacramentalist say, 'There is only bread and wine in the sacrament of the altar,' or 'Do

57. SC Baptism, 9–10. BC 359; BSELK 884.
58. "Last Sermon in Wittenberg (January 17, 1546)," LW 51:376; WA 51:129,4–12.
59. "Letter of Consolation to the Christians at Halle (1527)," LW 43:151; WA 23:413,7–12.
60. See, for example, "The Sacrament of the Body and Blood of Christ–Against the Fanatics (1526)," LW 36:335–36; WA 19:483,22–26; "Confession Concerning Christ's Supper (1528)," LW 37:304; WA 26:446,1–3.
61. "Report of the Marburg Colloquy (1529)," LW 38:67; WA 30.III:147,15–18.

you think that at your word Christ is going to descend from heaven into your mouth and your belly?' You just say to him, 'Ah, I like what you say; what a learned bride the devil has! But what do you say to this: "This is my beloved Son, listen to him?" And he says, "This is my body" [Matt 17:5; 26:26].'"[62] The correct understanding of the Lord's Supper was directly connected to the Word proclaimed and heard.

The injunction to "Listen to Him" was also prominent in confession and absolution. The penitent was to listen to the person proclaiming the absolution as if the penitent were listening to Christ himself. It is Christ, not the person speaking words of absolution, who speaks the words, "You are forgiven." Luther deliberately asked the one confessing, "Do you also believe that my forgiveness is God's forgiveness?" If they answered in the affirmative, then the person hearing the confession would proclaim that they were forgiven.[63] In his lectures on John's Gospel, Luther reminded the people that whenever they were uncertain that they were actually forgiven when the words of absolution were spoken, they should remember that these words came from Christ himself.[64] Thus he affirmed that "when the minister pronounces absolution, liberation from the devil and from sin is sure to follow. If the Holy Spirit grants you grace to believe, there He drives out Satan and death with one word. . . . For it has been determined by God that Christ wants to speak in His church and does not want to tolerate any other teacher, as the voice of the Father resounds from heaven: 'Listen to Him' (Matt 17:5)."[65] The authors of the Formula of Concord–Solid Declaration echoed Luther, stating, "Therefore, the eternal Father calls from heaven regarding his dear Son and all who proclaim repentance and forgiveness of sins in his name, 'Listen to him!' (Matt 17[:5])."[66] The person speaking the words of absolution to a person was only repeating what they heard from Christ.

THE LISTENING CHURCH ENGAGED IN LIFE

Listening to Christ is pivotal, to shape not only the theology of the church but also the life of its members. Luther the pastor interpreted the words from heaven spoken during the transfiguration of Christ in various ways.

---

62. "Last Sermon in Wittenberg (January 17, 1546)," LW 51:379; WA 51:133,30–35.
63. SC Baptism, 27–28. BC 361–62; BSELK 888.
64. "Sermons (1534)," LW 69:405; WA 37:381,8–18, and "Church Postils (1544)," LW 77:137; WA 49:139,14–26.
65. "Lectures on Genesis (1535–1545)," LW 8:271 WA 44:778,15–25.
66. FC-SD II:51. BC 554; BSELK 1370.

Hearing Christ's voice provided comfort to those with terrified consciences, shaped their way of living out the faith, removed doubts about predestination or election, revealed God's will, and helped them deal with civil authorities. "Listen to Him" was therefore very pragmatic advice.

The Wittenberg reformers were very concerned that life-giving pastoral care be provided for the community. Luther had this advice:

> To those who are afraid and have already been terrified by the burden of their sins Christ the Savior and the gift should be announced, not Christ the example and the lawgiver. But to those who are smug and stubborn the example of Christ should be set forth, lest they use the gospel as a pretext for the freedom of the flesh and thus become smug. Therefore let every Christian learn to be able to shake off the false idea of Christ that Satan urges upon him in his terror and affliction, and to say: "Satan, why are you debating with me now about deeds? I am already frightened and troubled enough because of my deeds and my sins. Indeed, since I am already troubled and burdened, let me hear, not you with your accusation and condemnation but Christ, the Savior of the human race, who says that He came into the world to save sinners (1 Tim 1:15), to comfort the despairing, and to proclaim release to the captives (Luke 4:18). This is the real Christ in the most precise sense of the word, and no one else besides Him. I can find an example of a holy life in Abraham, Isaiah, John the Baptist, Paul, and other saints. But they cannot forgive my sins, deliver me from your power and from death, save me, and give me life. Only Christ is qualified to do these things, He whom God the Father has marked with His seal. Therefore I shall not listen to you as my teacher; but I shall listen to Christ, of whom the Father has said (Matt 17:5): 'This is My beloved Son, with whom I am well pleased; listen to Him.'"[67]

When someone needed to hear the gospel, Luther's solution was simple: listen to Christ,[68] as God had instructed, and then the Gospel would be breathed upon them.

The reformers also knew that people struggle to know God's will for themselves and whether they are among God's elect. To such souls, Luther offered the same simple advice: listen to Christ. Referring to the voice from heaven that spoke on Mount Tabor, Luther stated,

> Now this is the will of the Father, that we be intent on hearing what the Man Christ has to say, that we listen to His Word. You must not cavil at His Word, find fault with it, and dispute it. Just hear it. Then the Holy Spirit will come and prepare your heart, that you may sincerely believe the preaching of the divine Word, even give up your life for it, and say: "This is God's Word

---

67. "Lectures on Galatians (1535)," LW 27:35; WA 40.II:43,15–44,11.
68. "Sermons on John (1537)," LW 22:119–120; WA 46:639,14–30.

and the pure truth." . . . [But if you listen to other voices, then] you are setting yourself up as its schoolmaster. In that way you will never discover the
meaning of Christ's Word or of His heavenly Father's will.[69]

Hearing God's voice puts everything into perspective. Said Luther: "Our
thoughts of God and our mode of dealing with Him begin where He
begins and directs us when, in the first place, He speaks from heaven and
declares (Matt 17:5): 'This is My beloved Son; listen to Him.'"[70] When a
person was assaulted by doubts about election and predestination, Luther's
advice remained the same: "I will fulfill your desire, in order that you may
be able to know whether you are predestined or not. Behold, this is My
Son; listen to Him (cf. Matt 17:5). Look at Him as He lies in the manger
and on the lap of His mother, as He hangs on the cross."[71] This voice from
heaven is the living, authoritative, life-giving voice of God spoken to the
person on the mountaintop, in the valley, at work, or in the sanctuary.
This voice speaks and breathes the Word of Life into individuals and into
the worshipping community.

Luther admonished those who faced challenges from society or civil
authorities to also listen to Christ, as the voice from heaven had instructed.
In his treatise, "Against the Robbing and Murdering Hordes of Peasants,"
he urged Christians to live according to Christ's teachings. In the dispute
over having property in common, he advised that the "Father commands
from heaven, saying, 'This is my beloved Son, listen to Him' [Matt 17:5],"
and then added, "For baptism does not make men free in body and property, but in soul; and the gospel does not make goods common, except
in the case of those who, of their own free will, do what the apostles and
disciples did in Acts 4 [:32–37]."[72] When listening to Christ, however, one
must distinguish whether Christ is speaking to the spiritual realm or the
temporal realm, speaking a word of law or a word of gospel. If the gospel is
forced, it becomes a law. Yet the key to Luther's approach remains the same:
listening to Christ, and then proceeding in an appropriate manner, is the
best way to proceed. The believer never goes wrong by listening to Him.

---

69. "Sermons on John (1530–1532)," LW 23:229; WA 33:362,20–363,2.
70. "Sermons on John (1537)," LW 24:58; WA 45:514,1–4. Caspar Cruciger also addressed the
question of predestination in his commentary on John 10:29. He pointed to the voice speaking
from heaven telling the questioning soul to "listen to Christ." Cruciger, *In Evangelivm Iohannis,*
484–88; in *John 1–12: New Testament,* vol. IV, Reformation Commentary on Scripture, eds.
Craig S. Farmer et al. (Downers Grove, IL: IVP Academic, 2014), 394–395.
71. "Lectures on Genesis (1535–1545)," LW 5:45; WA 43:459,26–29.
72. "Against the Robbing and Murdering Hordes of Peasants (1525)," LW 46:51; WA 18:359,3–7.

Sanct Lucas.   XLV.

Matth.
rliij.
Mar. vj
Joh. vj.

fieng an sich zu neigen/Da tratten zu jm die Zwelffe/vnd sprachen zu
jm/Las das volck von dir/das sie hin gehen jnn die merckte vmbher/
vnd jnn die dörffer/das sie herberge vnd speise finden/denn wir sind
hie jnn der wüsten. Er aber sprach zu jnen/Gebt jr jnen zu essen/Sie
sprachen/Wir haben nicht mehr denn fünff brod/vnd zween fisch/
Es sey denn/das wir hin gehen sollen/vnd speise keuffen fur so gros
volck (denn es waren bey fünff tausent man) Er sprach aber zu seinen
Jüngern/Lasset sie sich setzen bey schichten/ia funfftzig vnd funfftzig. Vnd sie thetten also/vnd satzten sich alle. Da nam er die fünff
brod/vnd zween fisch/vnd sahe auff gen himel/vnd dancket drüber/
brach sie/vnd gab sie den Jüngern/das sie dem volck furlegten. Vnd
sie assen vnd wurden alle sat/vnd wurden auffgehaben/das jnen vber
bleib von brocken/zwelff körbe.

Matth.
rvj.
Marci.
viij.

Vnd es begab sich/da er allein war vnd betet/vnd seine Jünger
bey jm/fraget er sie/vnd sprach/Wer sagen die leute das ich sey? Sie
antworten/vnd sprachen/Sie sagen/du seiest Johannes der Teuf-
fer/Etliche aber/du seiest Elias/Etliche aber/es sey der alten Propheten einer aufferstanden. Er aber sprach zu jnen/Wer saget jr aber
das ich sey? Da antwortet Petrus/vnd sprach/Du bist der Christ
Gottes. Vnd er bedrawet sie/vnd gepot/das sie das niemand sagten/
vnd sprach/Denn des menschen Son mus noch viel leiden/vnd verworffen werden von den Eltesten vnd hohen priestern vnd Schrifft-
gelerten/vnd getödtet werden/vnd am dritten tage aufferstehen.

Da sprach er zu jnen allen/Wer mir folgen wil/der verleugne sich
selbs/vnd neme sein creutz auff sich teglich/vnd folge mir nach/
Denn wer sein leben erhalten wil/der wird es verlieren/Wer aber sein
leben verleuret vmb meinen willen/der wirds erhalten. Vnd was nutz
hette der mensch/ob er die gantze welt gewünne/vnd verlöre sich
selbs/odder beschedigt sich selbs? Wer sich aber mein vnd meiner
wort schemet/des wird sich des menschen Son auch schemen/wenn
er komen wird jnn seiner Herrligkeit/vnd seines Vaters/vnd der heiligen Engel. Jch sage euch aber warlich/das etliche sind von denen/
die hie stehen/die den tod nicht schmecken werden/bis das sie das
Reich Gottes sehen.

Matth.
rvij.
Mat.ir.

Vnd es begab sich nach diesen reden bey acht tagen/das er zu sich
nam/Petron/Johannen vnd Jacoben/vnd gieng auff einen berg zu
beten/Vnd da er betet/ward die gestalt seines angesichts anders/vnd
sein kleid ward weis vnd glantzet. Vnd sihe/zween menner redeten
mit jm/welche waren Moses vnd Elias/die erschienen jnn klarheit/
vnd redeten von dem ausgang/welchen er solt erfüllen zu Jerusalem.
Petrus aber vnd die mit jm waren/waren vol schlaffs. Da sie aber
auffwachten/sahen sie seine klarheit/Vnd die zween menner bey jm
stehen.

(Ausgang)
Das ist/was er fur
ein ende nemen
würde.

Vnd es begab sich/da die von jm wichen/sprach Petrus zu Jhe-
su/Meister/hie ist gut sein/lasset vns drey hütten machen/dir eine/
Mosi eine/vnd Elias eine/vnd wuste nicht was er redet. Da er aber
solchs redet/kam eine wolcken/vnd vberschattet sie/Vnd sie erschra-
cken/da sie die wolcke vberzog. Vnd es fiel eine stimme aus der wol-
cken/die sprach/Dieser ist mein lieber Son/DEN SOLT IR
HOREN. Vnd jnn dem solche stimme geschach/funden sie Jhe-
                                    D iij   sum alleine.

"DEN SOLT IR HOREN" in Luke 9:35, 1534 Luther Bible.
(Reformation Historical Research Library Wittenberg—
Stiftung Luthergedenkstätten, LH, Kn D 254)

SUMMARY

While Luther's decision to highlight the words spoken by the voice in heaven during the transfiguration of Christ may have originally seemed surprising, it quickly becomes clear that the words, "Listen to Him," are prominent in his theology. When people listen, they hear the Word spoken as Law and Gospel, but always for the sake of breathing life into individuals and the community. Moreover, the church is founded on the Word who is Christ. The gathered community is called to listen to Christ in determining doctrine and faith. It is the starting point for preaching and the sacraments. Listening to Him is also the most important step in determining how to best provide pastoral care to a people in need. When the pastor or neighbor advises a troubled soul to listen to the Word of God spoken by Christ, fears, doubts, and terrified consciences are comforted. The key is to Listen to him, the Living Word, rather than to other voices. That way a church, a pastor, a community, or an individual does not go wrong.

The advice to listen to Christ alone, the living voice of the gospel, was taken seriously by the second generation of Lutherans as well. David Chytraeus aptly summarized the importance of listening to Christ when he wrote in the Formula of Concord–Solid Declaration:

> For our Lord and Savior Jesus Christ is our only teacher; concerning him this weighty command was given from heaven to all human beings, "*Hunc audite*" ("listen to him") [Matt 17:5]. He was not a mere human being or angel. He was not only truthful, wise, and powerful. He is the eternal truth and Wisdom itself, and almighty God. He knows very well what to say and how to say it, and he can accomplish through his power everything that he has said and promises, and can make it happen.[73]

God speaks Words of wisdom and promises to the world through the voice of Christ, the eternal and Living Word. The Word worth listening to proclaims the gospel. Moreover, this Word of gospel that the church is called to listen to is, first and foremost, the forgiveness of sin—which were the next words that Luther emphasized in the 1534 Bible. For when Christ speaks, we are to listen, as he declares to those in need, "your sins are forgiven you. Stand up and walk" (Matt 9:5). That is a word worth hearing.

73. FC-SD VII, 42–43. BC 600; BSELK 1470,1472.

7.

Luther's Emphasis on "Forgives Sin"

"Forgiveness of sins is not more than two words,
yet the entire realm of Christ is based upon them."[1]

"Where there is no gospel, there is also no forgiveness."[2]

INTRODUCTION

Luther's translation of Paul's letter to the Romans was the most controversial portion of his translation of the New Testament and served as a
lightning rod for criticism by his opponents. Jerome Emser, Duke George
of Saxony's secretary, claimed that among Luther's many translation errors,
the most blatant was the addition of *"allein"* (alone) to Romans 3:28.[3] It was
not just the addition of this word or the other "poor choices" in Luther's
translating of ideas rather than literally translating the words that made
his translation so controversial. Rather, Luther's translation of Romans
raised questions because he unequivocally emphasized that Romans was
the heart of the scriptures, and at the heart of Romans was its gospel message of forgiveness and justification by God's grace alone. In his "Preface

---

1. *"Vergebung der sunden sind nicht mehr denn zwey wort, daryn das gantz reich Christi steth."* "Sermon
on the Sunday after St. Michael's (1524)," WA 15:703,24–25. Obviously, *vergebung der sunden*
is three words here, not two. However, Luther was referring to the Latin Vulgate, in which
"forgiveness of sins" is only two words: *remissio peccatorum*. See also Martin Schloemann, "Die
Zwei Wörter: Luthers Notabene zu 'Mitte der Schrift,'" *Luther: Zeitschrift der Luther-Gesellshaft.*
65 No. 3 (1994), 117, n. 12.
2. LC II,55. BC 438; BSELK 1064, 1065.
3. Martin Brecht, *Martin Luther: The Preservation of the Church, 1532–1546*, trans. James L. Schaaf
(Minneapolis: Fortress Press, 1993), 107–8.

to Romans," Luther declared, "This epistle is really the chief part of the New Testament, and is truly the purest gospel."[4] The forgiveness of sin by Christ alone through grace alone, apart from any meritorious works or human actions meant to earn it, threatened the penitential system and the sale of indulgences. This message threatened the Roman church.

Paul's letter to the Romans was also the next place that the reader encounters Luther's deliberate capitalization of every letter in a word or phrase in order to emphasize his theological agenda. The two highlighted words, "FORGIVES SIN," are deliberately connected to the words that Luther had emphasized in the Wisdom of Solomon and the Synoptic Gospels. When Jesus was transfigured, a voice from heaven said to the disciples present, "Listen to Him." The One to be listened to was none other than the "Word," as emphasized in the Wisdom of Solomon. Furthermore, the human temptation to focus on the law too often overshadows the life-changing gospel message that Christ speaks. Thus, after highlighting "Word" and "Listen to Him," Luther also highlighted two words in Romans 3:25, "FORGIVES SIN" (*SUNDE VERGIBT*), beginning in his 1533 edition of the New Testament.[5] This was the content of the Gospel Word.

Luther's translation of Romans 3:25 was unique. His translation read: "God has set forth [Jesus] to be a throne of grace, through faith in his blood, so that God presents the righteousness that applies to him in that he forgives sin, which was pardoned under divine patience."[6] John Calvin translated the verse as "[Jesus], Whom God hath set forth to be a propitiation through faith in his blood, to declare his righteousness for the remission of sins that are past, through the forbearance of God."[7] He thus removed the sense of immediacy of and focus on forgiveness, as Luther had done. Calvin also emphasized the predestined aspect of God's actions.[8] Their translations of this verse also differ from contemporary English translations. The translation of Romans 3:25 in the New Revised

---

4. LB NT XCIXa; LW 35:365; WA DB 7:3,3–4.

5. LB NT CVIIa; WA DB 7:38. See also Hartmut Hövelmann, *Kernstellen der Lutherbibel: Eine Anleitung zum Schriftverständnis*. Texte und Arbeiten zur Bibel, Deutschen Bibelgesellschaft, Bd 5 (Bielefeld: Luther Verlag, 1989), 49.

6. "welchen Gott hat furgestellet zu einem Gnadenstuel durch den glauben inn seinem blut damit er die gerechtigkeit die fur im gilt darbiete inndem das er SVNDE VERGJBT welche bis an herbleiben war vnter Göttlicher gedult." LB NT CVIIa; LB DB 7:38, 39 (the highlighting is not present in the 1522 and 1545 editions of Romans 3:25).

7. "Quem proposuit Deus propitiatorium per fidem in sanguine ipsius, in demonstrationem justitiæ suæ, propter remissionem delictorum." John Calvin, *Commentary on the Epistle of Paul the Apostle to the Romans*, trans. John Owen (Grand Rapids: Baker, 1989), 139.

8. Calvin, *Commentary on Romans*, 141.

An die Römer.   CVII·

Jhesu geschehen ist / welchen Gott hat furgestellet zu einem Gna/
denstůl/durch den glauben jnn seinem blut/ damit er die gerechtig/
keit/die fur jm gilt/ darbiete/jnn dem/ das er SVNDE VER/
GJBT / welche bis ª an her blieben war/vnter Göttlicher gedult/
auff das er zu diesen zeiten darböte die gerechtigkeit/die fur jm gilt/
Auff das er allein gerecht sey/ vnd gerecht mache den/der da ist des
glaubens an Jhesu.

Wo ist denn nu dein rhum? Er ist aus/ Durch welch Gesetz?
durch der werck gesetz? Nicht also/sondern durch des glaubens ge/
setz.

So halten wir es nu/ das der mensch gerecht werde/on des Ge/
setzes werck/ allein durch den glauben. Odder ist Gott allein der Ju/
den Gott? Ist er nicht auch der Heiden Gott? Ja freilich auch der
Heiden Gott/ sintemal es ist ein einiger Gott/der da gerecht machet
die Beschneidung aus dem glauben / vnd die Vorhaut durch den
glauben. Wie? Heben wir denn das Gesetz auff/durch den glauben?
Das sey ferne/sondern wir richten das Gesetz auff.

IIII.

Gen.xv.

As sagen wir denn von vnserm vater Abraham/das
er funden habe nach dem fleisch? Das sagen wir. Ist
Abraham durch die werck gerecht/ so hat er wol
rhum/ aber nicht fur Gott. Was saget aber die
Schrifft? Abraham hat Gott geglenbet/ vnd das ist
jm zur gerechtigkeit gerechnet. Dem aber/der mit wer
cken vmbgehet/wird der lohn nicht aus gnade zu ge/
rechnet/sondern aus pflicht. Dem aber/der nicht mit wercken vmbge
het/ gleubet aber an den/ der die Gottlosen gerecht macht/dem wird
sein glaub gerechnet zur gerechtigkeit. Nach welcher weise auch Da/
uid sagt/das die seligkeit sey allein des menschen/ welchem Gott zu/
rechnet die gerechtigkeit/on zuthun der werck / da er spricht/Selig
Psalm. sind die/welchen jre vngerechtigkeit vergeben sind/ vnd welchen jre
xxxij. sunde bedecket sind/Selig ist der man/welchem Gott keine sunde zu/
rechnet.

Nu diese seligkeit/ gehet sie vber die Beschneidung odder vber die
Vorhaut? Wir müssen je sagen/das Abraham sey sein glaube zurge/
rechtigkeit gerechnet. Wie ist er jm denn zugerechnet/ jnn der Be/
schneidung? odder jnn der Vorhaut? On zweinel nicht jnn der Be/
scheidung/sondern jnn der Vorhaut.Das zeichen aber der Beschnei
dung empfieng er zum sigel der gerechtigkeit des glaubens/welchen
er noch jnn der Vorhaut hatte/auff das er würde ein vater aller/die
da gleuben jnn der Vorhaut/das den selbigen solches auch gerech/
net werde zur gerechtigkeit/vnd würde auch ein vater der Beschnei/
dung/nicht allein dere/die von der Beschneidung sind/sondern auch
dere/die wandeln jnn den fusstapffen des glaubens/welcher war jnn
der Vorhaut vnsers vaters Abrahams.

Denn die verheissung/ das er solte sein der welt erbe/ist nicht ge/
scheben Abraham oder seinem samen durchs Gesetz/sondern durch
die gerechtigkeit des glaubens/Denn wo die vom Gesetz erben sind/
so ist der glaub nichts/ vnd die verheissung ist abe/sintemal das Ge/
setz richtet nur zorn an/Denn wo das Gesetz nicht ist/da ist auch kei
ne vbertrettung / Derhalben mus die gerechtigkeit durch den glau/
                                 T ij   ben komen/

(margin notes:) der gantze schrifft. Nemlich/das alles sunde ist / was ni/ cht durch das blut Christi erlöset/im glauben gerecht wird. Darumb fa/ sse diesen text wol/ denn hie ligt dar/ nidder aller werck/ verdienst vn rhum/ wie er selbs hie sa/ get/vn bleibt alles ne lauter Gottes gnade vnd ehre.

ª (Bis an her) Die sunde kundre wed/ der Gesetz noch kein gut werck weg nemen/ Es muste Christus vnd die vergebung thun. (Richten auff) Der glaube erfül/ let alle gesetz/ Die werck erfullen kein titel des Gesetzes.

Die erweiset er mit zweien exempeln/ das verdienst ni/ chts sey/ sondern al lein Gottes gnade

Denn Abraham gleubet vnd ward gelobet fur gere/ cht/ehe denn er be/ schnitten ward/ Gene.xv.das je die gnade vor dem werck sein müsse.

"SUNDE VERGIBT" in Romans 3:25, 1534 Luther Bible.
(Reformation Historical Research Library Wittenberg—
Stiftung Luthergedenkstätten, LH, Kn D 254)

Standard Version replaces the words "forgives sins" with "passed over the sins." The subtle difference implies that sins are overlooked or not actually removed, rather than forgiven. Gone was Luther's conviction that the gospel proclamation has dealt with sin once and for all, thus reducing its power. Yet his emphasis on the power of the gospel became particularly important for his understanding of the efficacy of preaching to transform lives and the ability of the sacraments to forgive sin, and not just point to the one who forgives. The gospel proclaims that Christ forgives sin and does something to a person. A transfiguration takes place. No wonder these two words played a central role in Luther's theology.

FORGIVENESS AS THE WORK OF GOD ALONE

One of Luther's early battles with the Roman church addressed their understanding that through acts of love, people could cooperate with God in bringing about their justification. Proper contrition and acts of penance could contribute toward or even earn forgiveness. This approach, however, was contrary to Luther's radical understanding of the gospel, grace, and forgiveness. God's grace and forgiveness could not be earned; they were free and unmerited gifts. When forgiveness is not understood as a work of God alone, sinners are always looking for ways to earn their own forgiveness, thus breaking the first commandment by trying to be gods in God's place. Luther bluntly stated that "to forgive sins, justify, and save is the work of God; therefore, whoever attributes these works to himself and his own merit and righteousness makes himself God."[9] In the fifth petition of the Lord's Prayer ("forgive our sins as we forgive the sins of others"), Luther insisted that while people do not deserve or earn this forgiveness from God, once they are forgiven, they would "truly want to forgive heartily and to do good gladly to those who sin against us."[10] In his Genesis lectures, he stated, "For to forgive sins, to retain sins, to make alive, etc., are works of the Divine Majesty alone; nevertheless, the same works are given to human beings and are done through the Word which human beings teach."[11] If one listened to Christ's prayer, this would be clearly understood.

Luther wanted to emphasize the importance of forgiveness of sin as God's work alone because it underscored his contention that forgiveness was in God's very heart. Contrary to his initial view, God was not a wrathful God who delighted in accusing and damning him. Such a view only

9. "Sermons on John (1528–1529)," LW 69:231; WA 26:347–48.
10. SC III:16. BC 358; BSELK 878, 890.
11. "Lectures on Genesis (1535–1545)," LW 1:12; WA 42:10,38–40.

caused terror, making one unable to believe that God was merciful "and that He wants to forgive sins for the sake of Christ."[12] This wrathful view of God was based on human knowledge of God apart from the Word and was contrary to God's true nature.[13] Through the Word, Luther discovered that God's true nature, as revealed in Christ, was a God who forgives. He now heard Christ saying, "'Take courage, My son; your sins are forgiven you' [Matt 9:2]. With this word, Christ paints Himself in His true colors. This speech also truly expresses the character of His spirit, and out of the abundance of the heart His mouth speaks [cf. Matt 12:34]. That is: it is His every desire gladly to forgive sins and to free from punishment."[14] Johannes Bugenhagen echoed this view of the nature of God: "the gracious gospel is nothing else than that God wants to forgive sin, not for our sake, but for the sake of Jesus Christ who has suffered death for the sinners."[15] God wants to forgive sin. Thus, those who reject God's desire to forgive sins actually torture God by their wickedness,[16] since the natural working of God involves the forgiveness of sin and pronouncing sinners just, thus saving those who believe in Christ.[17] Unlike idols, God alone can sweep away sins "like a cloud."[18] That is God's nature. As Luther stated, "But God alone forgives sins and justifies. God alone liberates from death and eternal damnation. God alone gives the Holy Spirit. God alone is also truthful."[19] God, as a jealous God, reserves the right to justify and forgive sins and gives this right to no others. It is also what Christ does, since Christ has God's very nature. When Jesus forgave the man born lame, allowing him to walk again, his critics charged him with blasphemy, since they claimed that only God could forgive sin (Mark 2:1–12). Thus, Jesus reveals his divine identity by forgiving sin. It's in his heart.

THE GOSPEL AS THE FORGIVENESS OF SIN

Luther's simplest definition of the gospel was two words, "forgives sin." He repeatedly used this simple definition of the gospel. Commenting on the fifth petition of the Lord's Prayer ("Forgive us our

---

12. "Galatians Commentary (1535)," LW 26:318; WA 40.I.2:493,14–15.
13. "Galatians Commentary (1535)," LW 26:400; WA 40.I.2:608–25–609,11.
14. "Annotations on Matthew (1534–1535/1538)," LW 67:60; WA 38:476,38–42.
15. Johannes Bugenhagen, "A Christian Open Letter to Lady Anna," *Johannes Bugenhagen: Selected Writings*, vol. I & II, ed. Kurt K. Hendel (Minneapolis: Fortress Press, 2015), 385.
16. "Lectures on Genesis (1535–1545)," LW 2:22; WA 42: 277,19–22.
17. "Lectures on Psalms (1534)," LW 13:135; WA 40.III:584,11–14.
18. "Lectures on Isaiah (1527–1530)," LW 17:116; WA 31.II: 352,31–36.
19. "Lectures on Psalms (1532)," LW 12:55; WA 40.II.2:262,19–21.

sins"), he stated, "[God] gave us the gospel, in which there is nothing but forgiveness."[20] He also tied the gospel to listening to the voice of Christ: "the voice of the Gospel carries us and brings grace and forgiveness of sins."[21] He never tired of talking about how Christ forgives sins. In one sermon, he declared that "forgiveness of sins is not more than two words, yet the entire realm of Christ is based upon them."[22] This was the proper office of the gospel, and it happens "whenever the forgiveness of sins is proclaimed."[23] In another sermon, he stated, "Here you have the Gospel, which gives you forgiveness of sin."[24] The words "forgives sin" best captured the gospel, and so he capitalized every letter in the two words, "forgives sin," in Romans 3:25. This was simply good "gospel talk."

While the gospel could be defined most simply as "forgives sin," Luther realized that forgiveness was interwoven with the work of Christ and in relationship to both law and gospel. This gospel, claims Paul Althaus, "proclaims that all the law's demands have been met in Jesus Christ, that is, it preaches the forgiveness of sins. 'The gospel is the preaching of forgiveness of sins through the name of Jesus Christ.' Luther also adopts Paul's characterization of the gospel as 'promise.'"[25] The gospel promise, moreover, needs to be seen in relationship to justification, law, gospel, promise, and the person and work of Christ:

> The Gospel is a light that illumines hearts and makes them alive. It discloses what grace and the mercy of God are; what the forgiveness of sins, blessing, righteousness, life, and eternal salvation are; and how we are to attain to these. When we distinguish the Law from the Gospel this way, we attribute to

---

20. LC, II, 88. BC 452; BSELK 1100–1101. Even earlier, he had stated, "For what is the whole Gospel but the good tidings of the forgiveness of sins?" "Babylonian Captivity of the Church (1520)," LW 36:55; WA 6:525,36–37.

21. "Lectures on Isaiah (1527–1530)," LW 17:188; WA 31.II:408,22–23.

22. "Sermon (1524)," WA 15:703,24–25.

23. "Sermon on St. Thomas' Day (1516)," LW 51:20; WA 1:113,6–11. See also "Sermon on St. Mathias' Day (1525)," LW 51:126; WA 17.I:41,32–33; and "Sermon at the Baptism of Bernhard von Anhalt (1540)," LW 51:326; WA 49:132,32–35.

24. "Sermon on John (1530–1532);" LW 23:341; WA 33:549,26–28. In his Galatians commentary, he states, "Here comes the Gospel, which preaches the forgiveness of sins." "Galatians Commentary (1535)," LW 26:152; WA 40.I.2:262,20–21.

25. Paul Althaus, *The Theology of Martin Luther*, trans. Robert C. Schultz (Philadelphia: Fortress Press, 1966), 256. See also "Galatians Commentary (1519)," LW 27:184; WA 2:466,12–13. Luther elsewhere states, "The Gospel, properly defined, is the promise concerning Christ that frees from the terrors of the Law, from sin and death, and brings grace, forgiveness of sins, righteousness, and eternal life." "First Antinomian Disputation (1537)," LW 73:89; WA 39.I:387,2–4.

each its proper use and function. . . But when this distinction is recognized, the true meaning of justification is recognized.[26]

Forgiveness is pure gospel. Christ can grant this forgiveness because he has defeated sin, death, and the devil. The law no longer controls or dictates the human relationship with God. Though the law may drive one toward Christ and the gospel, it cannot give life. Nor can following the Law earn forgiveness. As Melanchthon claimed, "it is still necessary to attack and reject the opinion which imagines that [people] merit remission because of their contrition or that remission is given because of the worthiness of our contrition. But we must retain the voice of the Gospel which proclaims that sins are freely forgiven for the sake of the Son of God."[27] Luther's approach could be summarized by stating, "Unlike law with its voluminous books lining a lawyer's shelves, the Gospel is a short word: 'I forgive you.' Forgiveness turns a statement of fact, like 'Jesus Christ is Lord,' into a personal confession of faith: 'Jesus Christ is *my* Lord,' and that makes all the difference between theology and proclamation."[28] Luther translated the Bible so that it would elicit a confession of faith in the Living Word who is Christ.

FORGIVENESS AND THE CENTER OF SCRIPTURE

Luther was convinced that the forgiveness of sin was at the heart and center of the gospel.[29] Yet he also claimed that Christ and the gospel were the center of Scripture. He insisted, for example, that everything, including Scripture, is centered on Christ.[30] Both Scripture and the work of Christ make the gospel possible wherever people experience the forgiveness of sin. To speak of the one automatically included the others. "The gospel, then, is nothing but the preaching about Christ,"[31] and the "consolation of the gospel" was nothing other than "the forgiveness of sins in Christ."[32] To have Christ is to have the gospel, and to have the gospel is to have

---

26. "Galatians Commentary (1535)," LW 26:313; WA 40.I/.I:486,17–487,13.
27. Philip Melanchthon *Loci Communes, 1543*, trans. Jacob A. O. Preus (St. Louis: Concordia Publishing House, 1992), 158.
28. Steven D. Paulson, *Lutheran Theology*, Doing Theology Series (New York: Bloomsbury, 2011), 88.
29. LB NT CVIb-CVIIa; WA DB 7:38.
30. "Sermons on John (1537)," LW 22:168; WA 46:682,3.
31. LB NT *Vorrhede*; "Preface to the New Testament (1522/1545)," LW 35:360; WA DB 6:7,22–24.
32. "Church Postils (1544)," LW 79:33; WA 22:227,31–34. See also "Sermons on John (1529)," LW 69:370; WA 28:478,37–39; and "Sermon at the Baptism of Bernhard von Anhalt (1540)," LW 51:326; WA 49:132,30–35.

forgiveness of sins. Thus, the words, "FORGIVES SIN, which remain capitalized in the [Luther] Bible until 1545, signal the remedial and creative *pro me* of the gospel."[33] These two words perform the gospel upon the sinner. In hearing the proclamation of forgiveness, a sinner experiences the gospel in its full force. The chains of sin are removed and not just "passed over," and the promise of life with God and in community are made a present reality for those who are "in Christ." Thus, just as Jesus was transfigured on Mount Tabor, so all who believe in Him are transfigured when he speaks the words, "your sins are forgiven you." Those words of Christ give life since they proclaim the gospel.

For Luther, "the forgiveness of sins bestowed in Christ is the real center of the biblical witness."[34] But forgiveness is also at the heart of being justified by Christ alone. Being forgiven by Christ is nothing less than experiencing the gospel of being justified by God in God's presence. The gospel message of forgiveness, made possible for Christ, is thus very simple for Luther. God alone makes people righteous through Christ's death and resurrection. This resurrected Christ then forgives sinners so that they can experience life as it is meant to be. Luther emphasized this in his marginal note for Romans 3:23–26, next to where the words "forgives sin" are highlighted in the main text:

> Note this: when [Paul] says that (they are all sinners, etc. [v. 23]), it *is the centerpiece and heart of this epistle and of the entire scriptures*, namely that everything is sin which has not been redeemed through the blood of Christ and justified by faith. Therefore understand this text well, because here it undercuts the merit and fame of all works, as he himself says here, and the only thing that remains is God's grace and honor.[35]

While Luther does not mention the two words "forgives sin" directly in this marginal note, "forgives sin" is at the very heart of the gospel. Christ justifies the sinner by grace alone through faith alone, thus granting

33. Hövelmann, *Kernstellen der Lutherbibel*, 52.

34. Hans-Martin Barth, *The Theology of Martin Luther: A Critical Assessment* (Minneapolis: Fortress Press, 2013), 440.

35. Italics added. "*Merck diß, da er sagt, Sie sind alle sunder &c.. ist das hewbtstuck vnd der mittel platz dißer Epistel vnd der gantzen schrifft. Nemlich, das alles sund ist, was nicht durch das blut Christi erloset, ym glauben gerechtfertiget wirt, Drumb fasse disen text wol. Denn hie ligt darnyder aller werck verdienst vnd rhum, wie er selb hie sagt, vnd bleybt alleyn lautter gottis gnad vnd ehre.*" WA DB 7:38. These words were also found in the 1522 *Septembertestament*. Luther was not alone in considering this passage from Romans as the heart of Scripture. Calvin declared, "There is, perhaps, no passage in the whole of Scripture that illustrates in a more striking manner the efficacy of his righteousness." Calvin, *Commentary on Romans*, 61.

them forgiveness. No wonder Luther could claim that Christ, gospel, and forgiveness are all at the heart of Scripture.

Luther recognized that everyone has "sinned and fall short of the glory of God" (Rom 3:23). Everyone has "been made and declared sinners before God,"[36] and only Christ, through his death and resurrection, can change that reality. In the second article of the Augsburg Confession, Melanchthon also discussed sin, placing this article between the confession of the triune God and the article on Jesus the Christ, the source of forgiveness. Article 4 then notes that Christ alone declares and makes the person righteous through justification by God's grace alone through faith alone.[37] All attempts to deny human sinfulness—by claiming either that a person could be without sin or that sins can be overcome or removed by human actions—end in failure. The center of Scripture and the gospel is thus needed to keep things in proper perspective:

> Since the confessions extol the Gospel above the Law, it is not surprising to find that they regard the content of the Gospel as the real center of Scripture. What is the content of the Gospel? Luther describes it simply as the offer of "consolation and forgiveness . . . from the dreadful captivity of sin" (SA III, ii, 8), and Melanchthon similarly defines the Gospel as the promise of "forgiveness of sins, justification, and eternal life for his [Christ's] sake" (Ap IV, 5). In a phrase, the content of the Gospel and the center of all Scripture is the doctrine of justification "by grace for Christ's sake, through faith" (AC IV).[38]

The only escape from sin is found in the center of Scripture and the gospel. Through God's justifying actions, the forgiveness of sin reveals the foundational action of redemption in Christ and the basis of the good news, the gospel. The human condition of sin, as Luther noted in the marginal gloss, finds its resolution only in the Christ who forgives sins, as the sinner listens to Christ. Christ declares and makes the sinner righteous through a Word.[39] However, when Christ is not heard, forgiveness

---

36. "Romans Commentary (1515–1516)," LW 25:31; WA 56:37,8–9.
37. AC Art 1–4. BC 36–40; BSELK 92–99. In the gloss on Romans 3:23, Luther stated that people were *made* and *declared* sinners (*facti sunt et reputati peccatores*), while in Article 4 of the AC, Melanchthon stated that we *receive* forgiveness of sin (declared) and *become* (made) righteous (*wir vergebung der sunden bekommen und vor Got gerecht werhen*)—both conveying a "reckoned" sin and righteousness, and the sense of being made a sinner by the law and being made righteous through regeneration. AC 4, BC 38; BSELK 99; but a proper distinction between justification (declared righteousness) and sanctification (renewal) needs to be kept. FC-SD III:40 BC 569; BSELK 1405,1–2.
38. Ralph A. Bohlmann, *Principles of Biblical Interpretation in the Lutheran Confessions*, rev. ed. (St. Louis: Concordia, 1983), 69.
39. See, for example, AC IV; BC 38–40; BSELK 98:

is not heard or experienced. Humanity is therefore called to listen to this gospel proclamation. This was what Luther wanted to come through in his translation of the Bible. As he stated, "the ordinary man can be rescued from his former delusions, set on the right track, and taught what he is to look for in this book, so that he may not seek laws and commandments where he ought to be seeking the gospel and promises of God."[40] He constantly emphasized "what pushes Christ," since he understood Christ and his gospel of forgiveness as the center of Scripture.

FORGIVENESS AS THE FOUNDATION
OF THE CHURCH, WORD, AND SACRAMENT

Forgiveness is essential for healing and restoring broken relationships in the church. But relationships involve dialogue, and, for Luther, that meant healing required people to listen to—and experience—God's Word of the gospel. God speaks the gospel of forgiveness to humanity, inspiring those who hear Christ's voice to sing praises to God and to proclaim this same message of forgiveness to others. This task is not reserved to the individual, however: it is the primary function of the church. Luther stated:

> in this Christian church, you have "the forgiveness of sins." This term includes baptism, consolation upon a deathbed, the sacrament of the altar, absolution, and all the comforting passages [of the gospel]. In this term are included all the ministrations through which the church forgives sins, especially where the gospel, not laws or traditions, is preached. Outside of this church and these sacraments and [ministrations] there is no sanctification.[41]

The church and the sacraments are needed precisely because it is in the church and through the Word and sacraments that Christ, and Christ's gracious forgiveness of sins, are given.

The primary ministry of the church is to listen to Christ and then proclaim that forgiveness to others. By doing so, the church breathes the

---

40. "Prefaces to the New Testament (1546/1522)," LW 35:357, WA DB 6:3.8–11.
41. "Sermons on the Catechism [Creed] (1528)," LW 51:167; WA 30.I:92,18–93,3. In his Confession Concerning the Lord's Supper, Luther says: "In this Christian Church, wherever it exists, is to be found the forgiveness of sins, i.e., a kingdom of grace and of true pardon. For in it are found the gospel, baptism, and the sacrament of the altar, in which the forgiveness of sins is offered, obtained, and received. Moreover, Christ and his Spirit and God are there. Outside this Christian Church there is no salvation or forgiveness of sins, but everlasting death and damnation; even though there may be a magnificent appearance of holiness and many good works, it is all in vain." "Confession Concerning Christ's Supper (1528)," LW 37:367–8; WA 26:507b,7–13.

sanctifying breath of the Holy Spirit into the sinner and joins them to the body of Christ. As the Augsburg Confession notes, the primary "job description" of the church is to proclaim this gospel of the forgiveness of sins in Word and sacrament.[42] In the process, human lives will be changed. Luther insisted that the "primary function of the evangelical pastor is to convey the gospel of forgiveness in Jesus Christ to Christ's people."[43] Not only was this the pastor's primary function, but it was also a very powerful weapon. Luther observed that

> Christ and the apostles were supplied with no other arms than the Word, and today ministers come armed not with weapons but with the Word. It is a breath that is heard and goes forth from the mouth, and nevertheless underneath it there is great power, the power to forgive sins. Where sin has been taken away, death has no more right and might [cf. 1 Cor 15:55–57; 2 Tim 1:10]; the wrath of God and hell are closed up, and [there is] nothing but pure righteousness and life.[44]

Luther held the office of preaching in such high regard because its task was to proclaim the Word in any and all situations. Through the preacher, the gospel of forgiveness is announced and realized through Christ, to all who would listen to his voice. In a joint letter, Luther and Melanchthon declared,

> The preaching of the holy gospel itself is principally and actually an absolution in which forgiveness of sins is proclaimed in general and in public to many persons, or publicly or privately to one person alone. Therefore absolution may be used in public and in general, and in special cases also in private, just as the sermon may take place publicly or privately, and as one might comfort many people in public or someone individually in private.[45]

The purpose for such preaching was also clear: "Through this office of preaching and of forgiving sins, souls are resurrected here from sins and from death, and confidently await also the resurrection of the body and life everlasting through the same Holy Spirit who has now begun this in the soul."[46] Luther expressed this idea concisely when he stated that

---

42. AC V,1–2; VII 1–2. BC 40,42; BSELK 100, 102.
43. Robert Kolb, "The Doctrine of Ministry in Martin Luther and the Lutheran Confessions," in *Called and Ordained: Lutheran Perspectives on the Office of the Ministry*, ed. Todd Nichol and Marc Kolden (Eugene: Wipf & Stock, 2004), 60.
44. "Sermons on John (1528–1529)," LW 69:410; WA 41:541,27–542,2.
45. "Letter to City Council of Nürnberg (April 18, 1533)," LW 50:76; WA BR 6:454,6–12.
46. "Adoration of the Sacrament (1523)," LW 36:299: WA 11:451,14–17.

"where there is forgiveness of sins, there is life and salvation."[47] While he was referring to the Lord's Supper here, it was also true for preaching. Too often, following the penitential system and doing the right things to merit or earn this forgiveness meant that this focus on God's freely given forgiveness was overshadowed. Thus, it was important that the preacher clearly declare the gospel message of the complete forgiveness of sin through Christ. Luther never wanted people to forget that it was God's Word alone that brought about the forgiveness of their sin. The early twentieth century Lutheran theologian, James W. Richard, stated the position of the Wittenberg reformers well:

> What they were most deeply concerned about was that the Gospel be purely preached and that the sacraments be properly administered, as over against the "howl" and "the abomination of the Mass" in the Catholic Church. The center of the gospel they found in the promise of the forgiveness of sins for the sake of Christ. This was the supreme thought, and this thought permeated the Confession and the Apology from center to circumference.[48]

Thus, in the thought of the reformers, the principle of "what pushes Christ" called the preachers to proclaim Christ, who, by his death and resurrection, has offered to all the gospel of the forgiveness of sin.

The forgiveness of sin was also at the heart of the sacraments. Dennis Ngien has astutely observed that for Luther, "a sacrament is to be recognized by both its content, the same content that the Gospel has—the forgiveness of sin—and its external form in which God is present and active."[49] Luther ultimately decided that while confession and absolution was not a sacrament like baptism and the Lord's Supper, it was nevertheless an extension of the sacrament of baptism. The content of confession and absolution was clearly about the forgiveness of sin. It was not accidental that both Luther and Melanchthon placed the emphasis of this sacrament not on the action of confessing, but on the absolution proclaimed—the declaration that "Your sins are forgiven you." Even though Luther used the term "confession" in Article XI of the 1529 Marburg Agreement,[50] and Melanchthon used the same term in the Augsburg Confession,[51] their emphasis was not on confession or contrition, but on the proclamation

---

47. SC Sacrament of the Altar, 5–6. BC 362; BSELK 890.
48. James W. Richard, *The Confessional History of the Lutheran Church* (Philadelphia: Lutheran Publication Society, 1909), 281.
49. Dennis Ngien, *Luther as a Spiritual Adviser: The Interface of Theology and Piety in Luther's Devotional Writings* (Eugene: Wipf & Stock, 2007), 81–82.
50. "Marburg Agreement (1529)," LW 38:87; WA 30.III:166.,2–167,3.
51. AC XI.1. BC, 44; BSLK, 66, BSELK, 104.

of the word of absolution: "Your sins are forgiven you." Absolution was nothing less than the proclamation of the gospel. Melanchthon asserted that absolution was "a command of God—indeed, the very voice of the gospel—so that we may believe the absolution and regard as certain that the forgiveness of sins is given to us freely on account of Christ, and that we should maintain that we are truly reconciled to God by this faith."[52] Melanchthon also brilliantly shifted attention away from confession (which placed an emphasis on human actions), onto absolution (an action of God) in the Augsburg Confession when he noted, "concerning confession it is taught that private absolution should be retained and not abolished."[53] Absolution is the gospel proclaimed loudly. Moreover, the reformers also insisted that the office of the keys—the right and responsibility to forgive and retain the sins of others—was not the prerogative of the pope alone. The task was so important, and so central to the faith, that Luther insisted that this office of the keys belonged to the gathered worshipping community.

For both baptism and the sacrament of the altar, Luther claimed that Christ was present in the water and in the bread and wine. This presence meant that these sacraments gave what they promised: the forgiveness of sin. Both sacraments constituted a "speech act, as the Word that does what it says."[54] In the case of baptism, God does not just speak over the waters of baptism, but Christ actually enters the water, personally and directly encountering the one being baptized.[55] Luther's insistence on the real, bodily presence of Christ in the Lord's Supper is also well known and was at the center of his debates with Zwingli, Oecolampadius, and Karlstadt.[56] Christ's bodily, physical presence in the water, wine, and bread cannot be separated from the Word of promise: namely, the forgiveness of sin. Christ forgives sin and, wherever Christ is present, he is proclaiming

---

52. Ap. 11,2. BC 186; BSELK 428.

53. AC XI, 1. BC, 44, BSLK, 66; BSELK, 104–5.

54. Oswald Bayer, *Martin Luther's Theology: A Contemporary Interpretation*, trans. Thomas H. Trapp (Grand Rapids: Eerdmans, 2008), 52.

55. "Baptism must be a blessed affair, abounding in grace, since He not only provides His Word and office for it but also sinks and puts Himself into it and touches this water with His own holy body; indeed, He sanctifies it and fills it with blessing." "Baptism Sermons (1534)," LW 57:162; WA 37:647,11–14.

56. Luther insisted that in the meal, a person encounters the Christ: "it is the true body and blood of our Lord Jesus Christ under the bread and wine." SC Sacrament of the Altar, 1–2. BC 362; BSELK 888. "Christ himself comes to us in the meal, and "is just as near to us physically as he was to [the shepherds and Simeon at Christ's birth]." "That These Words of Christ (1527)," LW 37:94; WA 23:193,6–10.

and making the forgiveness of sin happen. This is what distinguished the baptism of John from that of Jesus. Luther stated:

> John points out the difference between Christ's Baptism and his own when he says: "I baptize with water, I do not confer the Holy Spirit. Thus I do not forgive sin. But the aim and end of my preaching is to lead men to repentance and to prepare them for the advent of the Lord, who is to bestow the forgiveness of sin on them." John points to Christ. He does not forgive sins, but he says: "After me will come one whose Baptism will not only serve the purpose of repentance but will carry with it the remission of sin." Thus John bore witness to Christ, and thus he was the forerunner of Christ the Lord.[57]

The main benefit of baptism, therefore, was that unlike John's baptism, the baptism of Jesus "brings about forgiveness of sins, redeems from death and the devil, and gives eternal salvation to all who believe, as the words and promise of God declare."[58] In Luther's mind, God wants people to experience the gospel of forgiveness in the water and word of baptism. Thus, Luther could claim that "[Christ] is able to forgive sins without Baptism, but He does not do so."[59] He knew people needed to experience the gospel of forgiveness through the physical touch of Christ's presence in the water.

Luther made the same basic claims for the Lord's Supper. Zwingli had argued that if salvation could be obtained through the word and sacraments, then repentance and faith were unnecessary. But the "flesh is of no avail." Thus, the Lord's Supper could not forgive sins. Luther, however, felt that God deliberately worked through the Word and the physical nature of the sacraments.[60] As he asserted, in responding to these Swiss reformers:

> Even if only bread and wine were there present, as they claim, as long as the word, "Take, eat, this is my body given for you," etc., is there, the forgiveness of sins, on account of this word, would be in the sacrament. Just as in the case of baptism we confess that only water is present, but since the Word of

---

57. "Lectures on John (1537)," LW 22:176; WA 46:689,7–14.

58. SC Baptism, 5–6. BC 359; BSELK 882.

59. "Lectures on Genesis (1535–1545)," LW 3:288; WA 43:81,27.

60. W.P. Stephens, *Zwingli: An Introduction to His Thought* (Oxford: Clarendon Press, 1994), 76. See also Ulrich Zwingli, "Commentary on True and False Religion (1525)," *The Latin Works and Correspondence of Huldreich Zwingli,* ed. Samuel Macauley Jackson, 3 vols. (New York: G.P. Putnam's Sons, 1912/Philadelphia: Heidelberg Press, 1922, 1929), 3:198–234, and *Friendly Exposition* (1527), and *Huldrych Zwingli: Writings,* eds. E. J. Furcha and H. Wayne Pipkin, 2 vols. (Allison Park, PA.: Pickwick, 1984), 2:233–385; and *Huldreich Zwinglis Sämtliche Werke,* ed. Emil Egli et al, *Corpus Reformatorum* 88–108 (Leipzig/Zürich: Heinsius/TVZ, 1905–2013), 5:562–762. This point is also raised in the introduction to "Confession Concerning Christ's Supper (1528)," LW 37:153.

God, which forgives sin, is connected with it, we readily say with St. Paul, that baptism is a bath of regeneration and renewal. Everything depends on the Word.[61]

For Luther, it was very simple: the Word cannot be separated from the bread, wine, or water. If a person listened to the Word, they would hear God speaking a Word of forgiveness through these elements. Moreover, the meal did not just point to Christ, saying, "go there and find forgiveness," but it proclaimed, "take, eat, . . . for the forgiveness of sins" (Matt 26:26–28). At the core of the sacrament of the altar was its promise that it provided "the bestowal of grace and the forgiveness of sins, i.e. the true gospel."[62] The words of institution for the Lord's Supper are, therefore, "the 'gospel in a nutshell,' offering forgiveness of sins, life and salvation. These convictions guided both his criticism and reform of the mass." [63] Not to be outdone, Herman Sasse stated,

"This Sacrament is the Gospel." Nowhere does the meaning of this statement of Luther become so clear as when we try to understand the words of Jesus: "Given for you," "shed for you," "shed for many," "for the remission of sins." For the Gospel is the forgiveness of sins, nothing else. It is not a theory about the possibility of forgiveness, not a religious message that there is a merciful God."[64]

Both claimed, with Luther, that this Gospel of forgiveness is nothing less than justification by grace alone through faith alone. The sacraments give what is unmerited and unearned—God's gift of the forgiveness of sins, life, and salvation. It is the central message of Scripture, the Word, and the sacraments, a message that comes through in the voice that believers are called to listen to because it is the voice of God that says, "Take, eat, for the forgiveness of sins." The sacraments are indeed the gospel in a nutshell.

FORGIVENESS IN THE CHRISTIAN LIFE

Forgiveness is foundational not only for the life of the church but also for human relationships with God and the world. As Luther stated, "Where there is forgiveness of sin, there is life and salvation" in God.[65] All human

61. "Against the Heavenly Prophets (1525)," LW 40:214; WA 18:204,15–21.
62. "Confession Concerning Christ's Supper (1528)," LW 36:325; WA 26:468b,32–4.
63. Vilmos Vajta, *Luther on Worship: An Interpretation* (Eugene: Wipf & Stock, 2004), 28.
64. Italics added. Hermann Sasse, *This Is My Body: Luther's Contention for the Real Presence in the Sacrament of the Altar* (Minneapolis: Augsburg Publishing House, 1959), 382.
65. SC V, 5–6. BC 362; BSELK 888, 890.

relationships—marriage, or in a congregation, or a community—require liberal doses of love and forgiveness to function in a healthy way. Relationships—even strong, loving relationships—can break or be subject to fracturing, and they need to be restored. Being joined to Christ through his death and resurrection means being placed into community with other sinners. In this community, forgiveness is constantly needed. As Luther stated, "Here there is full forgiveness of sins, both in that God forgives us and that we forgive, bear with, and aid one another."[66] God's actions make life in community possible and, even more, nurturing. Dietrich Bonhoeffer picked up on this theme, stating that "As Christ bore with us and accepted us as sinners, so we in his community may bear with sinners and accept them into the community of Jesus Christ through the forgiveness of sins."[67] Thus, when Luther wanted to define the gospel for the congregation engaged in the world, he called it simply the "forgiveness of sins." That is what he was concerned with: restoring broken relationships between God and the individual, and between the individual and the community. Today, Luther might have added the restoration of relationships between humanity and creation. God works to heal relationships by using the most powerful tool possible: the Word proclaiming forgiveness. If there is no need for forgiveness in community, then the gospel and the church are not present. As he poignantly stated it in a sermon on John's Gospel:

> May a merciful God preserve me from a Christian Church in which everyone is a saint! I want to be and remain in the church and little flock of the fainthearted, the feeble, and the ailing, who feel and recognize the wretchedness of their sins, who sigh and cry to God incessantly for comfort and help, who believe in the forgiveness of sin, and who suffer persecution for the sake of the Word, which they confess and teach purely and without adulteration. Satan is a cunning rogue. Through his fanatics he wants to trick the simple-minded into the belief that the preaching of the gospel is useless. "Greater effort" is necessary, they say. "We must lead a holy life, bear the cross, and endure persecution." And by such a semblance of self-styled holiness, which runs counter to the Word of God, many a person is misled.[68]

The church is the place where the gospel of the forgiveness of sins, rather than "self-styled holiness," is fully operative.

66. LC II, 55; BC 438; BSELK 1064, 1065.
67. Dietrich Bonhoeffer, *Life Together and Prayerbook of the Bible*, eds. Gerhard Ludwig Müller, Albrecht Schönherr, and Geffrey B. Kelly, trans. Daniel W. Bloesch and James H. Burtness Vol. 5, *Dietrich Bonhoeffer Works* (Minneapolis: Fortress Press, 1996), 102.
68. "Sermons on John (1537)," LW 22:55; WA 46:583,11–22.

Luther's emphasis on forgiveness, however, was not about the toleration of sin. Rather it was God's decisive action against sin and for life. To speak "you are forgiven" transfigured a person and a community from death into life because that person or community has been united with Christ in his death and resurrection. Being united in Christ through the gospel of the forgiveness of sins is essential in order to heal and reconcile the community. That is why preaching—and the sacraments—were so important for Luther: they fostered and nurtured life in community. In the sacrament of the altar, for example, the gathered community encountered the new covenant [promise], which is "the bestowal of grace and the forgiveness of sins, i.e., the true gospel."[69] In the community, the sacraments are present, "along with the gospel, in which the Holy Spirit richly offers, bestows and accomplishes the forgiveness of sins."[70] As Luther claimed, "In this Christian Church, wherever it exists, is to be found the forgiveness of sins, i.e., a kingdom of grace and of true pardon. For in it are found the gospel, baptism, and the sacrament of the altar, in which the forgiveness of sins is offered, obtained, and received."[71] Thus, the highlighting of the two words, "forgives sin," captured the very heart of Luther's community-grounded reformation theology, and he deliberately emphasized it so that the preachers would preach this gospel, and the hearers could hear God's voice and listen, making it possible for all to experience life in the community God has envisioned for everyone.

The gospel proclamation that Christ forgives sin also has a strong pastoral component. The bold proclamation that God forgives *your* sin can comfort troubled consciences afraid of the law, death, and condemnation *coram Deo* (in the presence of God).[72] Luther stated, "To put on Christ according to the gospel, therefore, is to put on, not the Law or works but an inestimable gift, namely, the forgiveness of sins, righteousness, peace, comfort, joy in the Holy Spirit, salvation, life and Christ himself."[73] The gospel not only stops the condemnation or breaks the restricting power of the law; it also comforts the afflicted soul with the forgiveness of sins and, thus, life and salvation.[74] Like the Hippocratic oath, the gospel not only prevents further harm (the negative aspect to the law) but also heals

69. "Confession Concerning Christ's Supper (1528)," LW 37:325; WA 26:468,32–34.

70. "Confession Concerning Christ's Supper (1528)," LW 37:370; WA 26:508,28–29.

71. "Confession Concerning Christ's Supper (1528)," LW 37:368; WA 26:507,7–13.

72. ". . . the Gospel does nothing else than liberate consciences from the fear of death so that we believe in the forgiveness of sins and hold fast the hope of eternal life." "Psalms Lectures (1532)," LW 12:19; WA 40.II.2:214,14–17.

73. "Galatians Commentary (1535)," LW 26:353; WA 40.I/II:541,17–20.

74. SC V, 5–6. BC 362; BSELK 888, 890.

and gives life (the life-giving, positive aspect of the gospel). In his commentary on the Creed in the Small Catechism, Luther made it clear that God's activities are "Gospel oriented." God proclaims and establishes the gospel by creating, nurturing, and sanctifying life.[75] This is further reinforced in the Large Catechism, when he stated:

> Therefore everything in this Christian community is so ordered that everyone may daily obtain full forgiveness of sins through the Word and signs [the sacraments] appointed to comfort and encourage our consciences as long as we live on earth. Although we have sin, the Holy Spirit sees to it that it does not harm us because we are a part of this Christian community. Here there is full forgiveness of sins, both in that God forgives us and that we forgive, bear with, and aid one another.[76]

This emphasis is also found in his explanations about the sacraments. By forgiving sin, God heals the brokenness of the world. Thus, the highlighting of the two words "forgives sin" in his translation of Romans 3:25 was more than a stylistic change. It was a compact yet profound statement about what was at the very heart of his Reformation theology.

SUMMARY

The emphasis on "Word" in Wisdom of Solomon identified the source of the gospel, and the highlighted words "Listen to Him" in Luther's 1534 Bible from the transfiguration accounts in the Synoptic Gospels directed attention to this voice, or Word, of the gospel. In Romans 3:25, however, the capitalization of every letter in the words "forgives sin" identified for Luther, in no uncertain terms, the *content* of the gospel. The voice of Christ that proclaimed "you are forgiven" was nothing less than the Holy Spirit breathing life into people condemned to death by their sin. True penance, as Luther stated in the first of the Ninety-Five Theses, was not about doing penance,[77] but about living lives in the forgiveness of sin offered freely by Christ. Proclaiming the Word audibly through reading the Scripture and preaching, and visibly through the sacraments, was all about declaring, "your sins are forgiven you." This is the message that gives life and healing to an individual and to a community of believers. A worship service without this message being proclaimed is not life-giving.

75. Luther makes this clear in his explanation to the three articles of the Creed in the Small Catechism. BC 354–56; BSELK 870–73.
76. LC, Creed, Ill, 55. BC 438; BSELK 1054.
77. "Disputation on the Power and Efficacy of Indulgences (1517)," LW 31:25; WA 1:233,10–11.

It might entertain or amuse, but without the proclamation of this gospel that Luther was so intent on highlighting, it would not be life-giving, truly liberating, or salvific. The translation of the 1534 Bible was, for Luther and his colleagues, one of the most important opportunities they had of proclaiming the gospel of forgiveness in clear, unmistakable words. It extended their preaching of the gospel of forgiveness beyond the pulpits and altars of their own local congregations to congregations and individuals throughout the land, in places where they might never have a chance to visit. The Word, which all are invited to listen to, declared the radical message of the forgiveness of sins by a God who does not wait for people to do what was "in them." This gospel was nothing less than the Word of Christ that justifies a person by grace alone through faith alone, apart from works of the law. The Word proclaims forgiveness and, in doing so, breathes life into the depths of tombs of sin and brings forgiven sinners to life. "You are forgiven" is the Word that Christ speaks to proclaim the gospel to people and to turn their world around. "Forgives sin" may be only two words, but these two words turn the world around. It is no wonder, therefore, that Luther emblazoned "forgives sin" in his translation by capitalizing every single letter of these two words.

8.

Luther's Emphasis on "Take"

"Here stand the lean and bare words of the gospel, 'Take, eat; this is my body, given for you. Take and drink, this is my blood, shed for you. This do in remembrance of me'."[1]

Martin Luther was first and foremost a pastor. His focus on what the gospel "does" to a person thus shaped his way of translating the Bible. For troubled human beings, simply hearing the gospel of the forgiveness of sins audibly proclaimed was not enough. Thus, God has determined that the gospel needs to reach a person's heart in multiple ways. People can "hear" the gospel through other sensory organs beside the ears, such as through tasting and touching this gospel made flesh and discovering that "it is good." This emphasis on the multiple ways of hearing led Luther to the final instance of highlighting in the 1534 Luther Bible, where the word "TAKE" (*NEMET*) is capitalized in 1 Corinthians 11:24–25.[2] Luther refers to the word "take" as commanded by Christ in the Lord's Supper, hundreds of times. In fact, when citing this passage from 1 Corinthians, Luther almost invariably included "Take, eat," as a part of the words of institution of the Lord's Supper. Apart from the command, the incarnational, real presence of Christ in the Lord's Supper could easily be pushed aside or misinterpreted. His inclusion of the word, "Take!" did not allow for the separation of the body and blood of Christ from the bread and wine of the meal, as the Swiss reformers had attempted.

---

1. "A Letter of Consolation to the Christians at Halle (1527)," LW 43:151; WA 23:414,22–24.
2. LB NT CXXIa. WA DB 7, containing both the 1522 and 1546 translations of the New Testament, does not mention the capitalization of all the letters in NEMET, even in a footnote.

An die Corinther. CXXI.

tung vnter euch/vnd zum teil gleube ichs. Denn es müssen rotten vnter euch sein/auff das die/so rechtschaffen sind/ offenbar vnter euch
werden. Wenn jr nu zu samen komet/so helt man da nicht des Herrn
abentmal/Denn so man das abentmal halten sol/nimpt ein jglicher
sein eigens vor hin. Vnd einer ist hungerig/der ander ist truncken.
Habt jr aber nicht heuser/da jr essen vnd trincken müget? oder verach-
tet jr die Gemeine Gottes/vn beschemet die/so da nichts haben? Was
sol ich euch sagen? Sol ich euch loben? Hie rinnen lobe ich euch nicht.

Ich hab es von dem Herrn empfangen/das ich euch gegeben ha-
be/Denn der Herr Jhesus inn der nacht da er verrhaten ward/nam
er das brod/dancket/vnd brachs/vnd sprach/NEMET/esset/das
ist mein leib/der fur euch gebrochen wird/Solches thut zu meinem
gedechtnis. Desselbigen gleichen auch den kelch/nach dem abent-
mal/vnd sprach/Dieser kelch ist das newe Testament inn meinem
blut/Solchs thut/so offt irs trincket/zu meinem gedechtnis.

Denn so offt jr von diesem brod esset/vnd von diesem kelch trin-
cket/solt jr des Herrn tod verkündigen/bis das er kompt. Welcher nu
vnwirdig von diesem brod isset/odder von dem kelch des Herrn trin-
cket/der ist schüldig an dem leib vnd blut des Herrn. Der mensch a
prüfe aber sich selbs/vnd also esse er von diesem brod/vnd trincke von
diesem kelch/Denn welcher vnwirdig isset vnd trincket/der isset vnd
trincket jm selber das gerichte/damit das er nicht b vnterscheidet den
leib des Herrn.

Darumb sind auch also viel schwachen vnd krancken vnter euch/
vnd ein gut teil schlaffen. Denn so wir vns selber richteten/so würden
wir nicht gerichtet. Wenn wir aber gerichtet werden/so werden wir
von dem Herrn gezüchtiget/auff das wir nicht sampt der welt ver-
dampt werden. Darumb/meine lieben Brüder/wenn jr zu samen ko-
met zu essen/so harret einer des andern. Hungert aber jemand/der
esse da heimen/auff das jr nicht zum gerichte zu samen kompt. Das
ander wil ich ordenen/wenn ich kome.

XII.

Von den geistlichen gaben aber/wil ich euch/lieben Brü-
der/nicht verhalten. Jr wisset c das jr Heiden seid gewe-
sen/vnd hin gegangen/zu den stummen götzen/wie jr
gefurt würdet/Darumb thu ich euch kund/das niemand Jhesum verfluchet/der durch den Geist Gottes
redet. Vnd niemand kan Jhesum einen Herrn heissen/
on durch den Heiligen geist.

Es sind d mancherley gaben/aber es ist ein Geist. Vnd es sind mancherley empter/aber es ist ein Herr. Vnd es sind mancherley krefften/
aber es ist ein Gott/der da wircket alles inn allen. Inn einem jglichen
erzeigen sich die gaben des Geistes/zum gemeinen nutz. Einem wird
gegeben durch den Geist zu reden von der weisheit/Dem andern
wird gegeben zu reden von der erkentnis/nach dem selbigen Geist.
Einem andern der glaube/inn dem selbigen Geist/Einem andern die
gabe gesund zu machen/inn dem selbigen Geist. Einem andern wunder zu thun/Einem andern weissagung/Einem andern geister zu vn-
terscheiden/Einem andern mancherley sprachen. Einem andern die
sprachen aus zu legen. Dis aber alles wircket der selbige einige Geist/
vnd teilet einem jglichen seines zu/nach dem er wil.

X iiij   Denn

(Marginal notes:)

a (prüffe) Das ist/ein jglicher sehe zu wie er gleube inn diesem abentmal was vnd wo zu ers empfahe.

b (nicht vnterscheidet) Der Christus leich nam handelt vnd damit vmb gehen/als achtet ers nicht mehr/denn ander speise.

c (das jr Heiden) Das ist/da jr Heiden waret/wustet jr nichts wedder von dem Christo noch von den heiligen geist/zu aber solt jr des Geistes gaben wissen/on welchen niemand Christum erkennet/sondern viel mehr verflucht.

d (mancherley) Es ist inn allen Christen ein geist/weisheit/erkentnis/glaube/krafft etc. Aber solchs geben ander vben vnd beweisen/ist nicht jederman. Son dern von weisheit reden/die da leren Gott erkennen. Vnd erkentnis reden die da leren eusserlich wesen vnd Christliche freiheit. Glauben beweisen/die in offentlich beken nen mit worten vnd wercken/als die merckerer. Geister vnterscheiden/die da prüfen die pro pheceien vnd leren.

"NEMET" in 1 Corinthians 11:24–25, 1534 Luther Bible.
(Reformation Historical Research Library Wittenberg—
Stiftung Luthergedenkstätten, LH, Kn D 254)

Luther first capitalized every letter in this word in the thoroughly revised 1530 translation of the New Testament, along with the words, "Listen to Him" from the transfiguration accounts.[3] As Hartmut Hövel- mann observes, the emphasis on "Take" was not merely to help the reader easily find the words of institution for the Lord's Supper. If that were the case, the word would also have been emphasized in the gospel accounts of the Last Supper (Matt 26:26–29; Mark 14:22–25; Luke 22:14–20). Rather, Luther wanted to emphasize that "the sacrament is a visible Word" and that in the Lord's Supper, nothing but gospel is heard and seen.[4] In the sacraments, a person encounters none other than Christ, the Living Word, breathing life into them.

THE THEOCENTRIC EMPHASIS OF "TAKE"

Luther's emphasis on the word "TAKE" continued his emphasis on the Word and the actions of God, rather than on human activities and attempts at self-justification. The Word and actions of God are paramount, and in his Copernican revolution of theology,[5] the actions of Christians are contingent on the actions of God. It cannot be otherwise. This is true not just of the doctrine of justification but also for Luther's theology of the sacraments. In his commentary on the imperial edict issued following the 1530 Diet of Augsburg, he emphasized God's actions and Word with regard to the sacrament of the altar:

> It has been, however, sufficiently proved . . . that the mass is God's Word and sacrament, which [Christ] tenders and gives us. For here stand the words, stark and clear, "Jesus took bread, gave thanks, and broke it, and gave it to the disciples, saying, 'Take, eat; this is my body which is given for you.' In the same manner also the cup," etc. With these words we remain, on these words we stand, in these words we shall (God willing) live and die, on these words is based the mass. Here you do not find that we should buy or sell the sacrament, or mass. Here you do not find that we are offering or giving something to God in the mass. Here you do not find that we are to honor the saints with it. Here you do not find that souls are to be bought out of purgatory with it.[6]

---

3. Hartmut Hövelmann, *Kernstellen der Lutherbibel: Eine Anleitung zum Schriftverständnis.* Texte und Arbeiten zur Bibel, Deutschen Bibelgesellschaft, Bd 5 (Bielefeld: Luther-Verlag, 1989), 49.

4. Hövelmann, *Kernstellen der Lutherbibel,* 53.

5. Philip S. Watson, *Let God Be God! An Interpretation of the Theology of Martin Luther* (London: Epworth Press, 1954), 33–38.

6. "Commentary on the Alleged Imperial Edict (1531)," LW 34:85; WA 30.III:355,16–356,8.

Luther could not make it much clearer. One does not buy or sell the sacrament of the altar. It is not an offering given by the gathered community to God, but a gift from God. Everything revolves around what God does. That is where God's unconditional grace is found.

Luther also emphasized the word "Take" because it is spoken to the gathered community by the very One that the community is called to "listen to" as the source of life and forgiveness. In his sermons on John, he insisted that the only voice the church should listen to is "Take, eat, drink," spoken by the Bridegroom.[7] The Bridegroom (Christ) speaks with authority when he says, "Take, eat, this is my body which is given for you,"[8] for these words are the Word of God, declaring the reality of Christ's presence in the bread and wine. Any attempts to downplay this claim, felt Luther, moved God out of the center of theology and turned God into a "God of the gaps" that fills in human gaps in knowledge or a God at the periphery,[9] as Bonhoeffer described: God and God's church "is the critical center. Where [one] is completely without a place, where [one is on] the periphery, there is [the] critical center of the world (*Galilee* in the Roman Empire or *Wittenberg*)."[10] It would be like assigning God a supporting role in the divine drama, rather than making Christ the key actor and center of all that is life.

The theocentric starting point also meant that Luther insisted that when God—the creator and source of life—spoke, things happen, whether it be creation, forgiveness, or justification. Thus, the God who created heaven and earth with a word could also, with a word, make bread and wine into Christ's body and blood. Even if human logic could not explain how this happened, what was important for Luther was that God's actions, not human thoughts, defined reality.[11] So when Christ says, "Take, eat, this is my body," one should not look at the bread or wine, but at the speaker who

---

7. "Sermons on John (1539)," LW 22:444; WA 47:159,13–15.
8. "Defense and Explanation of All the Articles (1521)," LW 32:16–17; WA 7:325,11–18.
9. DBW 8:405–406. *Letters and Papers from Prison.*
10. DBW 11:279. *Ecumenical, Academic, and Pastoral Work: 1931–1932.*
11. "Luther took the position that would occupy the remainder of the discussions: 'God is beyond all mathematics, and the words of God are to be revered and followed in awe. It is God who commands, "Take, eat, this is my body." I therefore demand compelling proof from the Scriptures to the contrary'." James M. Kittelson, *Luther the Reformer: The Story of the Man and His Career* (Minneapolis: Fortress Press, 1986), 223. See also "The Marburg Colloquy (1529)," LW 38:16, 75; WA 30.III:112,11–16; 153,9–13, where Luther insists that he isn't interested in listening to arguments based on human reason or mathematics. Rather, he is interested in what God declares. If God declares Christ can be both God and man, then that is the reality. He was concerned with divine omnipotence, not the mathematics of time and space.

declared it so.[12] It is the speaker, not the earthly elements or the recipient of the bread and wine, that is the center of attention. The Living Word who speaks makes things happen.

The emphasis on God's action in the Lord's Supper was entirely consistent with Luther's emphasis on justification as an action of God alone. In his debates over the sacrifice of the mass with the Roman church, Luther repeatedly used the passage from 1 Corinthians 11 to argue that the mass was not about priests sacrificing something to God, but, rather, it was about what God sacrificed for humanity. He commented, "[Christ] does not say, 'Offer or give me something in the mass,' but on the contrary, '*You* (not I) take, and *you* (not I) eat, *you* (not I) drink.' We, we are to receive and take, while he gives and bestows."[13] Furthermore,

> Paul does not command us to sacrifice anything or do anything but only to take, eat, and drink. But what we eat and drink we do not sacrifice; we keep it for ourselves and consume it.
>
> This is what I have taught: that one should not use the sacrament as a good work. They believed that whoever had confessed properly and knew of no mortal sin upon his conscience and so went to the sacrament was doing a precious, holy work, through which he merited heaven. If you wish to make the right use of it, you must not receive it in such a way that you say: "This I have done," just as if you had fasted or kept watch. But you ought to believe, not only that Christ is present with his body and blood, but also that he is given to you. You should always stand upon the words: "Take, eat, this is my body, which is given for you. Drink, this is my blood, which is poured out for you. Do this in remembrance of me." In these words his body and blood are given to us. So there are two things to be believed: that it is truly present, which the papists also believe; and that it is given to us, which they do not believe, and that we should use it as a gift.[14]

As with justification, the forgiveness bestowed in the Lord's Supper is not something earned, but a gift. God makes it so, and at the table the gathered community is commanded to take and eat what God has given: by doing so, they receive the gift of God's unmerited and unearned forgiveness. Treating the mass as something offered to God was completely contrary to Luther's theological approach that placed God's actions at the center of all life and faith.

12. "Eastertide Sermons (1544/1545)," LW 58:111; WA 49:405,29–32.
13. "Commentary on the Alleged Imperial Edict (1531)," LW 34:85; WA 30.III: 357,20–23.
14. "Against the Fanatics (1526)," LW 36:347–348; WA 19:502,24–503,18.

Luther also insisted that the verb "Take" was an imperative verb, which meant that what God gives in the meal is important, for God is giving something that people do not possess. Only God can bestow the life-giving, community-creating forgiveness of sin through word and sacrament. All people can do is to receive what God gives. Luther bluntly stated, "There you hear it, expressed in clear German: he commands you to take his body and blood. Why? For what reason? Because the body is given for you and the blood is poured out for you."[15] The only response possible to Christ's command is to take what is offered. The imperative verb "Take" gives no room to do anything else.[16] After all, "This word of God [Take, eat . . .] is the beginning, the foundation, the rock, upon which afterward all works, words, and thoughts of man must build. This word man must gratefully accept."[17] A correct understanding of the sacrament of the altar begins by listening to what God says and by seeing what God does. Luther focuses attention on the commanding actions of God, rather than on the actions of the recipient of the meal. It is all about God declaring, "Take, eat," not about screaming "without ceasing, 'Offer mass, offer mass.'"[18] He wanted to make sure that Lord's Supper is all about God's Word creating and bringing life and community into being.

For Luther, the incredible marvel of the Lord's Supper was that God chose to address human sin and death by becoming incarnate in the bread and wine, thus transforming the gathered community through the forgiveness of sin. Christ is not "sitting at the right hand of the Father" according to his human nature, as the Swiss and South German reformers insisted,[19] but God is becoming flesh, full of grace and truth (John 1:1, 14). The imperative, "Take," draws attention away from the actions of the

---

15. "Against the Fanatics (1526)," LW 36:348; WA 19:503,19–21.

16. Contradicting Zwingli, Luther insisted that "since it is written, 'Take, eat,' etc., it is to be done and to be believed altogether. One must do it." "The Marburg Colloquy (1529)," LW 38:54; WA 30.III:116,25.

17. "Treatise on the New Testament, That is, the Holy Mass (1520)," LW 35:82; WA 6:356,7–10.

18. "Commentary on the Alleged Imperial Edict (1531)," LW 34:86; WA 30.III, 357,26–27.

19. Zwingli stated, "Therefore when we read in Mark 16 that Christ was received up into heaven and sat on the right hand of God we have to refer this to his human nature, for according to his divine nature he is eternally omnipresent, etc. But the saying in Matthew 28: 'Lo, I am with you always, even unto the end of the world,' can refer only to his divine nature, for it is according to that nature that he is everywhere present to believers with his special gifts and comfort." G. W. Bromiley, ed., *Zwingli and Bullinger*, Library of Christian Classics (Philadelphia: Westminster, 1953), 213; "On the Lord's Supper (1526)." *Huldreich Zwinglis Sämtliche Werke*. Emil Egli et al, editors. *Corpus Reformatorum* 88–108, (Leipzig/Zürich: Heinsius/TVZ, 1905–2013), 4:828. Zwingli preferred the human Christ in the heavens over the Christ made flesh, especially when it implied incarnate in the bread and wine of the sacrament.

communicant, focusing instead on Christ's actions, who became human, reinforcing Luther's theocentric approach. Forgiveness of sins, life, and salvation revolve around what God declares in the Word—a Word that the gathered community are called to listen to. By emphasizing "Take," Luther was stating, "this is where it's at, regardless of what you are doing about it." It's not about the individual. It's about what God does to proclaim and push the Gospel into human hearts.

"TAKE, EAT," AND THE WORDS OF INSTITUTION

The imperative verb "Take," which Luther highlighted in his 1534 Bible translation, revealed a lot about his theocentric perspective. But it also said a great deal about his understanding of the words of institution. First, "Take" emphasized the inseparable connection of the Word of Christ to the sacrament. Even before the Lord's Supper controversy with the South German and Swiss theologians began, he insisted that the most important thing in the sacrament is "the word of Christ, when he says: 'Take and eat, this is my body which is given for you'."[20] The whole Gospel is to be found in the words, "Take and eat, this is my body."[21] "Everything depends on the Word,"[22] he said, for it proclaims the forgiveness of sin and makes forgiveness a reality. Thus, the Word added to the elements makes it a sacrament.[23] During the controversy over the meal of the Lord a few years later, Luther wrote a letter to the congregation in Halle following the murder of two supporters of the Reformation. He pointed the grieving people to the sacrament, because in the Eucharist they could come face-to-face with Christ and his gospel: "Here stand the lean and bare words of the gospel, 'Take, eat; this is my body, given for you'."[24] Even amid their grief, they could find the gospel. At the table, they could find Christ, the forgiveness of sin, life, and salvation in the sacrament. The Lord's Supper, unlike a memorial litany, actually does something to people. The gospel is distributed and given as people take the bread and cup.[25] The sacraments

---

20. "The Adoration of the Sacrament (1523)," LW 36:277; WA 11:432,10–12.
21. "The Adoration of the Sacrament, (1523)," LW 36:288; WA 11:442,12–13.
22. "Against the Heavenly Prophets (1525)," LW 40:214; WA 18:204,21.
23. SC, Baptism, 9–10; BC 359; BSELK 884; SC, Sacrament of the Altar, 7–8; BC 363; BSELK890.
24. "Letter of Consolation to All Christians at Halle (1527)," LW 43:151; WA 23:413,22–24.
25. Luther had stressed how the forgiveness won on the cross was distributed to the gathered community in the Lord's Supper in his polemical treatises against Zwingli, Oecolampadius and Karlstadt in the last half of the 1520s. See, for example, "Confession Concerning Christ's Supper (1528)," LW 37:192; WA 26:294,5–18. A few years later, in a hasty note written to Melanchthon, just before he went to Kassel to meet with Martin Bucer to discuss the Lord's

are resurrection events because God's life-giving Word is proclaimed. The Living Word breathes life into those who "take and eat."

Second, separating the imperatives "Take, eat" in the words of institution from the other words of institution ("This is my body . . . this is my blood") opened the door separating the bread and wine from the body and blood of Christ. When citing the words of institution, Luther invariably made sure that "take, eat" and "this is my body" were spoken with the same breath. Karlstadt and Zwingli had separated "take, eat" from "this is my body," which allowed them to speak of two disparate activities: the command and the declaration. In referring to Karlstadt, Luther stated, "He pretends that the passage, 'This is my body given for you,' does not belong to what immediately precedes, namely, 'Take, eat,' but is to be considered a new, independent, sentence. Yet he admits, and must admit, that this last passage, 'This do in remembrance of me,' belongs to the first words, 'Take, eat'."[26] Luther also complained that Zwingli did the same, separating the command, "Take, eat" from the narrative declaration, "This is my body."[27] In response, states Sasse, Luther challenged Zwingli:

> [Zwingli] ought to prove that they must be thus torn apart, even though they appear in a fine order in a single passage: "Take, eat, this is my body." And after all, they are not our words, but Christ's own words.
>
> Moreover, even though these words, "This is my body," are in themselves action-words, when they are torn out and detached from the others and imprisoned in solitary confinement, nevertheless they are purely and simply command-words, because they are embraced and embodied in command-words.[28]

By putting the command "Take, eat" into solitary confinement, Karlstadt and Zwingli decisively prevented the Lord's Supper from being a sacrament. For them, the Lord's Supper was not about God's actions of proclaiming and giving the gospel to people.[29] It also allowed Karlstadt to

Supper in December of 1534, Luther had stated, "Christ is truly presented, *distributed*, received and eaten" (*ferri, dari, accipi, manducari*). WA BR 12:160,66–67. When Christ's body and blood was distributed in the bread and wine, forgiveness of sins was distributed. See also Ap. X:1. BC 184; BSELK 424–25.

26. "Against the Heavenly Prophets (1525)," LW 40:172; WA 18:161,36–162,5.

27. According to Sasse, Luther felt that "the question is not whether the words are words of command or words of a historical statement, but whether or not they were true when Jesus spoke them." Further, if they were true when Jesus first spoke them, they would continue to be true, even today. Hermann Sasse, *This Is My Body: Luther's Contention for the Real Presence in the Sacrament of the Altar* (Minneapolis: Augsburg Publishing House, 1959), 166, n.70.

28. "Confession Concerning Christ's Supper (1528)," LW 37:182; WA 26:283,28–35.

29. Sasse, *This Is My Body*, 165–166.

separate what he treated as two, unrelated statements. The first statement, "Take, eat," was an invitation to join in a meal, and the second, "This is my body," was Jesus simply making a statement not about the bread, but about himself. Luther, however, insisted that the command to "Take, eat" was inexorably connected to Christ's body. It was not a simple reference to a piece of bread. The command was to take and eat his body, for the forgiveness of sin. The two statements could not be separated without robbing the sacrament of the good news of the gospel.

Third, the sacrament of the altar loudly and clearly proclaims the Gospel to the gathered community—not simply because the Word and the sacrament are inseparable, but because it is one of the two dominical commands that promise, and give, life and salvation. When God commands, that which is spoken happens. Luther stated his position in a sermon on baptism:

> It is the same in the Sacrament of Christ's body and blood: if the command and institution are not kept, it is not a Sacrament. For instance, if a man reads the Ten Commandments, the Creed, or some verse or psalm over the bread and wine on the altar; or again takes something else such as gold, silver, meat, oil, or water instead of bread and wine (even though he uses the right words of Christ's institution)—that would clearly not be Christ's body and blood. Even though God's Word and something created by God are present, it still is not a Sacrament, for His order and command, in which He referred to bread and wine and spoke the words "Take, eat; this is My body," etc., "Drink; this is My blood," etc., are not present. In short, you are not to make a choice or determination on your own about either Word or object, nor of your own accord to include or leave out any action whatsoever. Rather, His command and order should determine for you both Word and object, which you are to leave completely intact.[30]

The Dominical command "Take, eat, and drink" was an essential defining component of the sacrament of the altar, along with the elements themselves. They could not be separated. Here the Wittenberg reformers were simply echoing Augustine's famous dictum, "When the word comes to the element, it becomes a sacrament."[31] But the reformers made a clarification to Augustine's statement, suggesting that the Word in the sacrament was both command and promise. As Wengert astutely observes, "there were two definitions of sacraments rattling around Wittenberg, both dependent on the Augustinian and medieval tradition. One emphasized God's word connected to a physical element;

---

30. "Sermons on Holy Baptism (1534)," LW 57:153; WA 37:638,16–28.
31. Augustine, *Patrologiae cursus completus: Series Latina*, ed. J.-P. Migne. 221 Volumes (Paris: Garnier Fratries, 1844–64), 35:1840. "*Tractates on John*," 80.3.

the other stressed God's command connected with a divine promise."[32] Luther included both aspects of the Word (command and promise) in the Small Catechism when he stated, "Baptism is not simply plain water. Instead it is water enclosed in God's command and connected with God's Word," referring to both Matthew 28 (the command) and Mark 16 (the promise).[33] Melanchthon followed suit in the Apology to the Augsburg Confession, when he noted that a sacrament required "the expressed command of God and a clear promise of Grace."[34] In the Large Catechism, Luther stated that in the sacrament, "a promise is attached to the commandment,"[35] which, as he stated later, is also connected to the elements. The presence of the command was one of the markers of a sacrament in Luther's theology. A sacrament required a command, a promise, and an earthly element.

Fourth, Luther insisted that the command "Take, eat" must be connected to the other words of institution "This is my body . . . do this" because their interconnection was essential to understanding Christ's real presence in the sacrament. In the Babylonian Captivity of the Church, he noted that even though he could not understand how the bread is the body of Christ, he would simply cling "to his words, firmly believe not only that the body of Christ is in the bread, but that the bread is the body of Christ. My warrant for this is the words which say: 'He took bread, and when he had given thanks, he broke it and said, 'Take, eat, this (that is, this bread, which he had taken and broken) is my body" [1 Cor 11:23–24]'."[36] Six years later, in a treatise on the Sacrament, he stated,

> Just as little as you are able to say how it comes about that Christ is in so many thousands of hearts and dwells in them—Christ as he died and rose again—and yet no man knows how he gets in, so also here in the sacrament, it is incomprehensible how this comes about. But this I do know, that the word is there: "Take, eat, this is my body, given for you, this do in remembrance of me." When we say these words over the bread, then he is truly present, and yet it is a mere word and voice that one hears. Just as he enters the heart without breaking a hole in it, but is comprehended only through the Word and hearing, so also he enters into the bread without needing to make any hole in it."[37]

32. Timothy J. Wengert, *Martin Luther's Catechisms: Forming the Faith* (Minneapolis: Fortress Press, 2009), 108.
33. SC, Baptism, 1–8. BC 359; BSELK 882.
34. Ap. XIII,6. BC 220; BSELK 512.
35. LC, Sacrament of the Altar, 64. BC 473; BSELK 1150.
36. "Babylonian Captivity of the Church (1520)," LW 36:34; WA 6:511,18–28.
37. "Against the Fanatics (1526)," LW 36:341; WA 19:490,14–23.

Thus, one must always start with God's word rather than with human reason, in approaching the sacrament of the altar. Christ's command to take and eat of his body was also the most literal and simplest meaning of the sentence. In translating the Bible into German, Luther had always kept in mind that the words should speak clearly—rather than torturing the whole text and making it obscure and unintelligible, just so it would fit with human reason. Doing unnecessary linguistic gymnastics with the text leads only to injury to the faith. By trying to twist the words to say something else, whether it be Zwingli's "Take, eat; this represents my body," or Oecolampadius's "Take and eat, this is a sign of my body," Luther's opponents sought to deny the real presence of Christ in the bread and wine.[38] In Luther's view, Zwingli and Oecolampadius wanted to take Christ out of the supper and put him in heaven—but in doing so, they were denying the incarnation. Luther insisted that the words of institution demanded a bodily, physical, incarnate presence. On this point, the Wittenberg reformers were in full agreement with the Roman and Orthodox churches, as Melanchthon observed in the Apology of the Augsburg Confession.[39] The reformers rejected the Roman doctrine of transubstantiation as an adequate way to explain this real, bodily presence, but they did not reject the importance of Christ's presence in the meal. In the sacrament, the recipients encounter and experience the incarnated Christ himself. They actually participate "in the body of Christ (1 Cor 10:16). He does not say, 'in the bread there is,' but 'the bread itself is' the participation in the body of Christ."[40] The incarnation in the sacraments allows humanity to physically encounter a saving, life-giving, and ever-present God. Furthermore, if salvation is indeed found "in Christ," then to take Christ out of the sacrament would mean that the sacrament no longer delivered what it promised: the forgiveness of sins, life, and salvation, or, in short, the gospel. Melanchthon suggested that apart from the real presence of Christ in the meal, Christ would be absent and could not bear witness to the resurrection.[41] Treating the Lord's Supper as a memorial, based on John's words, "the flesh is of no

---

38. "That These Words of Christ (1527)," LW 37:30; WA 23:89,32–90,9.

39. ". . .we have ascertained that not only the Roman church affirms the bodily presence of Christ, but that the Greek church has always maintained the same position and still does so, *as the canon of the Mass among the Greeks testifies*." Ap. X,2. BC 184; BSELK 424.

40. "Babylonian Captivity of the Church (1520)," LW 36:34; WA 6:511,25.

41. Philip Melanchthon, "Letter to Osiander on the Lord's Supper (1529)," in *Selected Writings*, eds. Elmer Ellsworth Flack and Lowell J. Satre, trans. Charles Leander Hill (Minneapolis: Augsburg Publishing House, 1962), 126–27.

avail" (John 6:63),[42] simply does not help a person when it comes to human need. To thus rob the sacrament of Christ's real presence would be akin to taking from people an opportunity for experiencing life in Christ—not just spiritually but also physically. To deny Christ's presence in the meal was to rob people of hope, of a chance to experience what it meant to be fully human—not only in the future but also in the here and now. The command "Take, eat, this is my body" clearly indicated the real, bodily presence of Christ in the meal. Luther's authority for claiming this was nothing less than the Word proclaimed by Christ, a Word which the gathered community were commanded to listen to, as commanded by the voice from heaven. If a person wanted to receive the forgiveness of sins, they were to "Take and eat." If a person wanted Christ's presence, life, salvation, and forgiveness, then they could find it, in the bread and wine, the body and blood of Christ. That was Christ's command and promise, all rolled together.

A VITAL COMMAND FOR PASTORAL CARE

The Lutheran reformers insisted that the administration of the sacrament of the altar as a means of grace was a basic, and powerful, way of providing pastoral care to someone caught in sin or despair. The Augsburg Confession made it clear that the basic purpose of the office of preaching was to give the gospel and sacraments: "Through these, as through means, he gives the Holy Spirit who produces faith, when and where he wills, in those who hear the gospel."[43] Moreover, the message proclaimed by the office of ministry, and through preaching and the sacraments, was that "we have a gracious God, not through our merit but through Christ's merit, when we so believe."[44] Luther reiterated this view in the Schmalkald Articles, emphasizing that "God is extravagantly rich in his grace," which is given, among other ways, "through the holy Sacrament of the Altar."[45] Unfortunately, this gospel message was often overshadowed and forgotten

---

42. Much of the debate over the Lord's Supper between Zwingli and Luther, for example, hinged on the interpretation of the dialogue in the sixth chapter of John. Zwingli used this passage from John to interpret the texts of the Lord's Supper, thus arguing against the real, bodily presence of Christ in the meal (since it was of no avail), but Luther used the texts of the Lord's Supper, with Christ's command, to interpret John's text. See here Gordon A. Jensen, *The Wittenberg Concord: Creating Space for Dialogue* (Minneapolis: Fortress Press, 2018), 33–37, for a basic summary of their arguments.
43. AC V,1–2. BC 40; BSELK 100.
44. AC V,3. BC 40; BSELK 100.
45. SA III.4. BC 319; BSELK 764,766.

by a people that had been taught to focus on their unworthiness, God's judgment and wrath, and the dangers of eating and drinking at the Lord's Table without proper preparations. This sacred terror of the improper reception of the sacrament carried over into the reception of both kinds in the sacrament, and even into the practice of receiving the bread in the hand, rather than having the priest place it directly in a person's mouth.

One of the biggest challenges that faced the sixteenth century Wittenberg reformers was the reluctance of people to commune due to a sense of their own unworthiness. If people felt unworthy, they were reticent to "take" the forgiveness in Christ's body offered to them. After all, they had been taught that the improper reception of the sacrament brought judgment upon themselves. Captured by a medieval piety that constantly stressed their unworthiness and God's judgment had made early sixteenth century Germans reluctant to encounter and receive Christ's presence in the sacrament, since they expected only judgment. However, Luther the pastor invited people instead to focus on experiencing the Gospel proclaimed in the sacraments.[46] In the Large Catechism, he made his pastoral position very clear:

> For the Word by which it was constituted a sacrament is not rendered false because of an individual's unworthiness or unbelief. Christ does not say, "If you believe or if you are worthy, you have my body and blood," but rather, "Take, eat and drink, this is my body and blood." Likewise, when he says, "Do this" (namely, what I now do, what I institute, what I give you and bid you take), this is as much as to say, "No matter whether you are worthy or unworthy, you have here his body and blood by the power of these words that are connected to the bread and wine." Mark this and remember it well. For upon these words rest our whole argument, our protection and defense against all errors and deceptions that have ever arisen or may yet arise.[47]

46. At the time of the publication of the *Luther Bible* in 1534, Luther, Melanchthon, and Martin Bucer were beginning a debate over whether the piety of the recipient determined the Sacrament's efficacy. Bucer insisted that one's piety played a role, while the Wittenberg theologians insisted that God's actions were decisive. While the matter was "resolved" in the Wittenberg Concord two years later, by making a distinction between the pious and the unworthy (those recognizing their unworthiness as they stand before God) and the ungodly (those deliberately reject God). Yet this "solution" was not ultimately satisfactory to either party. See Jensen, *The Wittenberg Concord*, 99–102, and "Luther and Bucer on the Lord's Supper," *Lutheran Quarterly* 27, no 2 (Summer 2013), 167–87.

47. LC Sacrament of the Altar, 17–19. BC 468; BSELK 1136, 1138. This pastoral approach is repeated in the Solid Declaration in the Formula of Concord: "For the Word by which it was constituted and instituted a sacrament is not rendered false because of an individual's unworthiness or unbelief. Christ does not say, 'If you believe or if you are worthy, you have my body and blood,' but rather, 'Take, eat and drink, this is my body and blood.' Likewise, when he says,

Rather than focusing on the recipients' sense of worthiness, Luther turned their attention to what God commands, offers, and promises, wrapped in the bread and wine. Here is forgiveness; here is life; here is salvation, *for you*. "Mark this and remember it well," said Luther. God's Word could be trusted, unlike the inner voice within a person that all too often whispered only what the person wanted to hear.

In examining the texts concerning the Lord's Supper in Paul's first letter to the Corinthians, Luther observed that many in Corinth had trusted their own wisdom, rather than the voice of Christ. This, he recognized, was not a helpful practice. It took the focus away from God's gracious actions and placed it instead on the fickleness of human wisdom. But one did not find life and salvation in human actions or wisdom. As he commented, "everyone wanted to be the expert and do the teaching and make what he pleased of the gospel, the sacrament, and faith. Meanwhile they let the main thing drop—namely, that Christ is our salvation, righteousness, and redemption—as if they had long since outgrown it."[48] Failing to listen to Christ or changing the gospel message from its basic meaning of the proclamation of the forgiveness of sins to a focus on a person's adequate and worthy penitence smothered the good news of life found in the gospel wrapped up in the sacrament. When people listen to their own voice, they hear only what they expect to hear from a wrathful, judging God. To shatter this "curved inward" attitude in individuals and in the gathered community (an attitude Luther defined as sin) and to push Christ into their mouths and into their hearts, Luther turned their focus on the injunction to "Take, eat," in his translation of 1 Corinthians 11.

In contrast to Martin Bucer and others who had argued that only the godly or those believers who felt they were unworthy would receive Christ's true presence in the bread and wine, Luther claimed that the validity of the sacrament was not dependent on the piety of the recipient or the presider.[49] The strength of one's own faith did not make the Lord's Supper a sacrament. In fact, Luther stated that the proper reception of the sacrament didn't presuppose faith. As he stated, "Imperatives are of

'Do this' (namely, what I now do, what I institute, what I give you and bid you take), this is as much as to say, 'No matter whether you are worthy or unworthy, you have here his body and blood by the power of these words that are connected to the bread and wine.' Mark this and remember it well. For upon these words rests our whole argument, our protection and defense against all errors and deceptions that have ever arisen or may yet arise." FC-SD VII, 25–26. BC 597; BSELK 1464, 1466.

48. "Preface to 1 Corinthians, (1522 /1546)," LW 35:381; WA DB 7:85,5–9.
49. For a brief overview of this debate, see Jensen, *The Wittenberg Concord*, 99–102.

two kinds: one kind where faith is presupposed, such as Matthew 21[:21] on the moving of mountains. . . . The other kind comprises the passages where faith is not presupposed, such as these words in the Supper, 'Take, eat,' for here even the unworthy and unbelieving eat Christ's body, as Judas and many of the Corinthians did."[50] Making the sacrament of the altar dependent on the faith of the recipient implies that it is the person's faith—and not God's command and promise, as found in the bread and wine—that makes the Lord's Supper a life-giving sacrament. Depending on the strength of one's own faith only creates an ongoing, insurmountable doubt about whether a person has done enough to make the meal a valid sacrament. A word that a person speaks to themselves (*verbum internum*) always leaves doubts about the word's veracity and leads to despair. Much better, claimed Luther, to trust in the very words spoken by Christ, declaring what God was doing, and had done, in the sacrament. Because Christ declares that he was in bread and wine and that in him there is forgiveness of sins, life, and salvation; this external word (*verbum externum*) "Take" is the pure gospel, the promise from God, a promise that could be trusted absolutely.[51] Christ himself mediates his own self-revelation in the earthly elements of bread and wine, and this revelation and presence does what a sinful human most needs: forgiveness of sins (Rom 3:25).

Luther also reminded the gathered community that the words at the beginning of the words of institution, "Take, eat," were imperative verbs, commands of God that do not require a corresponding human response to be valid. Rather, its validity rested solely upon God acting to create a new reality and a new community—a community that was united and recognizable as the body of Christ.

The question about whether a person was worthy enough to receive the sacrament brought with it other pastoral questions. For example, could a person receive the sacrament without proper preparation? Would that not condemn them? If the focus was on human preparation, people would naturally ask, "So what must we do to make ourselves worthy to receive the real presence of Christ in the meal?" Luther addressed this in a very succinct, pastoral way in his Small Catechism, where he advised that "Fasting and bodily preparation are in fact a fine external discipline, but a person who has faith in these words, 'given for you' and 'shed for you for the forgiveness of sins,' is really

---

50. "Confession Concerning Christ's Supper (1528)," LW 37:188; WA 26:288,12–14.

51. Paul R. Hinlicky, *Lutheran Theology: A Critical Introduction*, Cascade Companions (Eugene: Cascade Books, 2020), 83.

worthy and well prepared. However, a person who does not believe these words or doubts them is unworthy and unprepared, because the words 'for you' require truly believing hearts."[52] What was important was not how much a person needed to do to adequately prepare for the Lord's Supper in a worthy manner, but God's actions: what God declares and what Christ offers. What Christ does and gives is what is transformative "for us human beings and for our salvation."[53] Luther recognized that in obeying the command to "Take" what is thrust into one's hands, God is giving the recipient the only proper preparation for the sacrament that they need. Christ is giving them himself. Thus, to "Take" and eat the bread and drink from the cup was nothing less than tasting the gospel and encountering Christ.

The debate over reception of the sacrament of the altar in "both kinds" (receiving both the bread and the cup) was also a pastoral care concern for the reformers. Again, the highlighted word of command, "Take," as found in 1 Corinthians 11:24 in the 1534 Bible, was important for the reformers in addressing this practice. Luther and his colleagues argued that the word "Take" applied to both the bread and the cup. Paul did not say, "Take and eat the bread, but leave the cup only to the priests."[54] To withhold the cup from the communicants was to "openly steal from God," making those who insisted on such practices "robbers of his Word and Sacrament."[55] In explaining his position to churches in other territories, Luther stated the practice they were following in Wittenberg:

> Here everything is done, first of all, according to the ordinance and command of Christ, so that it is offered and given to the church *under both kinds* on the basis of the words of Christ: "Take, eat, this is my body," etc., and "Do this in remembrance of me." The pastor does not receive [the cup] only for himself, as the pope's sacrilege does. He also does not sacrifice it to God for our sins and all kinds of needs [or] sell it to us as a good work to reconcile God . . . rather, he administers it to us for the comfort and strengthening of our faith. In this way Christ is made known and preached.[56]

Again, the *purpose* of the sacrament of the altar is clearly stressed; it is to comfort and strengthen the faith by making Christ known. Luther

52. SC Sacrament of the Altar, 9–10. BC 363; BSELK 890.
53. Nicene Creed, BC 22; BSELK 49.
54. "The Private Mass (1533)," LW 38:206; WA 38:244,37–245,2.
55. "Sermon for Trinity 23 (1535/1544)," LW 79:291; WA 37:603,28–29.
56. "The Private Mass (1533)." LW 38:209; WA 38:247,32–248,23. Italics added.

was also pragmatic about this, however. His advice to those who were preparing to move toward the practice of communing in both kinds involved education and respect. Evangelical freedom to commune with bread and cup was not to be abused by turning it into a law. Thus, those who went to communion in a congregation where only the bread was offered to the communicant were to take what was offered but not stir up a hornet's nest by demanding the cup as well, even though he suggested, that if asked, one could testify that receiving only the bread was not in "harmony with the gospel."[57] Likewise, if someone did not want to receive both kinds in the sacrament, "out of weakness and terror of conscience" (but not for reasons of obstinacy!), Luther advised that communing in both kinds should not be forced upon them.[58] To do so would be to turn the sacrament into something other than the liberating, life-giving gospel.

Luther also had to address the misconception among some of the more fervent that the command of Christ, "Take," meant that they were to take the host in their hand, rather than having the priest place it in their mouth, as was the common practice. To clarify his position, Luther simply stated, "though I am convinced beyond a doubt that the disciples of the Lord took it with their hands, and though I admit that you may do the same without committing sin, nevertheless I can neither make it compulsory nor defend it."[59] Likewise, one was not to make a law around the practice of wanting to take the chalice in one's own hands when receiving the meal. It made practical sense, in fact, for people to hold the chalice themselves, so the minister would not "miss my mouth."[60] As with the practice of receiving in both kinds, the guiding principle was to not abuse their evangelical freedom by making it a requirement. However, reformers did not consider the reception of the sacrament of the altar as optional. The use of imperative verbs by Jesus in relation to this sacrament, such as "take," "eat," "drink," and "do," is very specific.[61] Christ wants the sacrament to be received, not simply in obedience to his command, but because—and more importantly—it was beneficial and life-giving to those who received the promise of the gospel given by Christ in bread and wine.

57. "Receiving Both Kinds in the Sacrament (1522)," LW 36:254–55; WA 10.II:29,27–30,3.
58. "Instructions for the Visitors of Parish Pastors in Electoral Saxony (1528)," LW 40:289–90; WA 26:214,10–20.
59. "Invocavit Sermons (1522)," LW 51:89; WA 10.III:43,10–12.
60. "Table Talks (1542)," LW 54:417; WA TR 5:121,23–27, (No. 5390).
61. Samuel H. Nafzger et al., eds., *Confessing the Gospel: A Lutheran Approach to Systematic Theology* (St. Louis: Concordia, 2017), 860.

SUMMARY

The simple command of Christ in one of the words of institution, "Take," is important for Luther—not just for his understanding of the sacrament but also for his theology as a whole. Embedded in the command to "take" is the Word—a word not just of command, but a word that also speaks promise and life. It could be seen as a fervent plea by Christ for people to receive a gift of life, a gift made possible for all humanity through the incarnation of Christ. As with the Word that enters one's ears on the way to the heart, a word proclaiming the forgiveness of sins, so also the Word enters through a person's mouth on the way to their heart so that the person can experience the gospel. This emphasis on the dominical command to "Take" made it clear to the reformers that the forgiveness of sin was something God had already made possible through his death and resurrection. Human activities meant to make a person worthy of the sacrament do not make the sacrament efficacious. The Word spoken by Christ is what states the reality. God gives life in the sacrament because God chooses to do so through the beloved Son.

When the various instances of the highlighted "core places" are put together, a pattern emerges that together spell out Luther's theology. In the sacrament of the altar (1 Cor 11:24), the visible, tangible, and audible "Word," highlighted in Wisdom of Solomon (16:12 and 18:22), is to be "Listened to" (Matt 17:5 and parallels), for it declares the "forgiveness of sin" (Rom 3:25). This is the gospel, stripped down to its basics, which for Luther involved proclaiming and pushing (*was Christum treibet*), through Scripture, preaching, teaching, sacraments, and translating. In the interrelationship of these "core places" one discovers Luther's foundational principles for his translation of Scripture.[62] Proclaiming gospel through word and sacrament so that it can be experienced was what drove the Wittenberg "Sanhedrin" to translate the 1534 Bible and highlight its gospel message through the use of emphasizing the words identified by Luther. This translation was nothing less than a proclamation of the gospel in such a way that preachers throughout the land, along with anyone else who could read, would encounter and experience what it means to be "in Christ."

---

62. Hövelmann, *Kernstellen der Lutherbibel*, 53.

9.

After 1534: How the Luther Bible Developed and Changed

"If you would interpret well and confidently, set Christ before you, for he is the one to whom absolutely everything applies."[1]

INTRODUCTION

The publication of a Bible translated into German by Luther and his Wittenberg colleagues was a watershed moment in the history of the Reformation. Luther's dream was finally made a reality. Yet the Wittenberg reformers knew that their Bible translation was still a work in progress, despite its success in the marketplace. They realized that even more work had to be done to further improve the translation. For example, Job and the prophetic books still needed work. These books had proved the most challenging to translate, due to the complicated Hebrew texts,[2] and Luther and his colleagues would spend countless hours trying to improve the translation of these books.

The 1534 Luther Bible had collected the disparate earlier translation efforts by the translation team into one volume. There was an obvious lack of consistency, quality, and format. It looked like it was pieced together. For example, sections of the Old Testament were attached to each other without the use of continuous pagination. Typographical errors were also

---

1. "Preface to the Old Testament (1545)," TAL 6:61. See also LW 35:247; WA DB 8:29,32–33.
2. Philip Schaff, "*The Christian Church, Volume VII, Modern Christianity: The German Reformation* (Grand Rapids: Eerdmans, 1910), 354.

scattered throughout the text. Thus, as soon as the 1534 Bible came off
Lufft's press, a process of revising the text began. Sections of the Bible
were retranslated; errors and typos were corrected, and, as time went on,
additional important words and phrases were identified and highlighted
for each successive version, initially by capitalizing every letter in the
word or phrase and, later, by using a different font for the highlighted
sections. All these revisions were guided by Luther's insistence that the
translation make clear the gospel, as revealed in Christ Jesus. He wanted to
place Christ firmly in front of the reader and preacher of the Biblical text.

Luther and his colleagues did not have a monopoly on the German
Bible translation market. Nor were they the first to publish a complete
Bible translated by reformers. Printshops supportive of the Reformation rushed to publish complete bibles made up of previously translated
sections of the Bible in German that were already in print. One such
"combined" German translation of the Bible was published in 1529 by
Peter Schöffer at Worms, containing Luther's translation of the first three
parts of the Old Testament, the prophetic books translated by Ludwig
Hätzer and Hans Denck, Leo Judd's translation of the Apocrypha, and
Luther's translation of the New Testament.[3] Christopher Froschauer also
published a "Combined Bible" in the "true German language" (Swiss
German) in Zürich in 1530 and again in the summer of 1534, a month
or two before Luther's 1534 Bible was finally published.[4] In Strasbourg,
Wolfgang Köpfel published a "combined" Bible in 1529/1530.[5] It had
not taken publishers long to realize that there was a great demand for
the Bible in the language of the people.

Roman Catholic printers also began publishing their own "Catholic
Bibles." In 1534, the same year that the Zürich and Luther Bibles were
published, a Roman Catholic German Bible came out, combining Jerome
Emser's 1527 "plagiarized" version of Luther's New Testament with additional translation contributions by the Dominican Johann Dietenberger
and others. It was printed by Peter Quentel at Cologne.[6] Johannes Eck,

3. John L. Flood, "Martin Luther's Bible Translation in its German and European Context," in
   *The Bible in the Renaissance: Essays on Biblical Commentary and Translation in the Fifteenth
   Century*, ed. Richard Griffiths (Aldershot: Ashgate, 2001), 60–61. See also Hartmut Hövelmann, *Kernstellen der Lutherbibel: Eine Anleitung zum Schriftverständnis*. Texte und Arbeiten
   zur Bibel, Deutschen Bibelgesellschaft, Bd 5 (Bielefeld: Luther Verlag, 1989), 75–6.
4. Hövelmann, *Kernstellen der Lutherbibel*, 75–76.
5. "*Der gantze Bibel / der Ebraischen und Griechischen waarheyt nach /auf das aller trewlchest
   verteütschet* (1530)," as noted in Hövelmann, *Kernstellen der Lutherbibel*, 83–4. See also Flood,
   "Martin Luther's Bible Translation," 61.
6. Hövelmann, *Kernstellen der Lutherbibel*, 80–81. Timothy George comments, however, that it
   appeared that Quentel was "more concerned about making money than publishing correct

Luther's opponent at the Leipzig Disputations of 1519, also produced a combined German translation of the Bible in 1537, based on the Vulgate and the Emser/Luther New Testament. Eck's motivation for publishing his own edition was, in part, to correct Luther's mistakes that arose because of his abandonment of a word-for-word literal translation.[7] Dietenberger's translation remained the Roman Catholic translation of choice for nearly one hundred years.[8] Nevertheless, in publishing versions of the Bible that included Emser's New Testament translation, the Roman Catholics served to further circulate Luther's work, since Emser's version was basically Luther's translation, with only a few editorial changes.

There were also other Bible translation projects in Wittenberg that were not spearheaded by Luther. For example, in a bid to make the pure gospel available to those who spoke low German in northern Germany, Johann Bugenhagen provided annotations for a translation of the Lübeck Bible, which was also published in Wittenberg in 1541.[9] Bugenhagen was also instrumental in getting an adapted Bible for the Baltic regions published, beginning in 1528,[10] so that the people of his native land could hear and read the gospel.

While the primary goal of these Bible translations was to make the gospel clear to everyone who read or heard it, it also made the printing business very successful. As the nineteenth-century scholar Theophilous Stork noted, "In the course of forty years, one bookseller, Hans Lufft of Wittenberg, sold 100,000 copies; an astonishing number, when we consider the price of books in the sixteenth century."[11] The financiers for the Luther Bible printed by Lufft—namely, Moritz Golrz, Bartholomew Vogel, and Christoph Schramm—became the richest people in Wittenberg.[12] Nor were Lufft and his financial backers the only ones to profit from Luther's popularity. As Andrew Pettegree observes, Luther ensured that the printing jobs were spread around to all the printers in Wittenberg

theology." Timothy George, *Reading Scripture with the Reformers* (Downers Grove: InterVarsity Press, 2011), 201.

7. Hövelmann, *Kernstellen der Lutherbibel,* 81. See also Euan Cameron, "The Luther Bible," *The New Cambridge History of the Bible. Volume 3: From 1450 to 1750* (Cambridge: University of Cambridge Press, 2016), 235.

8. Cameron, "The Luther Bible," 235.

9. Kurt K. Hendel, ed., *Johannes Bugenhagen: Selected Writings* (Minneapolis: Fortress Press, 2015), 52.

10. Cameron, "The Luther Bible," 236.

11. Theophilus Stork, *Luther and the Bible* (Philadelphia: Lutheran Board of Publication, 1873), 142.

12. Martin Brecht, *Martin Luther: The Preservation of the Church, 1532–1546,* trans. James L. Schaaf (Minneapolis: Fortress Press, 1993), 100.

so that a monopoly by one publisher did not develop. Luther's insistence on spreading the work around was perhaps one reason Cranach decided to turn over his printshop to Joseph Klug.[13] Stork reported that "Luther's German Bible was received by the people with open hearts and hands."[14] The Luther Bible quickly became one of the most popular translations of the Bible in Germany, and it continues to be an important translation to this day. The most recent edition of the Luther Bible was published in 2017, commemorating the 500th anniversary of the beginning of the Reformation.

THE WITTENBERG BIBLE REVISION COMMITTEE

As already noted in the first chapter, Luther had long realized that the task of translating the whole of the Bible was beyond his scope as an individual. From a very early stage, he relied on a team to help translate and then revise the Bible. Even in preparing his New Testament translation for publication in September of 1522, he turned to his colleagues in Wittenberg to assist in the task. Thus, to assist him in this work, a "Revisions Committee" or Commission was formed by 1531. The core group was comprised of Matthew Aurogallus, Johannes Bugenhagen (also known as Pommer), Caspar Cruciger, Justus Jonas, Philipp Melanchthon, and the secretary Georg Rörer, with Bernhard Ziegler and Johann Förster occasionally present whenever they happened to be in Wittenberg.[15] Their original task had been to work on the translation of the Psalter in 1531. Later, they met to make final revisions to the 1534 Bible. They were reconvened again in 1539, where they oversaw the various revisions and updates to the Luther Bible. Michael Reu reports that "between 60 and 70 sessions of the commission were held from July 17, 1539, to Feb. 8, 1541, for the purpose of reviewing the canonical books of the Old Testament, to which the work was limited at this time."[16] In an illuminating insight, the former student and later biographer of Luther, Johannes Mathesius, who often observed the Revision Committee at work, described one of their typical sessions:

> The doctor entered the consistory with his old Latin and new German Bible [the 1539 edition]; he also always had the Hebrew text along. Master

13. Pettegree, *Brand Luther*, 268–69.
14. Stork, *Luther and the Bible*, 141.
15. Hövelmann, *Kernstellen der Lutherbibel*, 17.
16. Michael Reu, *Luther's German Bible: An Historical Presentation Together with a Collection of Sources*. (Columbus: Lutheran Book Concern, 1934), 234. See also WA DB 4:xxvii–xxxi.

Philip brought the Greek text with him. Dr. Cruciger brought the Chaldean Bible alongside the Hebrew. The professors had their rabbis with them. Dr. Pommer also had a Latin text before him, in which he was very well-versed. Everyone had prepared ahead of time for the text over which they were to deliberate and had read through Greek and Latin as well as Jewish expositors. Then [Luther] as presider proposed a translation, let the others vote in turn, and listened to what each had to say about it based on the nature of the language or the exposition from the old doctors.

Marvelously fine and instructive discussions must have taken place during this work, some of which Master Georg [Rörer] recorded and were later printed in the margins of the text as short glosses and explanations.[17]

This committee met weekly between 1539 and 1541 gathered around a table in the home of Luther. A glimpse of the proposed revisions by Luther himself is found in the margins of his 1539 Bible, and the committee decisions were also recorded in the "Protocols" by the committee secretary Rörer.[18] This committee worked on revising the Luther Bible, beginning with the preparation of the first edition in 1534 and continuing until Luther's death in 1546.

EDITIONS OF THE LUTHER BIBLE
DURING LUTHER'S LIFETIME

The German Bible that came off the printing presses in 1534 was only the first of many editions that Lufft printed during—and after—Luther's lifetime. The Luther Bible quickly became a very popular book, and it kept the printers busy. It is estimated that a half million partial or complete Bibles were distributed. Ten full Wittenberg Bibles were published during Luther's lifetime, and another edition came out shortly after his death in 1546. Another 110 editions of the Luther Bible were published up to the end of the Thirty Years War in 1648.[19] But the demand for German Bibles was not limited to those that came off the presses in Wittenberg. Brecht notes that there were

253 partial or complete editions that were printed elsewhere, and these contributed considerably to the circulation of the Luther Bible. This does not include the Low German versions or the translations done by Luther's Catholic opponents like Emser, Eck, and Dietenberger, which were based

17. LW CV 476–77.
18. These entries are marked "[Gl.]" in WA DB, Volumes 3 and 4.
19. Hövelmann, *Kernstellen der Lutherbibel*, 16.

on his. It is said that before Luther's death there were 430 complete or partial editions with a total of about a half million copies. Thus approximately ten percent of Luther imprints were Bibles.[20]

One would suspect that Luther would have appreciated being remembered primarily as a translator of the Bible into a German that was easy to read and understand by the people in his community. Understandable words meant that the Word, breathed by the Holy Spirit, more easily passed through the ears and eyes of the hearer or reader and into their heart.

Each successive edition of the Luther Bible brought about new changes meant to further emphasize the gospel message. Not only were the translations of the text itself revised, but glosses, marginal notes, illustrations, and even the innovative practice of highlighting important words and phrases using majuscules for every letter in the word or phrase constantly evolved. For example, Luther's glosses, along with the woodcuts he had selected, were replaced and eventually eliminated over time.[21] Thankfully, there are records that document many of the changes and why they were made. The primary source information about the earliest revisions to the 1534 Bible are found in Georg Rörer's "Protocols" and Luther's own entries in the margins of his 1539 Bible.[22] Thus, one can discover in the colophon to the 1541 edition noted by Rörer that Luther himself made the decision about what words and phrases should be highlighted through the use of majuscules or even larger or different fonts.[23] Records also provide occasional glimpses of proposed translations and revisions that were not accepted, helping later generations acquire a glimpse of the dynamic process of revision taking place among the Bible Revision Committee.

The first revision of the New Testament portion of the Luther Bible was printed in 1537. Minor changes to correct errors and typos were made to the translation. The number of highlighted texts also changed. The 1537 New Testament contained eleven highlighted phrases, up from the five New Testament highlighted instances of 1534 (the three transfiguration texts plus the texts from Rom 3 and 1 Cor 11). The newly capitalized, highlighted phrases in the 1537 New Testament were in the three Synoptic Gospel accounts of the baptism of Jesus. Now capitalized were the

20. Brecht, *Martin Luther: The Preservation of the Church,* 101–102. See also Hans Volz, *Martin Luthers deutsche Bibel: Entstehung and Geschichte der Lutherbibel* (Hamburg: Friedrich Wittig, 1978), 10.

21. Timothy J. Wengert, "Martin Luther's September Testament: The Untold Story," *The Report: A Journal of German-American History* 47 (2017), 60.

22. See here WA DB 3:167–577 and WA DB 4:1–278.

23. Reu, *Luther's German Bible,* 238–39. See also. Rörer's *Postfatio,* WA DB 7,xiii.

words, "This is my Son, the beloved, with whom I am well pleased" (Matt 3:17; Mark 1:11; Luke 3:22).[24] The other three newly highlighted phrases were the same words in the three Synoptic Gospel accounts of the transfiguration. In highlighting these phrases, Luther brought together the baptism and transfiguration accounts, while placing even more emphasis on the authority of Jesus given to him by the voice from heaven. Equally important, with this addition Luther drew attention to the fact that Jesus is *beloved* and *well-pleasing* to God. The voice of Jesus thus proclaims the beloved voice of God, highlighting why both the original and current disciples of Jesus ought to listen to him.

When the next edition of the Luther Bible came out in 1539, there were now a plethora of core places (*Kernstellen*) to catch the reader's eye.[25] The seven highlighted occurrences in the 1534 Bible are now expanded to "232 verses, words, or phrases printed with capital letters in the Bible in 1539."[26] The highlighted places in the Old Testament portion of the 1534 Bible grew from no instances of highlighting to seventy-five. In the Apocrypha, 2 Maccabees 3:15 (which foreshadows 1 Cor 15:57, according to Hövelmann) was also highlighted, bringing the total of highlighted words or phrases in the Apocrypha to three.[27] The largest increase in highlighted phrases, however, was found in the New Testament, where the original five instances are increased to one hundred fifty-four highlighted places. The Revisions Committee likely decided that the simplest and most effective way of drawing attention to certain texts was with the use of capitalizing the most important passages and words, and they took full advantage of this practice.[28] The plethora of highlighted words and phrases drew the reader's attention to important passages that emphasized the gospel. But the simple gospel message at the heart of the Lutheran Reformation, so clearly spelled out in the seven highlighted places of the 1534 Bible, was now in danger of being overshadowed by the multitude of highlighted instances. It was a shift from a minimalist approach that drew attention to the gospel, to an approach that attempted to show how the gospel is found everywhere in Scripture.

Another revised edition of the Luther Bible came out in 1540, a year after the first major revision had been published. In this edition, there was a slight increase of only five more highlighted words or phrases, with one

24. Hövelmann, *Kernstellen der Lutherbibel*, 49.
25. For a brief description of the numbers of highlighted words or phrases in the Bibles published during Luther's lifetime, see Appendix 2.
26. Hövelmann, *Kernstellen der Lutherbibel*, 53, 56.
27. Hövelmann, *Kernstellen der Lutherbibel*, 60.
28. Hövelmann, *Kernstellen der Lutherbibel*, 55–56.

addition in Isaiah and four additions in the Gospels and Acts.[29] However, the reader would have immediately noticed one of the most significant changes in the 1540 Bible: for the first time, each page was printed in two columns. This reflected the common practice of the pre-Lutheran German Bibles and the Latin Vulgates. Also, the printer, Lufft, used the Fraktur font in this edition, rather than the Schwabacher font of the earlier Luther Bibles. The woodcut illustrations were also changed. The woodcuts from the Cranach workshop, created by an artist with the monogram of MS, were replaced by woodcuts from the 1536 Low German Bible printed in Magdeburg by Georg Lemberger and Hans Brosamer. This new edition of the Bible also used twenty-six new woodcuts for the Revelation of John, created by an unknown artist who used the monogram of AW. Another change found in this edition was that for the first time the three parts of the Old Testament were joined together in one interconnected section and now had continuous page numbers and one index page.[30] This edition of the Bible also incorporated some of the earlier work of the Revisions Committee, which had begun work a year earlier.

In 1541, the first major revision of the Luther Bible took place, and it was easily distinguished from the previous versions. First, it reverted to the use of a single column of text on each page, and the woodcut illustrations again have the monogram of MS—most likely from the Cranach workshop, especially since there is a woodcut included by Lucas Cranach the Younger. Some new prefaces to individual books of the Bible were also added, along with a new, additional, preface for the Old Testament.

The printing of the 1541 Bible also began before all the revisions were completed. When Luther wanted to include some additional explanations to the new temple described in the last chapters of Ezekiel in April of 1541, the printers were already printing that book of the Bible. Lufft urged Luther to quickly finish his explanations so that they could be added within the text, but Luther complained in a letter to Melanchthon, who was attending the Regensburg Colloquy at the time, of "weakness of the brain," thus justifying his inability to complete his explanation at that time.[31] Eventually, his explanation of the new temple had to be added at the end of the book when the edition finally came out in September of that year.[32]

---

29. Hövelmann, *Kernstellen der Lutherbibel,* 55–56.
30. Volz, *Martin Luthers deutsche Bibel,* 155.
31. "Luther to Melanchthon (April 12, 1541)," WA BR 9:358,25–59,27, (No. 3592).
32. Scott H. Hendrix, *Martin Luther: Visionary Reformer* (New Haven: Yale University Press, 2015), 262–63.

The main changes introduced in the 1541 Luther Bible, however, were in the translation itself. This edition contained all the revisions made by the Revisions Committee in the previous few years. One other feature that set this Bible apart was that it was larger in size; the text area was increased from 13.6 × 24.3 cm per page to the medieval-styled format size of 16.7 × 28 cm per page. As with the 1534 Bible, it came out in September, in time for the annual autumn book fair in Leipzig, held in 1541 from October 2–9. Since the original print run for this Bible was only 1,500 copies, it also cost more than previous Luther Bibles, which had sold for three guilders. It also included the coats of arms of the electors and princes in the area, along with the first handwritten dedications.[33] The printer had originally intended this larger-sized version of the Bible to be a limited-edition Bible, with an even smaller print run. The printing was done on the much more expensive parchment, rather than on paper, with the elector and princes of Anhalt as its recipients. This version of the 1541 Bible was sold for sixty gulden each, making it far too expensive for most people to purchase. Part of the reason for this high price tag was the cost of binding the volume. The bookbinders in Wittenberg worked full-time throughout the fall of 1541 to complete their binding, and so Luther did not get the first of his own three copies until June of 1542. He also thought that this would be the final version of the Luther Bible.[34] A nicely printed and bound version of the Bible would have been an appropriate way to end this major project that had consumed so much of his time and energy.

Luther was justifiably proud of his work. Referring to the upcoming 1541 edition, he declared, "This German Bible (this is not praise for myself but the work praises itself) is so good and precious that it's better than all other versions, Greek and Latin, and one can find more in it than in all commentaries, for we are removing impediments and difficulties so that other people may read in it without hindrance."[35] He wanted nothing to get in the way of people being able to see, hear, grasp, and be transformed by the gospel in this translated Word of God. Compared to what else was available on the market at the time, the German Bible produced in Wittenberg set the standard for all other translations.

An interesting phenomenon also developed with the printing of the 1541 Bible: the desire for autographed copies from Luther. As Brecht describes it:

---

33. Volz, *Martin Luthers deutsche Bibel*, 155.
34. Brecht, *Martin Luther: The Preservation of the Church*, 107. See also LW 35:237–40; WA DB 8:14–16; WA DB 2:639; WA BR 9:564,1–565,32; and WA BR 10:110,4–111,13.
35. "Table Talks (Fall, 1540)," LW 54:408; WA TR 5:59,4–8, (No. 5324)

it became increasingly common for people to give Luther copies of the Bible and, occasionally, other books, and request that he inscribe them. The owners were mostly theologians and nobles, and sometimes burghers from the upper class. Luther usually wrote a Bible verse with a brief explanation, and signed his name. Almost three hundred such inscriptions are known, and they were soon collected and published. They are extremely personal documents of Luther's pious attitude toward the Bible and the Word, which have, undeservedly, been nearly forgotten.[36]

According to Brecht, most of the autographs that Luther provided reflected how he related his faith to the Word, which he invariably identified as present in the person of Christ.[37] This was the One who people are called to listen to, for Christ forgives sins and gives life and salvation whenever the gospel was proclaimed.

The major revisions made to the translation in the 1541 Bible were not the only significant changes that were made. Two other visual innovations showed up in this edition: the text was broken up into paragraphs for the first time, with "stylized initials at the beginning of each paragraph,"[38] and the highlighted (*Kernstellen*) texts were printed in the Fraktur font, and no longer in all capital letters, thus still setting them apart from the Schwabacher font used in the rest of the text.[39] This change in the way of highlighting the text also meant that the printers made a lot of use of the Fraktur font, since the number of highlighted texts in the 1541 edition of the Bible skyrocketed from 237 in the 1540 Bible to 825 instances in the 1541 edition. Most of the increases were found in the prophetic books (from 37 in 1540 to 117 in 1541) and in the Gospels and Acts (from 50 in 1540 to 349 in 1541).[40] Now, not just specific words and phrases were highlighted: whole sentences received special attention. Furthermore, the secretary of the Revision Commission fought but lost a battle for even more changes. Rörer wanted the 1541 and future editions of the Luther Bible to include interpretive tools to further help the reader and preacher identify law and gospel, God's wrath or comfort, and "Lutheran truth" or "Roman lies."[41] Rörer also proposed using the "home-grown" Gothic font to indicate passages that were comforting and containing the gospel,

---

36. Brecht, *Martin Luther: The Preservation of the Church,* 110–11. See here WA 48:1–297 in the notes for various instances of inscriptions Luther wrote for various people.

37. Brecht, *Martin Luther: The Preservation of the Church,* 113.

38. Willem Jan Kooiman, *Luther and the Bible,* trans. John Schmidt (Philadelphia: Muhlenberg, 1961), 182.

39. Hövelmann, *Kernstellen der Lutherbibel,* 53.

40. Hövelmann, *Kernstellen der Lutherbibel,* 55–56.

41. Flood, "Martin Luther's Bible Translation," 61–3.

while passages containing the law and God's wrath would be printed in the foreign, Latin or Roman fonts.[42] This was too much for Luther, who called this proposal by Rörer "fool's work."[43] Luther's opinion prevailed, and the proposed additions by Rörer were not included, at least at this time. Rörer was, however, at least very committed to the idea of properly distinguishing between law and gospel, something that Luther had insisted was essential to the proper preaching of the gospel.

The 1543 edition of the Bible contained very few changes, compared to the major overhaul of the Luther Bible that had occurred two years earlier. This edition followed its predecessor in both typesetting and design by using a single column of text on each page and by making use of the woodcuts by the artist with the monogram, MS.[44] The most significant change in the 1543 edition of the Luther Bible was that the number of highlighted texts or "core places" (*Kernstellen*) reached their peak, with 899 places now emphasized.[45] This was an increase of 74 core places from the 1541 edition of the Luther Bible. From this point forward, the number of highlighted places in the Biblical text would begin to decrease. For example, two years later, the number of emphasized, core places was reduced to 725, and the next year, in the 1546 edition of the Luther Bible, this number dropped dramatically to 272 highlighted places.[46] The "mass media" approach of emphasizing every place where the gospel was found began to be replaced with fewer instances, thus expecting the readers and preachers to be able to identify the law and gospel for themselves. It was time for the readers and preachers to do their own homework.

The 1545 Luther Bible was the last one that appeared during Luther's lifetime. The number of core places decreases to 725, with most of the reductions happening in the Psalter, Isaiah, and Matthew.[47] Hans Volz observed that:

> The tenth and last Wittenberg High German Bible edition in the reformer's lifetime appeared once again as a Medieval styled Bible in 1545. It contains only a few improvements traced back to Luther. Its design corresponds

---

42. Kooiman, *Luther and the Bible*, 182. Luther's opinion of this is captured by Lufft's assistant, Christoph Walther, in *Von der Biblia und Vorrede zu Jhena gedruckt.* (Wittenberg: Hans Lufft, 1564). Bl.A 4b. Printed in Joachim Christoph Bertram, *Litterische Abhandlungen* 1, (1781), 66–74.
43. Hövelmann, *Kernstellen der Lutherbibel*, 34. See also Otto Albrecht, "Das Luthersche Handexemplar des deutschen Neuen Testaments," *Theologische Studien und Kritiken* 87 (1914), 200.
44. Volz, *Martin Luthers deutsche Bibel*, 156.
45. Hövelmann, *Kernstellen der Lutherbibel*, 55–56.
46. Hövelmann, *Kernstellen der Lutherbibel*, 53.
47. Hövelmann, *Kernstellen der Lutherbibel*, 55–56.

basically to the single-column Bible of 1543, which had also served as a textual template. With this edition, which attained a certain canonical significance that has been in effect from the reformer's death to the present time, the text of the Luther Bible—with few exceptions—attained its final shape.[48]

This edition became, in many quarters, the authoritative "Luther Bible." It was not long, however, before a dispute arose over which edition was the "final" Luther Bible, the final edition that carried Luther's indisputable fingerprints in its pages. Were his fingerprints to be found on the 1546 Bible, and not just the Bible published in 1545 while he was still alive? The fact that many of the proposed revisions had already been made when Luther died in February 1546, only a few months before the 1546 Bible came out, meant that both editions of the Bible could claim to be the "last" Bible from Luther's hand.

At the heart of the controversy about whether the 1545 or the 1546 edition of the Luther Bible is Luther's "last, authoritative version" is the question of whether the 1546 version of the German Bible was in fact approved by Luther. Complicating matters is the fact that the 1546 Bible contains glosses and marginal notes that were obviously added by Georg Rörer rather than by Luther,[49] even though Rörer had, for some years, been the secretary for the Revision Committee. To make matters more complicated, it is nearly impossible to distinguish whether the handwritten revisions noted as early as in Luther's 1541 Bible were from the hand of Luther himself or added by Rörer. There is also an ecclesial-political component to this debate, since some scholars have claimed that Rörer's changes, made after Luther's death, reflect the views of Philip Melanchthon rather than of Luther, fueling the debate between the followers of Philip (the Philipists) and the "true Lutherans" (the Gnesio-Lutherans) who claimed to be the true keepers of Luther's theology.[50] While these political-theological differences had been simmering before Luther's death, after he died the divergent points of view emerged from the shadows. The Luther Bible was not immune to these differences of perspective.

THE LUTHER BIBLE SINCE 1546

Brian Gerrish has noted that Luther shared with Erasmus of Rotterdam a longing to combine good literature with sacred literature and that this

48. Hans Volz, *Martin Luthers deutsche Bibel: Entstehung und Geschichte der Luther-bibel* (Hamburg: Wittig, 1978), 156.
49. Hövelmann, *Kernstellen der Lutherbibel*, 33–34.
50. Hövelmann, *Kernstellen der Lutherbibel*, 34–36.

desire was fulfilled in the Luther Bible.[51] His translation was good sacred literature, one of the reasons it was so popular. Its popularity can also be partially attributed to the larger-than-life character that was bestowed upon Luther. However, what really gave the Luther Bible its "staying power" was the way this translation resonated with people. He had placed sacred literature into high-quality literature for the masses. The translation had a personal and relatable quality to it that made it attractive to others, even if they may not have been particularly enamored with Luther himself. For example, Emser's 1527 New Testament, a blatant copy of Luther's 1522 New Testament, attained a popularity among Roman Catholic readers. The personal and relatable characteristics of the translation also made the Luther Bible a popular source for new Bible translations into other languages. Thus, William Tyndale's English Bible, which was completed by Miles Coverdale when Tyndale was arrested in Antwerp, not only worked from the text of the Luther Bible but also tried to imitate Luther's translation methods, translating from "idea to idea" rather than "word for word."[52] Translations of the Luther Bible also showed up in the Scandinavian countries, England, the Low Countries such as the Netherlands, and in the Baltic and other regions of Eastern Europe.[53] It was a model to be copied.

Shortly after Luther died, the controversy over the 1546 Bible that included Rörer's changes, along with the release of Rörer's own edited version in 1547, led to an attempt to regulate and control the publication of an "authorized" Luther Bible. One of the advocates for this regulation was, according to John Hentz, a Gnesio-Lutheran called Melchior Goeze.[54] Goeze felt that Rörer's amendments betrayed the spirit of Luther, in favor of Melanchthon, even though this was disproved. Eventually, however, the disputes over the authorized text forced Elector George of Saxony to

51. Brian A. Gerrish, *Grace and Reason: A Study in the Theology of Luther* (Oxford: Oxford University Press, 1962), 171.

52. Gerald L. Bray, *Doing Theology with the Reformers* (Downers Grove: IVP Academic, 2019), 104. Ralph Werell, however, argues that there is little connection between the Tyndale and Luther Bibles, in *The Roots of William Tyndale's Theology* (Cambridge: Clarke, 2013).

53. See, for example, Birgit Stolt, "Luther's Faith of 'the Heart',"in *The Global Luther: A Theologian for Modern Times*, ed. Christine Helmer (Minneapolis: Fortress Press, 2009), 132; Theophilus Stork, *Luther and the Bible* (Philadelphia: Lutheran Board of Publication, 1873), 141–42; and "The Prussian-Vilnian Discussion (1560)," in *Reformed Confessions of the 16th and 17th Centuries in English Translation*, trans. James T. Dennison, Jr. (Grand Rapids: Reformation Heritage Books, 2008), 230.

54. It is unknown whether Hentz was referring here to Moritz Golrz, one of the financiers of Lufft's printing shop, especially since he would have greatly benefitted from a standardized version published by Lufft. John P. Hentz, *History of the Lutheran Version of the Bible* (Columbus: F.J. Heer, 1910), 140–41.

authorize a person named "Coelestinus to undertake a textual revision. This resulted in an edition which appeared in 1581 and which was called the 'Prince's Normal Bible'"[55] (*Die kursächsische Norm-Bibel*). This edition conformed closely to Luther's 1545 edition of the Bible.[56] This became the "officially" authorized version of the Luther Bible. However, apparently no one paid much attention to it, and so increasingly diverse "Luther Bibles" continued to roll off the presses. According to Hövelmann, ninety-one different versions of the Luther Bible were printed between Luther's death in 1546 and the end of the Thirty Years War in 1648.[57]

The Luther Bible finally gained some semblance of regulation due to two interrelated factors. First, General Superintendent Johann Dieckmann campaigned for an authorized version. He proposed his own, preferred version, known as the *Stade-Bibel,* named after Dietrich von Stade, and it would become the standard version.[58] Second, Lutherans were challenged to develop an organization to oversee the printing of authorized Luther Bibles. This challenge was met by Lutheran Pietism when the philanthropist Karl Hildebrand von Canstein, sympathetic to the Lutheran Pietist cause, decided to take up this task. He formed the first "Bible Society," with the express intent to make the Luther Bible the standard translation while also making it readily available to everyone. The reasoning was simple: if everyone had access to the same version, it would soon become the standard version. As Cameron reports,

> Karl Hildebrand von Canstein (1667–1719) consolidated and stabilised what became the received text of the Luther translation. Canstein fell under the influence of Philipp Jakob Spener and became a devout Pietist. He founded the "Cansteinschen Bibelanstalt," which began to supervise the issuing of large numbers of standard Luther Bibles in new editions from 1716 onwards. Within his lifetime it is estimated that at least 100,000 New Testaments and 40,000 complete bibles had been published; the number rose to approximately 3 million copies of New Testaments and complete bibles by 1800.[59]

Canstein made the printing of Bibles affordable for everyone by raising enough money to have the complete Bible typeset at once, with the

55. Hövelmann, *Kernstellen der Lutherbibel,* 46, 94–95.
56. Hentz, *History of the Lutheran Version of the Bible,* 141.
57. Hövelmann, *Kernstellen der Lutherbibel,* 90.
58. Hentz, *History of the Lutheran Version of the Bible,* 141; Hövelmann, *Kernstellen der Lutherbibel,* 158–59.
59. Cameron, "The Luther Bible," 235. For more information on the Canstein Bible Society, see O.M. Norlie, "Bible Societies," *The Translated Bible* (Philadelphia: United Lutheran Publication House, 1934), 200.

typesetting for each page permanently soldered together. Thus, printers did not have to follow the very time-consuming process of printing a few pages, breaking up the type, and then setting it up for the next few pages. With this new practice, whenever another printing was needed, the typesetting was already done and ready to use, which saved an incredible amount of time and money.

The Canstein society also needed a solid edition of the Luther Bible to publish. They first turned to Duke Eberhard Ludwig's court chaplain, John Henry Hedinger, who published a new edition of the Luther Bible in 1704 that included annotations by the Pietist leader August Hermann Francke of Halle. This Bible, which incorporated Pietist ideas into the text through annotations, became known as the Pietists' Bible.[60] Other attempts at a good, critical, and accurate version of Luther's Bible were by Johann Albrecht Bengel (1687–1752), John Frederick Meyer (1772–1849), and Rudolph Stier (1800–1862), but these attempts were criticized for using too many modern terms while at the same time retaining too many archaic terms.[61] The translators were quite inconsistent with their translations, despite their best intentions.

Despite the difficulty of finding a widely accepted edition of the Luther Bible, the Canstein Society had no trouble printing a multitude of copies of their own versions of the Luther Bible. By the time of Canstein's death in 1719, "eighty thousand bibles and a hundred thousand New Testaments had been sold in German-speaking territories."[62] The Canstein Society worked together with the Pietist foundation in Halle, so that by 1834 (the tricentennial anniversary of the first Luther Bible), over 2,700,000 copies of the Bible, and about two million copies of the New Testament, had been printed.[63] Not only was the Luther Bible now the most used version, it was doing what Luther had intended—proclaiming the Word far and wide.

By the middle of the nineteenth century, the lack of a standard version of the Luther Bible reflected the struggle the Lutherans had in sticking

60. Eric W. Gritsch, *A History of Lutheranism,* 2nd ed. (Minneapolis: Fortress Press, 2010), 159.
61. See here, John C. Wedborg, "Bengel, J(ohann) A(lbrecht) (1687–1752," *Historical Handbook of Major Biblical Interpreters,* Donald K. McKim, ed. (Downers Grove: InterVarsity Press, 1998), 292; and Hentz, *History of the Lutheran Bible,* 142–43.
62. Karl Krueger, "Bible Translations," *Dictionary of Luther and the Lutheran Traditions,* ed. Timothy J. Wengert (Grand Rapids: Baker Academic, 2017), 91.
63. Theophilus Stork, *Luther and the Bible* (Philadelphia: Lutheran Board of Publication, 1873), 141–42. Cameron suggests a more conservative estimate, suggesting that at least three million copies of the New Testament and complete Bible were printed by 1800. Cameron, "The Luther Bible," 235.

close to Luther's text while also using contemporary language—something that Luther and his colleagues had also wrestled with. Luther scholars wanted a Bible that was accurately reflective of Luther's theology as well as understandable to new generations of German-speaking people. This challenge was reflected by none other than Claus Harms, in his 95 Theses issued in 1817 (the tricentennial of the beginnings of the Reformation). These Theses were published as a response to Friedrich Wilhelm III's attempt to form a union church of Reformed and Lutheran to mark the anniversary. In theses 52 and 53, Harms made his case for needing new translations of the Luther Bible:

> 52. But a translation into a living language must be revised every hundred years, in order that it may remain in life.

> 53. The activity of religion has been retarded because this has not been done. The Bible societies should arrange for a revised Luther's Bible translation.[64]

Harms' calls for a thorough revision of the Luther Bible gained traction with the rediscovery of Codex Vaticanus, forgotten in the Vatican Library, and the discovery of Codex Sinaiticus in 1859 by Constantin von Tischendorf. The Eisenach Evangelical Church published a newly revised edition of the Luther Bible in 1883, the same year that the *Weimar Ausgabe* edition of Luther's Works began being published. Another more extensively edited and revised version came out in 1892, which included, among other things, a chronicle of Luther's family. It also continued the practice of including highlighted, or core, passages (*Kernstellen*) in the Bible.[65] Another revised edition of the Luther Bible come out in 1912/13, followed by a major revised version in 1956. This edition was then edited even further in 1964 and 1970. Finally, later editions came out in 1983 for the five hundredth anniversary of Luther's birth and again in 2017, to commemorate the quincentenary of the beginning of the Reformation. Not all the translation work took place in Germany. The first Luther Bible published in North America was brought out by Christopher Sauer (Saur) in Philadelphia (Germantown) in 1743, printed with type he had brought with him from Frankfurt. With this publication, he established himself as a leader in publishing

64. Claus Harms, "Theses of Claus Harms (1817)," *The Lutheran Cyclopedia*, ed. Henry Eyster Jacobs (New York: Charles Scribner's Sons, 1899), 513.
65. Hentz, *History of the Lutheran Bible*, 144–47; Hövelmann, *Kernstellen der Lutherbibel*, 241–66.

works for German readers.[66] After a wide variety of so-called Luther Bibles, no doubt capitalizing on Luther's name and reputation as a translator, if not also as a reformer, the involvement of the German Bible Society in publishing the standard editions of the Luther Bible helped standardize the fruits of the Bible Revision Committee that had so engaged Luther and his colleagues during his lifetime.

SUMMARY

There are many translations of the Bible in German available to purchase today, and yet the Luther Bible remains popular. In the 1930s, Dietrich Bonhoeffer considered it the best translation of the Bible in the German language.[67] Not all would concur with Bonhoeffer, however. Hartmann Grisar, a fierce early-twentieth-century critic of Luther, questioned Luther's motives for translating the Bible, suggesting he did not do it to place the Holy Word of God into the language of the people, but to use it as a platform to attack the pope and the Catholic Church.[68] While there is a grain of truth in this, at least with the woodcut in the book of Revelation in the 1522 *Septembertestament* that depicts the pope as the whore of Babylon, it was not the motive for Luther's translations. His concern was to proclaim the gospel as clearly as possible.

The Luther scholar Hans-Martin Barth raises other pertinent questions about the helpfulness of the translation in the Luther Bible, suggesting that "Luther's images and comparisons no longer have the same impact they once did. The agrarian-patriarchal culture of a small provincial Saxon town with, at the time, about two thousand inhabitants is most certainly not our own." He then adds that while the translation in the Luther Bible could be considered "modern" in the nineteenth century, today it would

---

66. Mark A. Noll, *A History of Christianity in the United States and Canada*. 2nd ed. (Grand Rapids: Eerdmans, 2019), 535. Sauer also published the first edition in North America of Luther's Small Catechism in German in 1744, with the support of Count Zinzendorf. The first "Lutheran approved" edition came in 1749, printed by none other than Benjamin Franklin and J. Boehm. Adolph Spaeth, "Catechism," *The Lutheran Cyclopedia*, eds. Henry Eyster Jacobs and John A.W. Haas (New York: Charles Scribner's Sons, 1899), 79.

67. Clifford J. Green and Michael P. DeJong, *The Bonhoeffer Reader* (Minneapolis: Fortress Press, 2013), 416.

68. Gustav Marius Bruce, *Luther as an Educator* (Minneapolis: Augsburg Publishing House, 1928), 147–48. See Hartmann Grisar, *Luther*, 6 Volumes, trans. E.M. Lamond (St. Louis: Herder, 1913–1917), 5:525–585.

be considered "premodern" or even "anti-modern."[69] Having said that, he also admits that the Luther Bible:

> with its prefaces and glosses, is an essential document for determining Luther's theological and historical position. It reflects specific situations, with their options and condemnations, together with the whole range of world, church, politics, and society. To a considerable extent, Luther's own church was molded by it, and thereby the Luther Bible became one of the fundamental pillars of the Lutheran church in Germany. In its substructure there were some things that were conditioned by the time, and some that were also theologically one-sided. With this Bible, nevertheless, the church was essentially built on its own solid foundation. Its verdict on conditions in the world around the church, including politics and society, is one that is neither approving on the one side nor condemnatory on the other, but one that must rather be characterized as open, sober, and critical. Neither the authority of the state nor the existence of social classes was accepted uncritically.[70]

Thus, as a theological and historical document, the Luther Bible continues to give insights into Luther and his context. However, in the final analysis, Barth questions whether a "*Bibel in gerechter Sprache*" (Bible in inclusive language) in today's world would be more consistent with Luther's original approach and goal in translating the Bible.[71] An ecumenical, standardized translation in German, he proposes, similar to the standardized texts of the Creed and the Lord's Prayer,[72] would better witness to the gospel in today's world. These suggestions by Barth are helpful, but perhaps not as attainable as one would hope. There is too much money to be made by offering a variety of translations of the Bible in any one language, and different translations impact people in different ways. If the goal of a translation is, according to Luther, to make sure the Word of gospel, the Word of Life, enters a person's ears in order to come into effect in the heart, then any translation that accomplishes this is a project worth its cost and time. A contemporary translation that vividly and clearly proclaims the gospel in today's context is something that Luther would most definitely approve of, since that was the foundational reason for his translation project from the very beginning.

---

69. Hans-Martin Barth, *The Theology of Martin Luther: A Critical Assessment* (Minneapolis: Fortress Press, 2013), 19.

70. Barth, *The Theology of Martin Luther*, 100.

71. Barth, *The Theology of Martin Luther*, 430.

72. Barth, *The Theology of Martin Luther*, 430.

Conclusion

"Yes, wherever there is faith, people cannot hold back. They cannot help but prove themselves, they cannot help but break out into good works, they cannot help but confess and teach this gospel before the people and stake their very lives on it. Every aspect of their life and everything that they do is directed to their neighbor's profit, in order to help them, not only to the attainment of this grace, but also for the sake of body, property, and honor. Seeing what Christ has done in this matter, they cannot help but follow Christ's example."[1]

Martin Luther was not content to simply translate the Bible from the Hebrew and Greek into readable German. He wanted to make reading and hearing Scripture a life-changing experience. Encountering Christ in Scripture and in the Living Word, he felt, would drive a person into living out this exciting, radical, and life-transforming message of abundant life in the community. He consciously translated the Scripture so that the gospel message proclaimed in the Bible would be experienced and not just meditated upon. The gospel was meant to be lived. Living and experiencing the gospel was, after all, the goal of any theologian worth their salt. Early in his career, he commented that it is by "Living, dying, and being damned, and not reading, speculating or understanding, that make the real theologian."[2] People are meant to experience the gospel, which drives them into the arms of Christ and into the community to live life to the fullest. This was what Luther had experienced, and this was the experience that he wanted for the readers and hearers of the Living Word.

1. "Prefaces to the New Testament (1546/1522)." Author's translation. See LW 35:361; WA DB 6:9,29–34. See also TAL 6:421.
2. "Second Psalms Commentary (1519/1522)," WA 5:163,28–29.

A year after the attempted siege of Vienna by the forces of Sultan Suleiman I in the fall of 1529, Luther decided to write a preface to a book that had been published between 1460 and 1480 and have it republished. The anonymous author of this book had escaped from twenty years of captivity by the Turkish Muslims. Luther felt the book was relevant because in 1530 the Holy Roman Empire was still facing the threat of a Turkish invasion on its eastern borders. Picking up his pen, the most valuable weapon he had, he focused his attention even more on completing his Bible Project. Yet despite the urgency Luther felt to finish the Bible Project translation, he still found time to write a preface to this anonymously authored book that he felt could prepare people to live under the rule of the Turkish Muslims if they successfully invaded the Holy Roman Empire. He wanted to prepare the German people to withstand the pressures that would be placed upon them by non-Christian rulers, and that meant equipping the followers of Christ with the gospel in their own language. Thus, his commitment to, and reason for, translating the Bible comes through in his preface to the "Pious Reader." As he stated:

> This is our purpose in publishing this book . . . so that . . . they may really *experience* and feel with their own hands that what the Gospel teaches is true, namely, that the Christian religion is something much different and far more sublime than fair-seeming ceremonies, tonsures, cowls, somber faces, fasts, festivals, canonical hours, and the whole façade of the Church of Rome throughout the world."[3]

Even though Luther named the Roman church here instead of the Turks, his agenda was still clear. He wanted to get the German people to *experience* the gospel through his translation, so they would know what was important and what was not important. Ceremonies and vestments would not protect them, but armed with the gospel and the Living Word, the people would be able to withstand anything that came their way. He wanted to help people, no matter what they were facing, to "experience and feel with their own hands that what the gospel teaches is true." That is why he dedicated so much time to translating the Bible into a language that people could understand and experience. Likewise, preachers, pastors, and, indeed, all the baptized were called to help each other *experience* this gospel, not just read it for themselves or hear it read out loud in the congregation. Luther made this intention clear in his Galatians commentary, stating that the proper task of the apostles, whom he identified here as the

---

3. "Preface to [George of Hungary,] Book on the Ceremonies and Customs of the Turks, Published Seventy Years Ago (1530)," LW 59:260; WA 30.II:206,23–28. Italics added.

preachers of the gospel, was to "illuminate the work and the glory of Christ and to strengthen and comfort troubled consciences."[4] The translation of the Bible was meant to accomplish the proper task of the apostles—to help people grasp and experience the gospel. The reason was simple: this gospel does something to people as individuals and as a community. He and his fellow reformer Melanchthon believed that the gospel sets people free to see, hear, and experience "Christ and his benefits"[5] for the sake of the whole community. As Timothy Wengert describes it,

> This twofold project—illumining Christ's work and giving comfort (*doctrina et usus*)—was at the heart of the Wittenberg Reformers' interpretation of Scripture and stood in direct conflict not only with Jerome and Erasmus—with scholastics and Romanists—but also with our own rather tame, law-centered approaches to texts that cannot believe Paul's own radical words and prefer the safety of interpretation that leaves people to their own devices as they stare into the modern or postmodern abyss.[6]

This twofold project is indeed as radical today as it was for Paul and for Luther. The 1534 Bible Project by the Lutheran reformers was not to simply make a nice-sounding German language translation of the Bible available to people so that they could merely read about what God had done for all creation in the past. Rather, it was so people could experience the gospel for themselves and in community. This gospel was embodied in Christ the Living Word who continues to come among us, "full of grace and truth" (John 1:14), so that anyone who has ears to hear and eyes to see this Word made flesh can experience life.

Luther's determination to translate the Bible in such a way that people could encounter and experience Christ the Living Word in its pages ought to be a helpful reminder to people seeking to understand Scripture and the Word in helpful and meaningful ways in today's world. It is clear, based on his understanding of Scripture and the Word, that he was not interested in trying to preserve the authority of the Bible by constructing fortresses that relied on theories of literal, errorless, or literal, word-for-word translations. Such an approach only places obstacles in the way of those seeking the Christ. Instead, he wanted the readers and hearers of Scripture to experience the "life-giving Word" who seeks them out and

4. "Galatians Commentary (1535)," LW 26:290. WA 40.I:451,25–27.
5. Melanchthon uses this phrase in AC XXIV, 24 (Latin text), BC 71; BSELK 145; as well as in Ap IV, 118, BC 139; BSELK 316.
6. Timothy J. Wengert, *Reading the Bible with Martin Luther: An Introductory Guide* (Grand Rapids: Baker Academic, 2013), 122.

gathers them into the community of the faithful. Thus, debates—debates which are still being carried on today—over whether sacred texts (e.g., Scripture) or leaders (e.g., the pope) are infallible and without error serve only to draw attention away from experiencing the Christ who comes to give people life through the Word of the gospel.

The Leipzig debate with Johannes Eck in 1519 had led Luther to realize that true authority was not located in a thing or in a person other than Christ, the Living Word.[7] This debate, held before Luther even began translating the New Testament, helped him to recognize that the problem with locating authority in a thing (*res*), whether it be a text, an institution, or a doctrine, was that it took attention away from an encounter with the One who speaks the Living Word with authority. Luther later reiterated this idea in the Schmalkald Articles, where he discussed who had the authority to establish articles of faith. He made a telling statement when he declared that "the Word of God—and *no one* else [*sonst niemand*], not even an angel—should establish articles of faith."[8] There was no reference to a text here. Rather, he deliberately stated that "the Word of God" (i.e., Christ) established articles of faith, not a text or a "thing" ("*nothing* else" [*sonst nichts*]). Any attempt to locate authority in a text could too easily turn the Bible into a historical document to be studied and dissected and all too often comes at the expense of ignoring the Living One behind the text and spoken of within the text of Scripture. Unfortunately, Luther's insights have been too often ignored by Lutherans in the last century and a half. Beginning in the early twentieth century, the draft articles on Scripture in Lutheran church constitutions reveal the "battle for the Bible" that went on between Lutheran church bodies that were in merger negotiations.[9] These inter-Lutheran debates over the infallibility and

7. See Mickey L. Mattox, Richard J. Serina, and Jonathan Mumme, eds. *Luther at Leipzig: Martin Luther, the Leipzig Debate, and the Sixteenth-Century Reformations* (Leiden: Brill, 2019) for a detailed description and analysis of the debates over authority at Leipzig.

8. SA II,2:15; BC 304, BSELK 734. As Kolb and Wengert note, this sentence was not in the original manuscript or in the copy made by Spalatin and subscribed to at Schmalkald in 1537. Luther inserted this paragraph into the text in 1538.

9. One of the first times that Holy Scripture is qualified by the terms "inerrant" or "infallible" is found in the *Articles of Union in the Norwegian Lutheran Church in America,* which in 1914 unanimously and unreservedly accepted "the canonical books of Holy Scriptures as the *inerrant* Word of God." J.A. Bergh, *The Union Documents of the Evangelical Lutheran Church with a Historical Survey of the Union Movement* (Minneapolis: Evangelical Lutheran Church, 1948), 58–59. The direction taken by the Norwegians was echoed in the "Chicago Theses of 1919, as the members of the National Lutheran Council tried to come to agreement on Scripture. It stated, "All Lutheran bodies represented by the National Lutheran Council are agreed in the fundamental doctrine that the canonical books of the Old and New Testaments are the inspired and *inerrant* Word of God, and the only rule of faith, doctrine and practice." *Proceedings*

inerrancy of Scripture (in the sense of "without error") have continued to cause tension among Lutherans, especially when discussions arise about what Scripture says about contemporary issues such as who can or cannot be ordained, how one defines marriage, or science, such as debates over the seven days of creation.

The Wittenberg reformers also realized that authority was misplaced when it was located in a person other than Christ the Living Word. This lay at the heart of the reformers' critiques of the claim that the pope was the only one who had the right (authority) to interpret Scripture. This evolved into claims of papal infallibility, since the Roman church claimed that "the pope cannot err in matters of faith."[10] While Luther addressed these claims of papal infallibility, they were not formalized as dogma until the First Vatican Council (1870). At Vatican I, one of the decrees declared that papal decrees were infallible when spoken *ex cathedra* (from the chair of Peter) by the pope.[11] The problem with these claims, the reformer would have asserted, was that locating authority in a text or in a person other than Christ the Living Word distracted people from what Luther wanted most—that they experience the gospel. All the claims to infallibility took attention away from the gospel proclamation.

Luther also knew the dangers of turning the Bible into a book of morality or a book of law, apart from gospel. When used as a book of rules

---

of the National Lutheran Council 1919 (MSS National Lutheran Council Library, New York), 11a. This statement formed the background for the statement on Scripture in the Minneapolis Theses of 1925, agreed to by merger commissioners of the Iowa, Ohio, and Buffalo Synods and the Norwegian Lutheran Church in America, and was sent to their church bodies for action. However, a controversy erupted over the statement on Scripture in the years 1926–1930, a controversy that took five years to resolve. It eventually culminated in the formation of The American Lutheran Church in 1930. While some were content with the wording from the *Formula of Concord*, the Norwegians preferred wording that included "inerrant," since many of their congregants, raised in Lutheran pietism, had been strongly influenced by the fundamentalist view of Scripture advocated by The Northwest Bible and Missionary School at Minneapolis. Fred W. Meuser, *The Formation of the American Lutheran Church* (Columbus: Wartburg Press, 1958), 185. The Ohio Synod journal, *Pastor's Monthly* V (1928), 439, in fact praised Fundamentalism's attitude toward the Bible. Meuser, *Formation*, 185 n. 31.

10. "To the Christian Nobility of the German Nation (1520)," LW 44:133–34; WA 6:411,8–35.
11. "We teach and define that it is a dogma Divinely revealed that the Roman pontiff when he speaks *ex cathedra*, that is when in discharge of the office of pastor and doctor of all Christians, by virtue of his supreme Apostolic authority, he defines a doctrine regarding faith or morals to be held by the universal Church, by the Divine assistance promised to him in Blessed Peter, is possessed of that infallibility with which the Divine Redeemer willed that his Church should be endowed in defining doctrine regarding faith or morals, and that therefore such definitions of the Roman pontiff are of themselves and not from the consent of the Church irreformable." See, *Pastor aeternus,* Vatican Council, Session IV, in Dom Cuthbert Butler, *The Vatican Council* (London: Collins and Harvill, 1962). 334.

and regulations, it all too often has been used to try to brow-beat people into proper moral behavior. Such shaming actions could drive people to despair rather than driving them to Christ and into an experience of the gospel—the goal of Luther's translation project. As church and society have been discovering, people do not relate well to authoritarian, moralistic language in today's world. Nor do many people—including those who are adherents of different faith traditions or those who reject all religious traditions—recognize Scripture as an authority for their lives. They are not interested in whether the Bible is an authoritative, errorless, inerrant text. Others, with roots in the Christian tradition, may consider Scripture as a historical, pre-modern text, with no contemporary relevance—a dead, irrelevant text. But that was not how Luther understood and experienced Scripture. In its pages, he encountered a living, breathing, life-giving gospel. Its authority came from the one who is proclaimed in Scripture, not from the text itself. The text is simply the manger that holds the Christ.

Luther believed that when the Bible is experienced by people, they experience the gospel incarnate—the "Word made flesh." This Word made flesh becomes incarnate, and becomes gospel, in the midst of people. Thus, the Wittenberg reformers, and not just Luther, wanted people to experience this gospel, not in isolation, but in the communities and places where they lived and breathed. He wanted people to experience gospel amidst the very brokenness at home or in the workplace. He wanted people to experience hope and the possibility of life in the very midst of seemingly hopeless dead ends. It was in these everyday human experiences that people encounter and experience the Word in full force, offering them a life-giving alternative to their encounters of despairing norms. Only when people experience this life-giving gospel can they honestly explore what drains life from them. Once people encounter the life-giving gospel in the pages of Scripture, their focus would fall, not on the letter of the text or the letter of the law, but on the Giver of Life—as Luther had intended. This was the purpose for his translation of the Bible into a language and vocabulary that could be understood by the German-speaking people. With this "Luther Bible" translated in a way that focused on Christ and his gospel, preachers could more easily proclaim a message that was experienced.

To help the preacher grasp the gospel proclamation in the Biblical text that he had translated, Luther went one step further. He deliberately highlighted seven specific words and phrases in the 1534 edition of his translation of the Bible, supported by the Wittenberg translation team. Luther began with emphasizing the Word (Wisdom of Solomon 16:12 and 18:22). This Word is the One who speaks a word to create life and heal all creation and conquer God's wrath. This Word of Life also calls people to hear for themselves the voice from heaven that instructs them to listen to the Beloved Son of God, which Luther had highlighted in each of the Synoptic Gospel accounts of the transfiguration of Jesus (Matt 17:5, Mark 9:7, and Luke 9:35). When people listen to this voice from heaven, they will hear the gospel message that Luther had highlighted, "Your sins are forgiven you" (Rom 3:25). This gospel message was loudly and frequently proclaimed by the Beloved Son of God who is the Living Word. But Luther had not yet finished his highlighting in the 1534 Luther Bible. He recognized that this word of forgiveness needs to be proclaimed both aurally and physically. Thus, his final highlighted word was "take" (1 Cor 11:24). In taking and eating the body and blood of Christ in the sacrament of the altar, the person experiences the gospel at a much deeper level than simply through hearing this Word of promise. The gospel is tasted, savored, and experienced, and this experience of the Gospel found in Christ the resurrected One transforms life. The Spirit is breathed-in and life happens. Thus, when the highlighted words and phrases are put together, a clear picture of Luther's goal for his Bible Project arises: that people would not just hear the Word of God in the Bible but that they would experience and encounter this Living Word through Word and sacrament. He wanted people to experience God and the gospel found in Christ when they read or hear the text of Scripture.

Luther was not content to simply have people experience this Living Word as they read, heard, or even tasted Christ and his gospel within the words of Scripture. He took his Bible Project one step further. When a person experiences the gospel for themselves in the Living Word proclaimed in Word and sacrament, they are then driven into the community to be "Christs one to another and do to our neighbors as Christ does to us."[12] Luther wanted others to also experience the gospel—not just through the Word and in the sacraments but also through the encounter with, and witness of, the community that is the body of Christ. He wanted people to encounter the One who gives life so that they, too, could experience life in its fulness.

The Wittenberg reformer also recognized the apostolic nature of proclaiming and living the gospel in his translating project. In a treatise written to respond to several questions about monastic vows, Luther identified this apostolic sense: "To serve God is to serve one's neighbor as Christ and the apostles did—they did not isolate and hide themselves forever in monasteries."[13] Instead, the apostles went out into society and

12. "The Freedom of a Christian (1520)," LW 31:368; WA 7:66,34–36.
13. "An Answer to Several Questions on Monastic Vows (1526)," LW 46:151; WA 19:290,34–35.

proclaimed the gospel. Thus, Luther translated the Bible so that people could experience the same thing the apostles experienced: that in Christ, there is life, and this life is lived in community. This is what made his translation of the Bible so unsettling to those who wanted to control access to this Living One through the strictures of the church. When people encounter and experience Christ in the manger, wrapped in the swaddling cloth of Scripture,[14] they cannot help but bow down and worship and then go and serve the neighbor—and, indeed, all creation—in ways that breathe life into their neighbors and into creation. The desired result for service to others and to creation was to see life springing forth as a result of experiencing the gospel. A cruciform way of life emerges, consisting of "abundant freedom"[15] and that is "the outcome of the faithful proclamation of the praise of God."[16] A cruciform life has a vertical dimension, where God shapes people through the gospel so that they can experience life as the Spirit breathes life into them. But it also has a horizontal dimension, where the people of God who have experienced Christ cannot help but seek ways for others to experience the gospel for themselves, even if it entails hardship. The Luther Bible was not just for reading. It was for living, for in the crucible of life, one experienced the gospel.[17] The ultimate aim of Luther's 1534 Bible Project was to allow readers to experience the gospel, and having experienced it, want to share this gospel so that others might experience Christ and the Word of life as well. This experiencing of the gospel through his Luther Bible translation did not always happen for the reader, admittedly. People could resist the Spirit breathing life into them. But his Bible translation project was meant to facilitate the Holy Spirit's inspiring transformation of people as they encountered and experienced God's actions of justifying them by grace through faith. Luther's translation of the Bible is a very deliberate proclamation of the gospel, a proclamation that was intended to do something to the reader and hearer, for their own sake and for the sake of all creation and the community.

---

14. "Sermon for the Second Day of Christmas (1540)," LW 75:254; WA 10.I.1:139,10–11. Luther also suggests that the Scriptures (the writings of Moses and the Prophets) are Christ's swaddling cloths and manger. See "A Brief Instruction on What to Look for and Expect in the Gospels (1521)," LW 35:122; WA 10.I:15,2–5.
15. Brett Muhlhan, *Being Shaped by Freedom: An Examination of Luther's Development of Christian Liberty, 1520–1525* (Eugene: Pickwick, 2012), 144.
16. Dennis Ngien, *Fruit for the Soul: Luther on the Lament Psalms* (Minneapolis: Fortress Press, 2015), 77.
17. "Second Psalms Commentary (1519/1522)," WA 5:163,28–29.

Appendix 1

Printed German Bibles Prior to 1522 [1]

Place Published[2]		Printer	Date of Publication	German Dialect
1.	[Strassburg]	[Johann Mentel]	[ca. 1466]	High
2.	[Strassburg]	[Heinrich Eggestein]	[ca. 1470]	High
3.	[Augsburg]	[Jodocus Pflanzmann]	[ca. 1475]	High
4.	Augsburg	[Günther Zainer]	1475 or 1476	High
5.	[Nuremberg]	[Johann Sensen-schmidt & Andreas Frisner]	[ca. 1476]	High
6.	Augsburg	[Günther Zainer]	1477	High
7.	Augsburg	Anton Sorg	June 20, 1477	High
8.	*Cologne*	*[Bartholomaeus von Unkel]*	*[1478]*	*Low Saxon*
9.	*Cologne*	*[Bartholomaeus von Unkel]*	*[1479]*	*West Low-German*

(*Continued*)

1. Compiled from Kenneth A. Strand, *German Bibles Before Luther: The Story of 14: High-German Editions* (Grand Rapids: Eerdmans, 1966), 24, and *Early Low-German Bibles: The Story of Four Pre-Lutheran Editions* (Grand Rapids: Eerdmans, 1967), 17–21.
2. Names and places in square brackets indicate uncertainty.

10. Augsburg	Anton Sorg	January 3, 1480	High
11. Nuremberg	Anton Koberger	February 17, 1483	High
12. Strassburg	Johann Reinhard Gruningen (Gruninger)	May 2, 1485	High
13. Augsburg	Johann Schönsperger	May 25, 1487	High
14. Augsburg	Johann Schönsperger	November 9, 1490	High
15. *Lübeck*	*Steffan Arndes*	*November 19, 1494*	*Low*
16. Augsburg	Hans Otmar	February 12, 1507	High
17. Augsburg	Hans Otmar	January 27, 1518	High
18. *Halberstadt*	*[Lorenz Stuchs]*	*July 8, 1522*	*Low*

Appendix 2

Highlighted Instances in the Luther Bibles, 1534–1546 [1]

Year	1534	1539	1540	1541	1543	1545	1546
Scripture (OT) [2]							
Historical	0	36	36	70	92	94	108
Poetical	0	3	3	63	86	8	11
Prophetic	0	36	37	117	152	111	113
Total: Scripture	*0*	*75*	*76*	*250*	*330*	*213*	*232*
Apocrypha	2	3	3	2	2	4	3
Kerygma or Proclamation (NT) [3]							
Gospels/Acts	3	44	50	349	367	311	37

(*Continued*)

1. Compiled from Hartmut Hövelmann, *Kernstellen Der Lutherbibel: Eine Anleitung zum Schrift-verständnis* (Bielefeld: Luther Verlag, 1989), 49–56.
2. Luther reserves the term, "Scripture" for the Old Testament, while calling the New Testament "proclamation." See "Advent Postil (1522)," LW 75:39; WA 10.1.2:34,27–35,3. See also William A Graham, *Beyond the Written Word: Oral Aspects of Scripture in the History of Religion* (Cambridge: Cambridge University Press, 1987), 145, and "Sermons on the First Epistle of Peter (1523)," LW 30:19; WA 12:275,5–15.
3. "And what is the New Testament but a public preaching and proclamation of Christ. . ." "Prefaces to the Old Testament (1545/1523)," LW 35:236; WA DB 8:11,19–20.

Letters	2	88	86	201	172	171	0
unnumbered[4]	0	22	22	23	28	21	0
Total: Kerygma	*5*	*154*	*158*	*573*	*567*	*503*	*37*
Total: Bible	**7**	**232**	**237**	**825**	**899**	**720**	**272**

4. Hebrews, James, Jude, and Revelation were not given numbers in the Table of Contents for the New Testament of the 1534 Luther Bible.

Bibliography

Albrecht, Otto. "Das Lutherische Handexemplar des deutschen Neuen Testaments." *Theologische Studien und Kritiken* 87 (1914): 153–208.

Althaus, Paul. "Der Geist der Lutherbibel." *Lutherjahrbuch* 16 (1934): 1–26.

_____. *The Theology of Martin Luther*. Translated by Robert C. Schultz. Philadelphia: Fortress Press, 1966.

Appold, Kenneth G. "The Importance of the Bible for Early Lutheran Theology." In *The New Cambridge History of the Bible. Volume 3: From 1450 to 1750*. Four Volumes. Edited by Euan Cameron, 3:439–61. Cambridge. University of Cambridge Press, 2016.

Arblaster, Paul, Gergely Juhász, and Guido Latré, eds. *Tyndale's Testament*. Turnhout: Brepols, 2002.

Bach, Adolf. *Geschichte der deutschen Sprache*, 7th ed. Heidelberg: Quelle und Meyer, 1961.

Bachmann, Paul. "Response to Luther's Open Letter to Albert of Mainz (1530)." In *Luther as Heretic: Ten Catholic Responses to Martin Luther, 1518–1541*, translated by William R. Russell, edited by M. Patrick Graham and David Bagchi, 186–99. Eugene, OR: Pickwick, 2019.

Bagchi, David. *Luther's Earliest Opponents: Catholic Controversialists, 1518–1525*. Minneapolis: Fortress Press, 1991.

Bainton, Roland H. "The Bible in the Reformation." In *The Cambridge History of the Bible, Volume 3: The West from the Reformation to the Present Day*. Three Volumes. Edited by S.L. Greenslade, 3:1–37. Cambridge: Cambridge University Press, 1963.

_____. *Here I Stand: A Life of Martin Luther*. Nashville: Abingdon, 1950; Festival Edition, 1978.

Barth, Hans-Martin. *The Theology of Martin Luther: A Critical Assessment*. Minneapolis: Fortress Press, 2013.

Batka, L'ubomír. "Luther's Theology of the Word in the Exposition of Psalms 1–25 at Coburg (1530)." *Canon & Culture*,11 No. 2 (2017). 35–62.

Bayer, Oswald. *Martin Luther's Theology: A Contemporary Interpretation.* Translated by Thomas H. Trapp. Grand Rapids: Eerdmans, 2008.

_____. *Promissio. Geschichte der reformatorischen Wende in Luthers Theologie,* 2nd ed. Darmstadt: Wissenschaftliche Buchgesellschaft, 1989.

Beintker, Horst. "Luthers Anteil an der Sprachwendung des Neuhochdeutschen und dessen möglicher Ermittlung durch lexikalische Untersuchungen." *Muttersprache* 76 (1966), 228–34.

Bentzinger, Rudolf. "Zur spätmittelalterlichen deutschen Bibelübersetzung. Versuch eines Überblicks," Irmtraud Rösler, editor. In *"Ik lerde kunst dor lust." Ältere Sprache und Literatur in Forschung und Lehre.* Festschrift Christa Baufeld. Rostocker Beiträge zur Sprachwissenschaft 7, 29–41. Rostock: Universität Rostock, 1999.

Bergh, J.A. *The Union Documents of the Evangelical Lutheran Church with a Historical Survey of the Union Movement.* Minneapolis: Evangelical Lutheran Church, 1948.

Beutel, Albrecht. *Luther Handbuch.* Tübingen: Mohr Siebeck, 2017.

Bielfeldt, Dennis, Mickey L. Mattox, and Paul R. Hinlicky. *The Substance of the Faith: Luther's Doctrinal Theology for Today.* Minneapolis: Fortress Press, 2008.

Bluhm, Heinz. "The Literary Quality of Luther's *Septembertestament.*" *PMLA* 81 no. 5 (1966). 327–333.

_____. "Luther's German Bible." In *Seven-Headed Luther: Essays in Commemoration of a Quincentenary 1483–1983,* edited by Peter Newman Brooks, 177–94. Oxford: Clarendon Press, 1983.

_____. "Martin Luther and the Pre-Lutheran Low German Bibles." *The Modern Language Review,* 62 no. 4 (1967): 642–53.

_____. "Martin Luther as a Creative Bible Translator." *Andrews University Seminary Studies,* 22 no. 1 (Spring 1984): 35–44.

_____. *Martin Luther: Creative Translator.* St. Louis: Concordia, 1965.

Boehmer, Heinrich. *Luther and the Reformation in the Light of Modern Research.* Translated by Eva Suzette Gertrude Potter. London: George Bell and Sons, 1930.

Bohlmann, Ralph A. *Principles of Biblical Interpretation in the Lutheran Confessions.* Rev. Ed. St. Louis: Concordia, 1983.

Bonhoeffer, Dietrich. *Life Together and Prayerbook of the Bible, Volume 5. Dietrich Bonhoeffer Works.* Edited by Gerhard Ludwig Müller,

Albrecht Schönherr, and Geffrey B. Kelly, translated by Daniel W. Bloesch and James H. Burtness. Minneapolis: Fortress Press, 1996.

Bornkamm, Heinrich. *Luther and the Old Testament.* Translated by Eric W. Gritsch and Ruth C. Gritsch. Philadelphia: Fortress Press, 1969.

————. *Luthers Lehre von den zwei Reichen im Zusammenhang seiner Theologie,* 2nd ed. Gütersloh: Mohn, 1960.

————. Die Vorlagen zu Luthers Übersetzungen des Neuen Testaments." *Theologische Literaturzeitung* 72 (1947): 23–28.

Bottigheimer, Ruth B. "Bible Reading, 'Bibles' and the Bible for Children in Early Modern Germany," *Past and Present* 139 (May 1993): 66–89.

Braaten, Carl E. "Prolegomena to Christian Dogmatics." In *Christian Dogmatics,* Volume 1, edited by Carl E. Braaten and Robert W. Jenson. Two Volumes. Philadelphia: Fortress Press, 1984.

Bray, Gerald L. *Doing Theology with the Reformers.* Downers Grove: IVP Academic, 2019.

Brecht, Martin. *Martin Luther: His Road to Reformation, 1483–1521.* Translated by James L. Schaaf. Minneapolis: Fortress Press, 1985.

————. *Martin Luther: Shaping and Defining the Reformation 1521–1532.* Translated by James L. Schaaf. Minneapolis: Fortress Press, 1990.

————. *Martin Luther: The Preservation of the Church, 1532–1546.* Translated by James L. Schaaf. Minneapolis: Fortress Press, 1993.

Bromiley, G. W., ed. *Zwingli and Bullinger.* Library of Christian Classics. Philadelphia: Westminster, 1953.

Brown, John. *The History of the English Bible.* Cambridge: Cambridge University Press, 1912.

Bruce, Gustav Marius. *Luther As an Educator.* Minneapolis: Augsburg Publishing House, 1928.

Buber, Martin. *I and Thou.* Translated by Walter Kaufmann. New York: Simon & Schuster, 1970.

Buchwald, Georg. *Doktor Martin Luther: Ein Lebensbild für das deutsche Haus, mit zahlreichen Abbildungen im Text, sowie dem Bildnis Luthers nach einem Gemälde von L. Cranach zu Nürnberg.* Leipzig & Berlin: Teubner, 1902.

Bugenhagen, Johannes. *Johannes Bugenhagen: Selected Writings.* 2 Volumes. Edited by Kurt K. Hendel. Minneapolis: Fortress Press, 2015.

Butler, Dom Cuthbert. *The Vatican Council*. London: Collins and Harvill, 1962.

Cairns, Earle E. *Christianity Through the Centuries: A History of the Christian Church*. 3rd ed. Grand Rapids: Zondervan, 1996.

Calvin, John. *Commentary on the Epistle of Paul the Apostle to the Romans*. Translated by John Owen. Grand Rapids: Baker, 1989.

————. *Ioannis Calvini Opera Quae Supersunt Omnia*, Vol 49. Edited by G. Baum, E. Cunitz, and E. Reuss. New York: Johnson, 1964.

Cameron, Euan. "The Luther Bible." In *The New Cambridge History of the Bible. Volume 3: From 1450 to 1750*. Four Volumes. Edited by Euan Cameron, 3:217–38. Cambridge. University of Cambridge Press, 2016.

Campbell, W. Gordon. "The 'Last Word' in Pictures: Enhanced Visual Interpretation of Revelation in Luther's High German Bible (1534)." *Postscripts* 11 no. 1 (2020): 5–33.

Christensen, Carl C. "Luther and the Woodcuts to the 1534 Bible" *Lutheran Quarterly* 19 no. 4 (Winter 2005): 392–413.

Cusa: Nicholas. *Writings on Church and Reform*. Translated and edited by Thomas Izbicki. Cambridge: Harvard University Press, 2008.

Deanesly, Margaret. *The Lollard Bible and Other Medieval Versions*. Cambridge: Cambridge University Press, 1920.

Dempster, Stephen G. "Canon and Old Testament Interpretation." In *Hearing the Old Testament: Listening for God's Address*, edited by Craig G. Bartholomew and David J. H. Beldman, 154–79. Grand Rapids: Eerdmans, 2012.

Dennison, Jr., James Ted. *Reformed Confessions of the 16th and 17th Centuries in English Translation*. Grand Rapids: Reformation Heritage Books, 2008.

Diehl, Emil. "Herstellung und Verbreitung der Lutherbibel im Wandel der Jahrhunderte." In *Die Lutherbibel: Festschrft zum vierhundertjähren Jubiläum der Lutherbibel*. Edited by Adolf Risch und Emil Zweynert, 89–115. Stuttgart: Steinkopf, 1934.

Duchrow, Ulrich. *Christenheit und Weltverantwortung. Traditionsgeschichte und systematische Struktur der Zweireichelehre*. 2nd ed. Stuttgart: Klett-Cotta, 1983.

————. *Two Kingdoms: The Use and Misuse of a Lutheran Theological Concept*. Geneva: Lutheran World Federation, 1977.

Duerden, Richard. "Equivalence or Power? Authority and Reformation Bible Translation." In *Reformation*, edited by Orlaith O'Sullivan, 9–23. London: British Library, 2000.

Eck, Johannis. *De primate Petri adversus Ludderum Joannis Eckii libri très.* Paris: Pierre Vikoue, 1521.

Emser, Hieronymus. *Auß was gründ || vnnd vrsach || Luthers dolmatschung/ vber das || nawe testament/dem gemeinē man || billich vorbotten worden sey.|| Mit scheynbarlicher anzeygung/wie/wo/vnd || an wölchen stellen/Luther den text vorkert/vnd || vngetrewlich gehandelt . . . || hab.|| . . . ||.* Leipzig: Wolfgang Stöckel, 1523.

Eusebius. *The History of the Church from Christ to Constantine.* Translated by G. A. Williamson. Harmondsworth: Penguin, 1965; reprint, Minneapolis: Augsburg, 1975.

Flood, John L. "Martin Luther's Bible Translation in its German and European Context." In *The Bible in the Renaissance: Essays on Biblical Commentary and Translation in the Fifteenth Century*, edited by Richard Griffiths, 45–70. Aldershot: Ashgate, 2001.

Forde, Gerhard O. *A More Radical Gospel: Essays on Eschatology, Authority, Atonement, and Ecumenism.* Edited by Paul Rorem et al. Lutheran Quarterly Books. Minneapolis: Fortress Press, 2017.

_____. *Theology Is for Proclamation.* Minneapolis: Fortress Press, 1990.

_____. *Where God meets Man: Luther's Down-to-Earth Approach to the Gospel.* Minneapolis: Augsburg Publishing House, 1972.

Füssel, Stephan. *Gutenberg and the Impact of Printing.* Translated by Douglas Martin. Aldershot: Ashgate, 2005.

_____. *The Bible in Pictures: From the Workshop of Lucas Cranach (1534).* Cologne: Taschen, 2009.

Gärtner, Kurt. "Die erste deutsche Bibel? Zum Bibelwerk des österreichischen Bibelübersetzers aus der ersten Hälfte d es 14. Jahrhunderts. Mit zwei neuen Handschriftenfunden zum Klosterneuburger Evangelienwerk und zum Psalmenkommentar." In *Wissensliteratur im Mittelalter und in der frühen Neuzeit. Bedingungen, Typen, Publikum, Sprache*, edited by Horst Brunner and Norbert Richard Wolf, 273–295. Wiesbaden: Reichert, 1993.

Gawthrup, Richard and Gerald Strauss. "Protestantism and Literacy in Early Modern Germany." *Past and Present* no. 104 (August 1984): 31–55.

Gelhaus, Hermann. *Der Streit um Luthers Bibelverdeutschung im 16. und 17. Jahrhundert.* Tübingen: Max Niemeyer, 1989.

George, Timothy. *Reading Scripture with the Reformers.* Downers Grove: InterVarsity Press, 2011.

Gerrish, Brian A. *Grace and Reason: A Study in the Theology of Luther.* Oxford: Oxford University Press, 1962.

_____. *The Old Protestantism and the New: Essays on the Reformation Heritage.* Chicago: University of Chicago Press, 1982.

Gilmont, Jean-François. *The Reformation and the Book.* St. Andrews Studies in Reformation History. Translated by Karin Maag. London: Routledge, 2016.

Gordon, Bruce. "Teaching the Church: Protestant Bibles and Their Readers." In *The People's Book: The Reformation and the Bible,* edited by Jennifer Powell McNutt and David Lauber, 15–26. Chicago: InterVarsity, 2017.

Gow, Andrew C. "The Bible in Germanic." In *The New Cambridge History of the Bible: Volume 2: From 600 to 1450,* Four Volumes, edited by Richard Marsden and E. Ann Matter, 2:198–216. Cambridge: Cambridge University Press, 2012.

_____. "The Contested History of a Book: The German Bibles of the Later Middle Ages and Reformation in Legend, Ideology, and Scholarship." *Analecta Gorgiana,* 263–300 Piscataway, N.J.: Gorgias Press, 2012.

Graham, William A. *Beyond the Written Word: Oral Aspects of Scripture in the History of Religion.* Cambridge: Cambridge University Press, 1987.

Granquist, Mark. *Lutherans in America: A New History.* Minneapolis: Fortress Press, 2015.

Green, Clifford J., and Michael P. DeJong. *The Bonhoeffer Reader.* Minneapolis: Fortress Press, 2013.

Greiling, Werner, Uwe Schirmer and Elke Anna Werner, eds. *Luther auf der Wartburg, 1521/22. Bibelübersetzungen—Bibeldruck— Wirkungsgeschichte.* Quellen und Forschungen zu Thüringen im Zeitalter der Reformation. Wein, Köln: Böhlau Verlag, 2023.

Griffiths, Richard, ed. *The Bible in the Renaissance: Essays on Biblical Commentary and Translation in the Fifteenth Century.* Aldershot: Ashgate, 2001.

Grisar, Hartmann. *Luther,* Six Volumes. Translated by E.M. Lamond. St. Louis: Herder, 1913–1917.

Gritsch, Eric W. *A History of Lutheranism.* 2nd ed. Minneapolis: Fortress Press, 2010.

Gritsch, Eric W. and Robert W. Jenson. *Lutheranism: The Theological Movement and Its Confessional Writings.* Philadelphia: Fortress Press, 1976.

Grobien, Gifford A. "What is the Natural Law? Medieval Foundations and Luther's Appropriations." In *Natural Law: A Lutheran*

Reappraisal, edited by Roland Cap Ehlke, 17–38. St. Louis: Concordia, 2011.

Haemig, Mary Jane. "Luther on Translating the Bible." *Word and World* 31 no. 3 (2011): 255–62.

Hagen, Hulda. *Die Spreche des jungen Luther und ihr Verhältnis zu Kanzleisprache seiner Zeit*. Diss. Phil. Greifswald, 1922.

Hahn, Sönke. *Luthers Übersetzungsweise im Septembertestament von 1522. Untersuchungen zu Luthers Übersetzung des Römerbriefs im Vergleich mit Übersetzungen vor ihm*. Hamburger philologische Studien 29. Hamburg: Helmut Buske Verlag, 1973.

Haile, H. G. "Luther and Literacy." *PMLA* 91 no. 5 (1976): 816–28.

Hall, H. Ashley. "Catholicism." In *Dictionary of Luther and the Lutheran Traditions*, edited by Timothy J. Wengert, 132–36. Grand Rapids: Baker Academic, 2017.

Haralambous, Yannis. "Typesetting in Old German: Fraktur, Schwabacher, Gotisch and Initials." *TEX 90 Conference Proceedings*. Providence: TEX Users Group, 1991.

Harms, Claus. "Theses of Claus Harms (1817)." In *The Lutheran Cyclopedia*, edited by Henry Eyster Jacobs, 512–14. New York: Charles Scribner's Sons, 1899.

Harrisville, Roy A. "Apocrypha and Pseudepigrapha." In *Dictionary of Luther and the Lutheran Traditions*, edited by Timothy J. Wengert. Grand Rapids: Baker Academic, 2017.

Heckel, Johannes. *Lex Charitatis: A Juristic Disquisition on Law in the Theology of Martin Luther*. Edited and translated by Gottfried G. Krodel. Grand Rapids: Eerdmans, 2010.

Heiderhoff, Horst. *Antiqua oder Fraktur? Zur Problemgeschichte eines Streits*. Frankfurt: Polygraph Verlag, 1971.

Helmer, Christine. *The Trinity and Martin Luther*, rev. ed. Bellingham: Lexham Press, 2017.

Hendrix, Scott H. *Martin Luther: Visionary Reformer*. New Haven: Yale University Press, 2015.

Hentz, John P. *History of the Lutheran Version of the Bible*. Columbus: F.J. Heer, 1910.

Higman, Francis. *Censorship and the Sorbonne; A Bibliographical Study of Books in French Censored by the Faculty of Theology in the University of Paris, 1520–1551*. Travaux d'Humanisme et Renaissance 172. Geneva: Librairie Droz, 1979.

Hinlicky, Paul R. *Luther and the Beloved Community: A Path for Christian Theology after Christendom*. Grand Rapids: Eerdmans, 2010.

_____. *Lutheran Theology: A Critical Introduction*. Cascade Companions. Eugene: Cascade Books, 2020.

Hirsch, Emmanuel. *Luthers Deutsche Bibel: ein Betrage zur Frage ihrer Durchsist*. Munich: Raiser, 1928.

Hövelmann, Hartmut. *Kernstellen der Lutherbibel: Eine Anleitung zum Schriftverständnis*. Texte und Arbeiten zur Bibel, Deutschen Bibelgesellschaft, Band 5. Bielefeld: Luther Verlag, 1989.

Hunter, M.J. "The Vernacular Scriptures: The Gothic Bible." In *The Cambridge History of the Bible*, Three Volumes, edited by G.H.W. Lampe, 2: 338–62. Cambridge: Cambridge University Press, 1969.

Jensen, Gordon A. "Highlighting in the 1534 'Luther Bible,'" *Lutheran Quarterly* 35 No. 2 (Summer 2021): 125–144.

_____. "Luther and the Lord's Supper." In *The Oxford Handbook of Martin Luther's Theology*, edited by Robert Kolb, Irene Dingel, and L'ubomír Batka, 322–32. Oxford: Oxford University Press, 2014.

_____. *The Wittenberg Concord: Making Space for Dialogue*. Lutheran Quarterly Books. Edited by Paul Rorem. Minneapolis: Fortress Press, 2018.

Jungel, Eberhard. *Justification: The Heart of the Christian Faith. A Theological Study with an Ecumenical Perspective*. Translated by Jeffery F. Cayzer. Edinburgh: T & T Clark, 2001.

Junghans, Helmar. "The Center of the Theology of Martin Luther." In *And Every Tongue Confess: Essays in Honor of Norman Nagel on the Occasion of his Sixty-Fifth Birthday*, 179–94 Dearborn: Nagel Festschrift Committee. 1990.

_____. "Interpunktion und Großschreibung in Texten der Lutherzeit." *Lutherjahrbuch* 74 (2007): 153–180.

_____. "Luther als Bibelhumanist." *Luther*, 53 no. 1 (1982): 1–9.

_____. *Wittenberg als Lutherstadt*. 2nd ed. Berlin: Union-Verlag, 1982.

Kässmann Margot, and Rösel Martin, editors. *Die Bibel Martin Luthers: Ein Buch Und Seine Geschichte*. Stuttgart: Deutsche Bibelgesellschaft, 2016.

Kaufmann, Thomas. "Vorreformatorische Laienbibel und reformatorisches Evangelium," *Zeitschrift für Theologie und Kirche* 101 (2004): 138–174.

Kolb, Robert. "The Enduring Word of God, in Wittenberg." *Lutheran Quarterly* 30 No. 2 (Summer 2016): 193–204.

_____. "Luther's Hermeneutics of Distinctions: Law and Gospel, Two Kinds of Righteousness, Two Realms, Freedom and Bondage." In *The Oxford Handbook of Martin Luther's Theology*, edited by

Robert Kolb, Irene Dingel, and L'ubomír Batka, 168–84. Oxford: Oxford University Press, 2014.

————. *Luther's Wittenberg World: The Reformer's Family, Friends, Followers, and Foes.* Minneapolis: Fortress Press, 2018.

————. *Martin Luther: Confessor of the Faith,* Christian Theology in Context. Oxford: Oxford University Press, 2009.

————. *Martin Luther and the Enduring Word of God: The Wittenberg School and Its Scripture-Centered Proclamation.* Grand Rapids: Baker Academic, 2016.

————. *Martin Luther as He Lived and Breathed: Recollections of the Reformer.* Eugene: Cascade, Books, 2018.

————. *Martin Luther as Prophet, Teacher and Hero: Images of the Reformer 1520–1620.* Grand Rapids: Baker Books, 1999.

———— "Two Realms." In *Dictionary of Luther and the Lutheran Traditions,* edited by Timothy J. Wengert, 756–57. Grand Rapids: Baker Academic, 2017.

Kolb, Robert and Charles P. Arand. *The Genius of Luther's Theology: A Wittenberg Way of Thinking for the Contemporary Church.* Grand Rapids: Baker Academic, 2008.

Kooiman, Willem Jan. *Luther and the Bible.* Translated by John Schmidt. Philadelphia: Muhlenberg, 1961.

Köstlin, Julius. *Life of Luther.* 2nd ed. London: Longmans, Green, and Co., 1895.

Krafft, Wilhelm Ludwig. *Die deutsche Bibel vor Luther: sein Verhältnis zu derselben und seine Verdienste um die deutsche Bibelübersetzung.* Bonn: Carl Georgi, 1883.

————. *Ueber die deutsche Bibel vor Luther und dessen Verdienste um die Bibelübersetzung.* Dissertation. Bonn: Formis Caroli Georgi University, 1883.

Kretzmann, Paul Edward. "German Versions Since 1534." In *The Translated Bible, 1534–1934: Commemorating the Four Hundredth Anniversary of the Translation of the Bible by Martin Luther,* edited by Olaf M. Norlie, 114–21. Philadelphia: United Luther Publication House, 1934.

Kühne Heinrich. "Der Wittenberger Buch- und Papierhandel im 16. Jahrhundert." In *Vierhundertfünfzig Jahre Reformation,* edited by Leo Stern and Max Steinmetz, 301–21. Berlin: Deutscher Verlag der Wissenschaften, 1967.

Kuntze, Simon. *Die Mündlichkeit der Schrift: Eine Rekonstruktion des lutherischen Schriftprinzips.* Leipzig: Evangelische Verlagsanstalt, 2020.

Lau, Franz. *Luthers Lehre von den beiden Reichen*. Berlin: Evangelische Verlagsanstalt, 1952.

Leaver, Robin A. *Luther's Liturgical Music: Principles and Implications*. Edited by Paul Rorem, Lutheran Quarterly Books. Minneapolis: Fortress, 2017.

Leppin, Volker. "Biblia, das ist die ganze Heilige Schrift deutsch" Luthers Bibelübersetzung zwischen Sakralität und Profanität." In *Protestantismus und deutsche Literatur*, edited by Jan Rohls and Gunther Wenz, 13–26. Göttingen: Vandenhoeck und Ruprecht Unipress, 2004.

_____. "Papst, Konzil und Kirchenväter: Die Autoritätenfrage in der Leipziger Disputation." In *Die Leipziger Disputation 1519*, edited by Markus Hein and Armin Kohnle, 117–24. Leipzig: Evangelische Verlanganstalt, 2011.

Levy, Ian Christopher. "The Leipzig Disputation: Masters of the Sacred Page and the Authority of Scripture." In *Luther at Leipzig: Martin Luther, the Leipzig Debate, and the Sixteenth Century Reformations*, edited by Mickey L. Mattox, Richard J. Serina, Jr, and Jonathan Mumme, 115–44. Studies in Medieval and Reformation Traditions 218, Andrew Colin Gow, general editor. Leiden: Brill, 2019.

van Liere, Frans. "The Latin Bible, c. 900 to the Council of Trent, 1546." In *The New Cambridge History of the Bible: Volume 2: From 600 to 1450*, Four Volumes, edited by Richard Marsden and E. Ann Matter, 2:93–109. Cambridge: Cambridge University Press, 2012.

Linebaugh, Jonathan A. *God, Grace, and Righteousness in Wisdom of Solomon and Paul's Letter to the Romans*. Texts in Conversation. Novum Testamentum, Supplements, 152. M.M. Mitchell and D.P. Moessner, general editors. Leiden: Brill, 2013.

Lockwood, William B. "Vernacular Scriptures in Germany and the Low Countries before 1500." In *The Cambridge History of the Bible. Volume 2: The West From the Fathers to the Reformation*, Three Volumes, edited by G.H.W. Lampe, 2: 415–435. Cambridge: Cambridge University Press, 1969.

Lohse, Bernhard. *Martin Luther's Theology: Its Historical and Systematic Development*. Translated by Roy A. Harrisville. Minneapolis: Fortress Press, 1999.

Losch, Richard R. *All the People in the Bible: An A–Z Guide to the Saints, Scoundrels, and Other Characters in Scripture*. Grand Rapids: Eerdmans, 2008.

Löser, Freimut. Deutsche Bibelübersetzungen im 14. Jahrhundert. Zwölf Fragen," *Jahrbuch der Oswald von Wolkenstein Gesellschaft* 12 (2000): 311–323.

Lundeen, Erik T. "Luther's Messianic Translations of the Hebrew Bible." *Lutheran Quarterly* 34 no. 1 (2020): 24–41.

Lutheran Church-Missouri Synod. *Die Neue Verfassung oder Constitution der deutschen evangelisch-lutherischen synod von Missouri, Ohio, u. a. Staaten.* St. Louis: LC-MS, 1855.

Luttor, Franz J., ed. *Biblia Pauperum: Studie zur Herstellung eines inneren Systems; mit dem Texte der in der Wiener k. k. Hofbibliothek aufbewahrten Handschrift und einem Lichtdruck.* Veszprém: Opitz, 1912.

Mantey, Volker. *Zwei Schwerter—Zwei Reiche. Martin Luthers Zwei-Reiche-Lehre vor ihrem spätmittelalterlichen Hintergrund.* Tübingen: Mohr/Siebeck, 2005.

Mathesius, Johannes. *Historia Vnsers Lieben herren vnd Heylands Jesu Christi . . . auß den heilgen Euangelisten genommen.* Nuremberg: Gerlatz, 1568.

Mattox, Mickey L., Richard J. Serina, and Jonathan Mumme, eds. *Luther at Leipzig: Martin Luther, the Leipzig Debate, and the Sixteenth-Century Reformations.* Leiden: Brill, 2019.

McGrath, Alister E. *The Intellectual Origins of the European Reformation.* New York: Blackwell, 1987.

Melanchthon, Philip. *Loci Communes, 1543.* Translated by Jacob A.O. Preus. St. Louis: Concordia, 1992.

———. *"Loci Communes Theologici," Melanchthon and Bucer.* Library of Christian Classics, Volume XIX. Edited by Wilhelm Pauck, 3–152. Philadelphia: Westminster, 1969.

———. *Loci communes theologici, 1555.* Translated and edited by Clyde L. Manschreck. New York: Oxford University Press, 1965.

———. *Selected Writings.* Edited by Elmer Ellsworth Flack and Lowell J. Satre. Translated by Charles Leander Hill. Minneapolis: Augsburg Publishing House, 1962.

Meurer, Siegfried, ed. *"Was Christum Treibet": Martin Luther Und Seine Bibelübersetzung.* Bibel Im Gespräch 4. Stuttgart: Deutsche Bibelgesellschaft, 1996.

Meuser, Fred W. *The Formation of the American Lutheran Church.* Columbus: Wartburg Press, 1958.

Milburn, R.L.P. "The 'People's Bible:' Artists and Commentators." In *The Cambridge History of the Bible, Volume 2: The West from the Fathers to the Reformation*, Three Volumes, edited by G.W.H. Lampe, 2:280–308. Cambridge: Cambridge University Press, 1969.

Muhlhan, Brett. *Being Shaped by Freedom: An Examination of Luther's Development of Christian Liberty, 1520–1525*. Eugene: Pickwick, 2012.

Mülhaupt, Erwin. "Bibel und Buchdruckerkunst vor Luther," *Die Bibel in der Welt* 6 (1955): 8–14.

Muller, Richard A. *Dictionary of Latin and Greek Theological Terms: Drawn Principally from Protestant Scholastic Theology*. Grand Rapids: Baker Book House, 1985.

Nafzger, Samuel H. et al., eds. *Confessing the Gospel: A Lutheran Approach to Systematic Theology*, Two Volumes. St. Louis: Concordia, 2017.

Nettelhorst, Leopold. *Schrift muss passen: Schriftwahl und Schriftausdruck in der Werbung, Handbuch für die Gestaltungsarbeit an Werbenmitteln*. Essen: Wirtschaft & Werbung Verlagsgesellschaft, 1959.

Newman, Jane O. "The Word Made Print: Luther's 1522 New Testament in an Age of Mechanical Reproduction," *Representations* 11 (1985): 95–133.

Ngien, Dennis. *Fruit for the Soul: Luther on the Lament Psalms*. Minneapolis: Fortress Press, 2015.

_____. *Luther as a Spiritual Adviser: The Interface of Theology and Piety in Luther's Devotional Writings*. Eugene: Wipf & Stock, 2007.

Nietzsche, Friedrich. "Jenseits von Gut und Böse," in *Werke in drei Bänden*. 7th ed. Karl Schlechta, ed. Munich: Carl Hanser, 1973.

Niggemann, Andrew J. "Martin Luther's Use of Blended Hebrew and German Idioms in His Translation of the Hebrew Bible." *Harvard Theological Review* 113, no. 4 (2020): 483–97.

Noll, Mark A. *A History of Christianity in the United States and Canada*. 2nd ed. Grand Rapids: Eerdmans, 2019.

Norlie, O.M. "Bible Societies." In *The Translated Bible*, edited by O.M. Norlie, 200–205. Philadelphia: United Lutheran Publication House, 1934.

Nygren, Anders. *Agape and Eros: A Study of the Christian Idea of Love*. Translated by Philip Watson. Philadelphia: Westminster Press, 1953.

Oberman, Heiko. A. *The Two Reformations. The Journey from the Last Days to the New World,* Edited by Donald Weinstein. New Haven and London: Yale University Press, 2003.

Otwinowska, Barbara. "Der »gemeine Mann« als Adressat der volkssprachlichen Literatur in der Renaissance." In *Renaissanceliteratur und frühbürgerliche Revolution, Studien zu den social- und ideologiegeschichtlichen Grundlagen europäischer Nationalliterturen*, edited by Robert Weimann, et al., 194–202. Berlin: Aufbau-Verlag, 1976.

Ozment, Steven. *The Age of Reform, 1250–1550: An Intellectual and Religious History of Late Medieval and Reformation Europe*. New Haven: Yale University Press, 1980.

Paret, Oscar. *Die Überlieferung der Bibel*. Stuttgart: Württembergische Bibelanstalt, 1963.

Pauck, Wilhelm, ed. *Melanchthon and Bucer*. Philadelphia: Westminster Press, 1969.

Paulson, Steven D. *Lutheran Theology*. Doing Theology Series. London: T & T Clark, 2011.

Pelikan, Jaroslav. *Luther the Expositor: Introduction to the Reformer's Exegetical Writings*. Luther's Works Companion Volume. St. Louis: Concordia, 1959.

————. *Reformation of Church and Dogma (1300–1700)*. The Christian Tradition: A History of the Development of Doctrine. Volume 4. Five Volumes. Chicago: University of Chicago Press, 1983.

Pettegree, Andrew. *Brand Luther: How an Unheralded Monk Turned His Small Town into a Center of Publishing, Made Himself the Most Famous Man in Europe—and Started the Protestant Reformation*. New York: Penguin Press, 2015.

————. "Publishing in Print: Technology and Trade." In *The New Cambridge History of the Bible. Volume 3: From 1450 to 1750*, Four Volumes, edited by Euan Cameron, 3:159–86. Cambridge. University of Cambridge Press, 2016.

Piepkorn, Arthur Carl, *The Sacred Scriptures and The Lutheran Confessions: Selected Writings of Arthur Carl Piepkorn*, Volume 2. Edited by Philip J. Secker. Mansfield: CEC Press, 2007.

Reinitzer, Heimo. *Biblia Deutsch: Luthers Bibelübersetzung und ihre Tradition*. Wolfenbüttel: Herzog August Bibliothek, 1983.

Reu, Michael. *Luther's German Bible: An Historical Presentation Together with a Collection of Sources*. Columbus: Lutheran Book Concern, 1934.

Richard, James W. *The Confessional History of the Lutheran Church*. Philadelphia: Lutheran Publication Society, 1909.

Risch, Adolf. *Luthers Bibelverdeutschung*. Leipzig: Heinsius, 1922.

Risse, Ursula. *Untersuchungen zum Gebrauch der Majuskel in deutschsprachigen Bibeln des 16. Jahrhunderts: ein historischer Beitrag zur Diskussion um die Substanzgroßschreibung.* Dissertation. Heidelberg: Winter, 1980.

Roper, Lyndal. *Martin Luther: Renegade and Prophet.* London: Vintage, 2017.

Root, Michael. "The Catholic Reception of the Leipzig Disputation." In *Luther at Leipzig: Martin Luther, the Leipzig Debate, and the Sixteenth Century Reformations,* edited by Mickey L. Mattox, Richard J. Serina, Jr, and Jonathan Mumme, 288–319. Studies in Medieval and Reformation Traditions 218, Andrew Colin Gow, general editor. Leiden: Brill, 2019.

Rost, Hans. *Die Bibel im Mittelalter. Beiträge zur Geschichte und Bibliographie der Bibel.* Augsburg: M. Seitz, 1939.

Ruge-Jones, Philip. *Cross in Tensions: Luther's Theology of the Cross as Theologico-Social Critique.* Princeton Theological Monograph Series. Edited by K. C. Hanson, Charles M. Collier, and D. Christopher Spinks. Eugene: Pickwick Publications, 2008.

Sasse, Herman. *This Is My Body: Luther's Contention for the Real Presence in the Sacrament of the Altar.* Minneapolis: Augsburg Publishing House, 1959.

Shaff, Philip. *The Christian Church. Volume VII, Modern Christianity, The German Reformation.* Grand Rapids: Eerdmans, 1910.

Schild, Maurice E. *Abendländische Bibelvorreden bis zur Lutherbibel,* Quellen und Forschungen zur Reformationsgeschichte, Volume 39. Gütersloh: G. Mohn, 1970.

Schloemann, Martin. "Die Zwei Wörter: Luthers Notabene zu 'Mitte der Schrift,'" *Luther: Zeitschrift der Luther-Gesellshaft.* 65 No. 3 (1994):110–23.

Schmidt, Philipp. *Die Illustration der Lutherbibel 1522–1700: ein Stuck abendlandische Kultur-und Kirchengeschiclite mit Verzeichenissen der Bibeln, Bilder und Kunstler, 400 Abbildungen.* Basel: Friedrich, 1962.

Schrey, Horst, editor. *Reich Gottes und Welt. Die Lehre Luthers von den zwei Reichen* Darmstadt: Wissenschaftliche Buchgesellschaft, 1969.

Schwarz, Reinhard. *Luther.* Die Kirche in ihrer Geschichte. Edited by Bernd Moeller. 3 no. 1. Göttingen: Vandenhoeck & Ruprecht, 1986.

Schwarz, Werner. *Principles and Problems of Biblical Translation: Some Reformation Controversies and their Background.* Cambridge: Cambridge University Press, 2009.

Schwarzwäller, Klaus. "Justification and Reality." In *Justification is for Preaching*, edited by Virgil Thompson, 102–22. Eugene: Pickwick, 2012.

Sehling, Emil, editor. *Die evangelischen Kirchenordnungen des XVI. Jahrhunderts,* Bands 1–5. Leipzig: Reisland, 1902–11.

Spaeth, Adolph. "Catechism." In *The Lutheran Cyclopedia*, edited by Henry Eyster Jacobs and John A.W. Haas, 77–79. New York: Charles Scribner's Sons, 1899.

Spener, Philip Jacob. *Pia Desideria*, Theodore G. Tappert, translator. Philadelphia: Fortress Press, 1964.

Stählin, Wilhelm. "Einheit der Bibel," *Freiheit und Ordnung*, Symbolon 4. Edited by Reinhard Mumm, 44–48. Frankfurt am Main: Evangelische Verlag Werke, 1980.

Stephens, W.P. *Zwingli: An Introduction to His Thought.* Oxford: Clarendon Press, 1994.

Stolt, Birgit. "Luther's Faith of 'the Heart:' Experience, Emotion and Reason." In *The Global Luther: A Theologian for Modern Times*, edited by Christine Helmer, 131–50. Minneapolis: Fortress Press, 2009.

_____. *Martin Luthers Rhetorik des Herzens.* Tübingen: Mohr Siebeck, 2000.

_____. "Luther's Translation of the Bible." *Lutheran Quarterly* 28 No. 4 (Winter 2014): 373–400.

_____. "Luthers Übersetzungtheorie und Übersetzungpraxis." In *Leben und Werk Martin Luthers von 1526–1546: Festgabe zu seinemn 500. Geburtstag*, edited by Helmar Junghans, 240–52. Berlin. Evangelische Verlaganstalt, 1983.

Stork, Theophilus. *Luther and the Bible.* Philadelphia: Lutheran Board of Publication, 1873.

Strand, Kenneth A. *Catholic German Bibles of the Reformation Era: The Versions of Emser, Dietenberg, Eck and Others.* Naples: Ann Arbor Publications, 1982.

_____. *German Bibles Before Luther: The Story of 14 High German Editions.* Grand Rapids: Eerdmans, 1966.

_____. *Early Low-German Bibles: The Story of Four Pre-Lutheran Bibles.* Grand Rapids: Eerdmans, 1967.

_____. *Reformation Bibles in the Crossfire: The Story of Jerome Emser, His Anti-Lutheran Critique, and His Catholic Bible Version.* Ann Arbor: Ann Arbor Publishers, 1961.

Streitberg, Wilhelm. *Die Gotische Bibel* (Reprint). Charleston: Nabu Press, 2010.

String, Tatiana C. "Politics and Polemics in English and German Bible Translations." In *Reformation*, edited by Orlaith O'Sullivan, 137–43. London: British Library, 2000.

Tanner, Norman P.S, ed. Decrees of the Ecumenical Councils: 2 Volumes. Washington: Georgetown University Press, 1990.

Thompson, Mark D. *A Sure Ground on Which to Stand: The Relation of Authority and Interpretive Method in Luther's Approach to Scripture.* Studies in Christian History and Thought. Eugene: Wipf & Stock, 2006.

Törnvall, Gustaf. *Geistliches und weltliches Regiment bei Luther. Studien zu Luther's Weltbild und Gesellschaftsverständnis.* Munich: Kaiser, 1947.

Trueman, Carl R. *Luther on the Christian Life: Cross and Freedom.* Edited by Stephen J. Nichols and Justin Taylor. Theologians on the Christian Life. Wheaton: Crossway, 2015.

Vajta, Vilmos. *Luther on Worship: An Interpretation.* Philadelphia: Fortress Press, 1958.

Volz, Hans. "Continental Versions to c. 1600: German Versions-Luther." In *The Cambridge History of the Bible: The West from the Reformation to the Present Day*, edited by S.L. Greenslade, 94–103. Cambridge: Cambridge University Press, 1963.

_____. *Hundert Jahre Wittenberger Bibeldruck 1522–1626.* Arbeiten aus der Staats- und Universitätsbibliothek Göttingen: Hainberg-schriften, n.s. Volume 1 Göttingen: L. Hantzschel, 1954.

_____. *Martin Luthers deutsche Bibel: Entstehung and Geschichte der Lutherbibel.* Hamburg: Friedrich Wittig, 1978.

_____. "Melanchthons Anteil an der Lutherbibel." *Archiv für Reformationsgeschichte* 45 no. 2 (1954): 196–233.

Walther, Wilhelm. *Die Deutsche Bibelübersetzung des Mittelalters*, 3 Volumes. Braunschweig: n.p., 1889–1892.

_____. *Luthers deutsche Bibel: Festschrift zur Jahrhundertfeier der Reformation.* Berlin: Mittler, 1917.

Watson, Philip S. *Let God Be God! An Interpretation of the Theology of Martin Luther.* London: Epworth Press, 1954.

Wedborg, John C. "Bengel, J(ohann) A(lbrecht) (1687–1752)." In *Historical Handbook of Major Biblical Interpreters*. Edited by Donald K. McKim. Downers Grove: InterVarsity Press, 1998.

Wengert, Timothy J. *Martin Luther's Catechisms: Forming the Faith.* Minneapolis: Fortress Press, 2009.

————. "Martin Luther's September Testament: The Untold Story." *The Report: A Journal of German-American History* 47 (2017): 51–61.

————. *Reading the Bible with Martin Luther: An Introductory Guide.* Grand Rapids: Baker Academic, 2013.

————. *Word of Life: Introducing Lutheran Hermeneutics.* Minneapolis: Fortress Press, 2019.

Wentz, Abdel Ross. "Luther and his Methods of Translating." *The Bible Translator* 4 no. 1 (1953): 27–32.

Werell, Ralph. *The Roots of William Tyndale's Theology.* Cambridge: Clarke, 2013.

Wolf, Herbert. *Martin Luther: eine Einführung in germanistische Luther-Studien.* Stuttgart: Metzler, 1980.

Wolf, Richard C., ed. *Documents of Lutheran Unity in America.* Philadelphia: Fortress Press, 1966.

Wolgast, Eike. "Luther's Treatment of Political and Societal Life." In *The Oxford Handbook of Martin Luther's Theology,* edited by Robert Kolb, Irene Dingel, and L'ubomír Batka, 397–413. Oxford: Oxford University Press, 2014.

Wormald, Francis. "Bible Illustration in Medieval Manuscripts." In *The Cambridge History of the Bible, Volume 2: The West from the Fathers to the Reformation,* Three Volumes, edited by G.W.H. Lampe, 2:309–37. Cambridge: Cambridge University Press, 1969.

Wrede, Adolph, ed. *Deutsche Reichstagsakten unter Kaiser Karl V, II. Band 1520–1521.* Gotha: Perthes, 1896.

Zwingli, Ulrich. *Huldreich Zwinglis Sämtliche Werke.* Edited by Emil Egli et al., *Corpus Reformatorum,* 88–108. Leipzig/Zürich: Heinsius/TVZ, 1905–2013.

————. *Huldrych Zwingli: Writings.* Edited by E. J. Furcha and H. Wayne Pipkin. 2 Volumes. Allison Park, PA.: Pickwick, 1984.

————. *The Latin Works and Correspondence of Huldreich Zwingli.* Edited by Samuel Macauley Jackson. 3 Volumes. New York: G.P. Putnam's Sons, 1912/Philadelphia: Heidelberg Press, 1922, 1929.

Index

absolution, 91, 104, 110, 124–26
    as voice of the Gospel, 120–21, 127
    commanded, 127
    not to be abolished, 127
allein ("only" or "alone": Luther's
    addition to Romans 3:28), 2, 26,
    67, 115
Althaus, Paul, 120
Amsdorf, Nicholas von, 26–28, 62
annotations, 37, 155, 167
antisacramentalists, 109
Apocalyptic Books, 54
Apocrypha, 44, 65, 69, 74, 80–81, 95,
    154, 159, 181
Apology to the Augsburg Confession,
    144
Appold, Kenneth, 49
Aquinas, Thomas, 15
Arndes, Steffan. *See under* printers:
    other printers
Augsburg, 15, 45, 179
Augsburg Confession, 92, 107–8, 123,
    125–27, 146
Augsburg, Diet of, 137
Augustine of Hippo, 14, 143
Aurogallus, Matthew, 28–29, 67, 70,
    156
authority

of apostles, 107
canonical, 69
of Christ/Gospel, 5, 17–19, 21, 85,
    98–99, 138, 159, 174–5
of Luther, 146
Papal, 15, 17, 51
of Scripture, 11, 13–19, 21, 51,
    173–74, 176
of state, 170
autographed Bibles 161–62

Bach, Adolf, 47
Bachmann, Paul, 66
Bainton, Roland, 23
banned Bibles, 40, 48–53, 56
baptism
    gives forgiveness/absolution
        of Jesus, 98–99, 128, 158
        of John, 128
    sacrament of, 104, 107–9, 112, 124,
        126–29, 131, 143–44, 159
Barth, Hans-Martin, 11–12, 20, 25,
    36, 169–70
Batka, L'ubomír, 89
Bayer, Oswald, 87
Beintker, Horst, 47
Bengel, Johann Albrecht, 167
Berlepsch, Hans von, 64

Lutheran Quarterly Books

Living by Faith: Justification and Sanctification, by Oswald Bayer (2003).

Harvesting Martin Luther's Reflections on Theology, Ethics and the Church, essays from *Lutheran Quarterly*, edited by Timothy J. Wengert, with foreword by David C. Steinmetz (2004).

A More Radical Gospel: Essays on Eschatology, Authority, Atonement, and Ecumenism, by Gerhard O. Forde, edited by Mark Mattes and Steven Paulson (2004).

The Role of Justification in Contemporary Theology, by Mark C. Mattes (2004).

The Captivation of the Will: Luther vs. Erasmus on Freedom and Bondage, by Gerhard O. Forde (2005).

Bound Choice, Election, and Wittenberg Theological Method: From Martin Luther to the Formula of Concord, by Roberg Kolb (2005).

A Formula for Parish Practice: Using the Formula of Concord in Congregations, by Timothy J. Wengert (2006).

Luther's Liturgical Music: Principles and Implications, by Robin A Leaver (2006).

The Preached God: Proclamation in Word and Sacrament, by Gerhard O. Forde, edited by Mark C. Mattes and Steven D. Paulson (2007).

Theology the Lutheran Way, by Oswald Bayer (2007).

A Time for Confessing, by Robert W. Bertram (2008).

The Pastoral Luther: Essays on Martin Luther's Pastoral Theology, edited by Timothy J. Wengert (2009).

Preaching from Home: The Stories of Seven Lutheran Women Hymn Writers, by Gracia Grindal (2011).

The Early Luther: Stages in a Reformation Reorientation, by Berndt Hamm (2013).

The Life, Works, and Witness of Tsehay Tolessa and Gudina Tumsa, the Ethiopian Bonhoeffer, edited by Samuel Yonas Deressa and Sarah Hinlicky (2017).

The Wittenberg Concord: Creating Space for Dialogue, by Gordon A. Jensen (2018).